Dwelling in the Text

Dwelling in the Text

Houses in American Fiction

Marilyn R. Chandler

University of California Press
Berkeley   Los Angeles   Oxford

University of California Press
Berkeley and Los Angeles, California

University of California Press, Ltd.
Oxford, England

Library of Congress Cataloging-in-Publication Data

Dwelling in the text : houses in American fiction / Marilyn R.
Chandler.
  p.   cm.
Includes bibliographical references and index.
ISBN 0–520–07363–0 (cloth)
1. American fiction—History and criticism. 2. Setting
(Literature) 3. Dwellings in literature. 4. Domestic fiction,
American—History and criticism. 5. Home in literature.
PS374.S45D87 1991
813.009'355—dc20   91–3635
                                                        CIP

Illustrations for chapters 1, 4, 5, 6, 7, 9, 10, and 11 from *The American House* (1980)
by Mary Mix Foley; drawings by Madelaine Thatcher, used by permission of Harper
and Row, Publishers. Illustration for chapter 2 from *Guy Mannerling* (1879) by Sir
Walter Scott, George Routledge and Sons, Publishers. Permission to reprint sections
of chapter 10 from Marilyn Chandler, "Voices Crying in the Wilderness" in *Suburbia
Re-examined*, ed. Barbara Kelly (1989), granted by Greenwood Press.

Printed in the United States of America

1 2 3 4 5 6 7 8 9

The paper used in this publication meets the minimum requirements of American
National Standard for Information Sciences—Permanence of Paper for Printed
Library Materials, ANSI Z39.48–1984 ⊗

Contents

Acknowledgments

This book has reminded me of two truths about authorship: that writing is a joyful but isolating business and that at the same time every book is a collaborative effort. I owe much to many who contributed new perspectives, advice, patience, love, and much listening time as this book took shape.

I first want to thank Patricia Troxel for our long conversations about American fiction and culture in which the idea for this book was born and began to take shape. Many others participated along the way with good ideas, helpful criticism, and an occasional admonishment to get on with it. Among those I wish especially to thank are Kathryn Reiss and Tom Strychacz, David Troxel, Vicki Reback, Bill Howarth, Karl Zender, Kevin Clark, Laura Jason, Kearnon Kanne, and the students in my course on architecture and fiction. The backdrop to all those conversations was my own valuable experience of what home, housekeeping, and homemaking meant, gathered in the years I spent with my reflective and articulate parents, Mary and Le-Gare Chandler.

I am grateful to the National Endowment for the Humanities for a summer grant that gave me time and means to take a closer look at historic houses in New England as well as a long second look at my manuscript and to the Arnold Graves Foundation for funding a sabbatical leave that brought the work near completion.

Thanks also to Doris Kretschmer for her editorial assistance and to Carol Lennox and Richard Povall in the Mills College faculty computer center, who provided invaluable assistance in preparation of the manuscript.

Finally, I am most grateful to my daughters, Mary, Elizabeth, and Margaret, for the extraordinary understanding with which they saw me through every stage of this effort and all the life changes that accompanied it; and to Michael, my best critic, my teacher in much, my partner in everything, without whom "all I do at piling stone on stone . . . is roofless around nothing." To the four of them this book is dedicated with much love.

Introduction

It is hardly possible to cast the mind's eye over the broad landscape of American literature without seeing a series of imposing houses rising in curious shapes along its horizons: Thoreau's cabin at Walden Pond, the dreary house of Usher, the House of the Seven Gables, Uncle Tom's cabin, Edna Pontellier's "pigeon house," Gatsby's mansion, the lonely and defiant house of Faulkner's Thomas Sutpen, Cheever's suburban Cape Cods, or, more recently, the haunted white clapboard in Morrison's *Beloved*. Our literature reiterates with remarkable consistency the centrality of the house in American cultural life and imagination. In many of our major novels a house stands at stage center as a unifying symbolic structure that represents and defines the relationships of the central characters to one another, to themselves, and to the world and raises a wide range of questions starting with Thoreau's deceptively simple "What is a house?"

Houses occupy this prominent place in American novels for a number of reasons. In a country whose history has been focused for so long on the business of settlement and "development," the issue of how to stake out territory, clear it, cultivate it, and build on it has been of major economic, political, and psychological consequence. For settlers, building on this land meant using native materials on "virgin territory" without established architectural context; arriving at some compromise between architectural ideas and designs imported from Europe and innovative, indigenous forms; and producing rough, hybrid constructions from what was available. Building here also meant suppressing the guilt attached to violent expropriation of land and entering a long struggle over the relations between political rights and property ownership.

"The American dream" still expresses itself in the hope of owning a freestanding single-family dwelling, which to many remains the most significant measure of the cultural enfranchisement that comes with being an independent, self-sufficient (traditionally male) individual in full possession and control of

1

home and family. The seldom-realized ideal is for the house-holder to have designed and built this house with his own hands; Jefferson's Monticello stands on its hill in Charlottesville in stately tribute to this mythic possibility. Behind the myth lies the enduring idea that a man's house represents his self (the relation of women to houses is a different issue) and becomes, as it grows into a home, a direct extension of that self into the enduring media of wood and stone.

Establishing a home is an indirect object of most other forms of work—a person works in order to afford a home and make it comfortable; conversely, the project of creating and inhabiting a living space serves as a model for other endeavors. Writers have thus frequently defined their work as demarcating, designing, and inhabiting space. As Alfred Kazin has observed, "One writes to make a home for oneself, on paper." The blueprints for those homes on paper are frequently borrowed directly from the world of architecture. Ellen Eve Frank, whose *Literary Architecture* explores in wide, cross-cultural terms the relations between the two disciplines, speaks of "the architecture of literature as external configuration, as form and embodiment, of consciousness," summing up neatly in that formulation a way of thinking about literal and imaginary structures that has deep roots in tradition and that precedes by many years the theoretical elaborations of structural or phenomenological criticism.[1] She observes, moreover, that "a building is not an object (product) only; it is, importantly, an activity" (4), which involves, as writing involves for writers, not only a variety of practical, economic, and aesthetic concerns but a continuing scrutiny of the interrelations of those concerns (3).

American writers as diverse as James, Cather, Wharton, and Faulkner repeatedly use architectural metaphors to describe their work and their idea of the text as something that can best be understood spatially and structurally. In explaining their craft, they speak of surfaces and interiors, rooms and foyers, thresholds and windows, and furnishings. James, in perhaps the most famous use of this conceit, likens the writer to a craftsman building a "house of fiction" with "a thousand windows." In her essay on "the unfurnished novel," Cather shifts the metaphor slightly with her focus on issues of "interior decoration." Faulkner frequently speaks of his writing as carpentry, of the business of crafting sentences as one no less exacting than the hewing and honing and joining that enable a structure to stand free and bear weight.

The houses in their novels thus reflect not only the psychological structure of the main character or the social structures in which he or she is entrapped but the structure of the text itself, thereby setting up a four-way, and ultimately self-referential, analogy among writer, text, character, and house. The same architectural habit of mind that designs and builds a house both to reflect patterns of life within it and to configure life in certain patterns may design a narrative to reflect and recast what the author conceives to be the essential structures of our lives.

This book is an exploration of the ways in which a number of our major writers have appropriated houses as structural, psychological, metaphysical, and literary metaphors, constructing complex analogies between house and psyche, house and family structure, house and social environment, house and text. Just as the history of the United States is a story of settling, building homes, domesticating land, and defining space, our fiction is, among other things, a history of the project of American self-definition wherein house-building, and for women, housekeeping, have been recognized as a kind of autobiographical enterprise—a visible and concrete means of defining and articulating the self. The semiotic significance of architecture as one of the most visible and multifaceted indices of cultural values has been heightened in the United States by our tendency to treat the visible world as a readable text, to define the structures we live in as mutable and meaningful, and to conflate aesthetic and moral categories. Fitzgerald's observation that "America is an idea" applies by extension to the way we tend to regard our social, economic, and artistic lives—as outward and visible manifestations of the ideas we believe bind us together as a people.

The spaces we create and inhabit in our imagination are particularly fraught with significance, unlimited as they are by practical constraints of material and context but informed by the natural and architectural features of our actual environment. Space is an ideologically weighted "product," and the idea of space is a highly charged issue for theorists and artists. In our fiction we find a composite representation of our eclectic architectural history and the dream material of our culture wherein houses figure not simply as historically accurate settings or stage props but as powerful, value-laden, animated agents of fate looming in the foreground, not the background, of human action; our novels are about houses and homes as much as they are about the people who inhabit them.

There are some significant consistencies in the ways the image of the house functions in American fiction and differs from analogous images in European novels. One of those differences lies in the characteristic tension in American culture between the project of building and settlement and the romantic image of the homeless, rootless, nomadic hero whose roof is the sky and whose bed is the open prairie, the meandering river, or the boundless sea. The "civilizing" process in this country has involved both overt and covert conflict over the tremendous psychic costs of "civilization" and domestication—a conflict generating the sort of apprehension that leads Huck Finn to resolve to "light out for the territory" before the Widow Douglas succeeds in "sivilizing" him. Enclosure in a house and in the structures of town or city life runs counter to the inherent romanticism of some of our most deeply held collective values: autonomy, self-determination, mobility. The heroic representation of nomadic life or certain forms of homelessness in our fiction can thus be seen as a powerful counterforce to the images of settlement and home-building that expresses not only the appeal of what is natural, wild, and unknown but also a deep and pervasive ambivalence about settlement. Paradoxically, in "nomadic" literature the issue of finding and defining home is, if anything, intensified. Other structures metonymically replace the house and its formative and expressive functions—for example, the ship in Melville's *Moby-Dick*, the raft in Twain's *Huckleberry Finn*, the homemade camper truck in Steinbeck's *Travels with Charlie*, the car in Kerouac's *On the Road*, or the motorcycle in Pirsig's *Zen and the Art of Motorcycle Maintenance*. In these works, too, the dwelling or vehicle becomes a home, assumes an inclusive symbolic importance, and defines the boundaries and practical challenges of a microcosmic private world.

The list of works in which the house (or an analogous structure) serves as governing metaphor comprises most of the traditional canon. This book aims at placing some of those works in the context of the development of American architecture, of urbanization and suburbanization, and of the politics as well as the poetics of space: Who owns or controls domestic space? Who designs it? Who decorates it? Who inhabits it, and what do they do there? A second aim is to pay attention to the language with which Americans have referred to "home," the values implicit in that language, and the social implications of those values, particularly as they affect expectations of family life, the shapes of women's lives, and adaptation to changing social and economic conditions. The chapters that follow trace a chronological trajectory that roughly corresponds to the movement from settlement to unsettlement, from rooting to rootlessness, and from transcendental romanticism to realism, irony, and nostalgia in American culture.

What unifies the novels studied here and many others in the American canon, broadly defined, is a complex of related conflicts and tensions that have been widely regarded as the defining strain in American mythology. One of the most fundamental of these conflicts is that between spiritual and material aims implicit in the convergence of Christianity and capitalism: God and mammon were never less comfortable together than in the American pantheon. Translated into secular terms, that conflict became a central principle in the development of American romanticism, where virtual worship of the ideas of nature, rusticity, and "wild" innocence coincided with an accelerating urban industrialism and a defiant cosmopolitanism that both rejected and emulated the overcivilized excesses of Europe. As the frontier moved west and the ideals of innocence and freedom became more deeply tainted with economic and political compromise, our mythology of radical opposition to the European model of civilization found nostalgic expression in the apotheosis of the nomadic hero resisting the diminishing confinements of domestic life, involved as it was in a worldly economy of wages and women. And, of course, the issue of gender, now a focus of much revaluation of our cultural history, has defined a field of tension between what have been perceived as opposed masculine and feminine objectives and modes of experience, most frequently expressed as the drive toward freedom, separation, and conquest in contest with the domesticating, and civilizing, impulse to put down roots and claim a spot of earth to inhabit and improve.[2]

Each of these conflicts is fundamentally the same conflict cast in new terms, and in each of its changing manifestations the business of building, buying, and maintaining a home has been a focal problem. Houses give us roots but also mire us in worldly concerns; they are indices of initiative and achievement but also of capitulation to the immediacies of temporal life that divert us from the nobler pursuits of mind and spirit. They are, after all, embodiments—incarnations that threaten to become incarcerations, doubling the stakes of the precarious human condition that entraps the spirit in the corruption of the flesh and bone or wood and stone. Inseparable from theological or metaphysical issues, houses are also the stage on which the dramas of sexual politics and class warfare are played out. Houses, as much as the wide wilderness and open spaces by which we have defined the reaches of our collective imagination and identity, are the locus of the central conflicts of American life.

The same ideological forces that shaped domestic architecture in the United States also shaped other forms of cultural expression, including, of course, our literature. The way we build and inhabit our houses has a good deal to do with the way we tell our stories. The history of architectural ideas in the United States closely parallels the history of literary theory or of the doctrines that define the conventions and appropriate uses of fiction and poetry. The parallel histories of these closely related enterprises can be roughly characterized as having moved from emulation of European models to the development of indigenous forms, which in revitalizing, recasting, or rejecting those models made something new of them. In both architectural and literary theory ongoing debates have focused on tensions between apparently opposed principles: beauty and utility, simplicity and decorativeness, imitation and originality, convention and experimentation. Both architecture and literature are simultaneously reflective and formative social forces. In both, implicit issues of gender and class lie behind the politics of style.

Both architects and writers have sustained some conflicting pressures in the matter of self-definition: whether to consider themselves artists or artisans, how much to conform to popular taste, how to survive in the marketplace while maintaining some degree of "artistic purity" of intention and practice. The author's conception of the audience and the domestic architect's conception of the family have been based on similar mixtures of idealization and observation. And what Michel Foucault would call a "bourgeois ideal of single authorship," with its attendant emphasis on distinctiveness, integrity, and originality, has dominated both art forms. Personality and process matter as well as product; we like to know (or think we know) who built the house we inhabit and wrote the book we are reading, believing moralistically that the worth of the product may be understood and judged by the virtue and character of the maker.

The issues that material culture, including architecture, has raised in the United States must be partly understood in relation to the iconoclastic stringencies of the Puritan theology that continued to dominate American values and public policy long after it had devolved into a variety of modified denominational modes and secular habits of mind. The iconoclastic heritage of Puritan Christianity was a significant factor in the development of architecture, as well as other arts, in the United States. In a religion that regarded economy, simplicity, and industry as the habits that led most directly to heaven, aesthetic considerations were suspect as seductive or distracting—likely to undermine the higher goods of utility, frugality, and discipline. Even Americans several generations removed from their Puritan forebears have had significant difficulties separating aesthetic from moral judgment. When Emerson declaims in his poem "Rhodora" that beauty is "its own excuse for being," he is refuting the deeply and widely held theological position that only the good is beautiful and that to judge things in purely aesthetic terms, and therefore to absent moral and utilitarian criteria, is at best suspect and at worst sinful. Moreover, Emerson's proclamation that beauty is self-justifying refers specifically to the beautiful as it occurs in nature, not to the products of manufacture. One way, therefore, to derive an acceptable aesthetic is to imitate nature, which comes from the hand of God and therefore offers a perfect model of beauty that deserves imitation and will edify as it delights.

Insofar as religion has had to do with how people live, domestic architecture has naturally been and continues to be fundamentally related to moral doctrine and behavioral ideals. In the 1820s and 1830s Horace Bushnell, a Congregational minister, popularized the concept of "home religion." He also idealized the "age of homespun," which represented the house as the center of training, production, and consumption and as such a centripetal moral force where all energies could be channeled. The immediate authority and supervision in the home would presumably foster a one-to-one relationship between the individual and his or her work and minimize distraction and temptation from "the world." Indeed, the biblical notion of the "world" as the devil's domain reinforced the idea that the home was a place of protection where one could be "in the world but not of it." Implied, too, was that the home should ideally be an Edenic retreat. The fall-to-redemption drama of salvation history was to be played out on each domestic stage. The home, in this light, was the outward form or mold for the soul of the unformed child in a precarious state of original sin.

The tensions that characterized American theology found direct material expression in architecture, interior decoration, and domestic science. Though the sacraments were attenuated in Protestant practice, the idea of the sacramental value of the material world retained considerable importance. Regarded as sacramental objects, a house and its furnishings not only reflected but formed character. Their presence and possession could "uplift" the owner and user and make him or her aspire to finer things. The tendency to allegorize and to regard the material world as emblematic lay deep in Christian tradition, and the home and its many objects and activities provided a convenient literalization of the divisions and forms of Christian life and morality. Nevertheless, because the material world was by definition a source of temptation, possession and decoration had to be rationalized and legitimized in moral terms and the pleasure they gave represented as spiritually uplifting. But that very process of intellectual and moral justification bred its opposite, a deeply resentful and rebellious anti-intellectual sentimentality about the heart as the source of truth, and an old epistemological quarrel reached a new peak in the decades of high romanticism. These tensions put architects, along with other artists and designers, in the delicate position of having to appeal to a people who wanted theory to morally justify practice and at the same time distrusted theory and were ambivalent about their own ambitions.

Because aesthetic values assumed the force of moral dicta or even doctrine, and because these values were essentially based on a romantic myth of an innocent past and a desire to reclaim that innocence, it was hard to incorporate the ideal of progress that also belonged to Christian eschatological tradition. Each step in technological progress needed moral justification. By the time of Harriet Beecher Stowe and Catherine Ward Beecher, whose book *The American Woman's Home* set new standards for middle-class home economics, we see this legitimation of domestic technology at work in the equation of such values as heightened efficiency with old Puritan virtues of industry and frugality. It is not irrelevant that these two intrepid women sprang from the oldest and sturdiest preacherly clan in New England.

So popular understanding of the function of architecture in the nineteenth century held that it was to reflect and enforce traditional virtues: simplicity, unity, humility, piety (often expressed in references to the hearth as a family altar), hard work, and purity. Like their Puritan forebears, who assumed that parents would teach their children reading, writing, and religion, nineteenth-century New Englanders regarded the home as the primary locus of moral and intellectual training, an enterprise in which both parents were expected to participate.[3] The theme of home as moral and spiritual center appeared frequently in popular literature such as *Mother's Magazine*, *Family Circle*, and *Happy Home and Parlor Magazine*. In 1823 John Howard Payne wrote "Home Sweet Home," which summarized sentimentalized attitudes toward the home as the seat of virtue and comfort in a dreary world.

Some architects, most notably Andrew Jackson Downing (1815–1852), specifically undertook to "elevate" the American public by producing architecture modeled on European refinements but adapted to American sensibilities. Downing's own writings borrow their rhetoric from sermons, often jeremiads admonishing the wayward to consider their pure origins and return to them, and the design of his houses literalizes notions of organicism, individual privacy, and the hearth as a kind of family altar. This is quintessential romanticism: an elevation of nature as a standard for all human manufacture, a generalized notion of God as expressed in nature and human institutions, and a tendency to validate sensibility—often sentimentality—over reason.

The popular notion that environment formed character had enormous impact on areas of social theory from education to criminology. Poe's dissolute life was explained by some contemporary biographers as a result of his having been orphaned and having had no real home. Especially in punishment of juveniles, crimes believed to have resulted from a poor home environment were to be rectified by sending the young miscreants to "houses of refuge" or "houses of reform," where they lived not in dormitories but in cottages where a master and mistress presided in family style. There these juveniles were literally given refuge against the incriminating environment with the expectation that the changed surroundings would have a transformative or redemptive effect. These effects extended to bodily health as well as to moral formation. William Alcott and other popular health reformers stressed quality of air, lighting, regulated temperature, and other factors in public buildings, schools, and prisons that had direct implications for house design. Typically, health and morals were regarded as analogous, and even in some respects synonymous, concerns.

American writers have generally portrayed the structures an individual inhabits as bearing a direct relationship or resemblance to the structure of his or her psyche and inner life and as constituting a concrete manifestation of specific values. The house is frequently treated as a schematic reiteration of the character of the central figure in a story. Poe's labyrinthine houses mirror the twisted minds of his crazed narrators; Uncle Tom's cabin translates his virtues into the simplicity and cleanliness of a humble dwelling; Isabel Archer's conjoined duplex reflects her ambivalent nature; Jay Gatsby's large, glamorous, empty shell, like the man himself, is mostly facade, a decontextualized imitation of a French villa, inauthentic for all its calculated fashionable rightness. Bent to its owner's monomaniacal purpose, it becomes an insidious mockery of what it purports to be.

Alternatively, as in Cather's *The Professor's House*, the house can become a three-dimensional graph of the dynamics of family life. In that novel the upper, lower, and middle portions of the decaying Victorian dwelling locate the family members in assigned positions and establish boundaries among them that are particularly hard to transgress by climbing a flight of stairs because the different floors of the house represent the rigid separations and stratifications that have riven the family for many years. The move to a new house, which is the underlying action of this story, brings two distinct sets of values into open conflict. Wharton similarly uses houses as indices of both her characters' individual psychologies and their familial and social relations; she frames the action of her stories in rooms and hallways minutely described in Ibsenesque detail that invites, even demands, close semiotic scrutiny and becomes at times emblematic.

This symbolic treatment of houses is not simply a literary fancy: houses in their various ways are obviously visible histories of personal and collective life. One of the problems that preoccupied writers and artists throughout the nineteenth century was that our collective identity had rather shallow roots; we had, as a nation, no significant past. For that reason, artists tended to mythologize the immediate and personal past, looking at it as through the wrong end of a telescope and, borrowing a note from the Puritans who so profoundly formed our habits of imagination, regarding both American history and personal history as reiterations of the timeless cycle of salvation history. Works such as Hawthorne's *House of the Seven Gables* or Faulkner's *Absalom, Absalom!* recall the double meaning of the word *house*—a structure and a family—a structure that absorbs and records and reveals the rise and fall of a family's fortunes as well as its moral degeneration.

The close association of the house with the human soul and body is by no means a peculiarly American idea. Freud points out that universally, in dreams, "the one typical . . .

representation of the human figure as a whole is a house"; he also claims rather unequivocally that "windows, doors and gates stood for openings in the body and that facades of houses were either smooth or provided with balconies and projections to hold on to."[4] Those with smooth walls he recognizes as male; those with balconies and projections, female. Gaston Bachelard's *The Poetics of Space* assigns the house a similarly fundamental status in the psychic economy by claiming that houses, like all "great, simple images, reveal a psychic state" and by reminding us that "our soul is an abode. And by remembering 'houses' and 'rooms' we learn to 'abide' within ourselves."[5] Moreover, just as houses embody characteristics of gender and psychic structure, so they also provide convenient diagrams of value relations. Upper, middle, and lower stories, basements and attics, niches and hallways, and thresholds and hearths allow us to situate events and people in spatial relations that dramatically express their relative importance. The houses we live in form our sense of space. The basic English "hall and parlor" construction that dominated middle-class domestic architecture in England and the United States from the late Renaissance into the eighteenth century located the room with the hearth at the center of a structure that could be elaborated and expanded outward in any direction without losing its "center." The logic of this simple, functional style not only had pragmatic rationale and practical effects but also contributed to shaping domestic activity and notions of privacy, intimacy, and comfort. Space, in any case, is never neutral; it is filled with ideologies.

The ideologies attaching to the design of domestic space are public and political as well as personal and psychological. Dolores Hayden, in her study of housing and family life in the United States, claims that "vernacular house forms are economic diagrams of the reproduction of the human race; they are also aesthetic essays on the meaning of life within a particular culture, its joys and rituals, its superstitions and stigmas. House forms cannot be separated from their physical and social contexts."[6] Similarly, the noted contemporary architect Christopher Alexander laments that "in almost all present-day forms of housing production, the public land or common land is controlled by public agencies remote from the people who will actually live there and use it" and that the bureaucratic process by which land for housing is laid out "in its nature, precludes any possible human feeling." The result is abstract arrangements such as the rigid grid—a "mechanical and abstract array of houses, independent of human social groups, with no congruent social structure."[7]

Just as home design became a focal point for debates over theology, pedagogy, and theories of health, so it also became a subject of political debate and a means of articulating political philosophies. In the United States the ideal of a self-contained and self-sufficient house, a simple, sturdy articulation of individualism and industry, early gained ascendancy over the ideal of a well-planned and structured town as notions of democracy and individualism won out over more collectively focused utopian visions. Thomas Jefferson, for instance, whom Hayden calls "the first mainstream American political theorist to attempt a schematic spatial representation of a national ideal of democracy," favored the family farm, rather than the model village, as the basic political unit.[8] Utopian experiments in collectivism have consistently failed in an environment where "independent," "self-reliant," and "self-sufficient" have been the watchwords of respectability and even heroism. The emphasis Thomas Jefferson and other early architects in this country placed on classical style had much to do with their political ideology, which envisioned the adoption of classical models for American life.

The quest for a style appropriate to the new country and its ideals was quite self-conscious, especially in the erection of public buildings in the postrevolutionary decades. The American virtue of independence idealized in the image of the settler was later transformed into new terms: home ownership became the essential symbol of an independent life. In the 1830s building and loan associations began to thrive; they gained considerable political power in the latter half of the century when the ideal of home ownership became a matter of political pride. Insofar as residences were public, they, too, were subject to ideological scrutiny. The campaign in the 1850s to restore George Washington's home at Mt. Vernon as a national monument and symbol met with hot debate because it included slave quarters and was therefore considered an inappropriate symbol of the union. Moreover, Mt. Vernon bespoke an aristocratic way of life inimical to northern, more egalitarian sensibilities.

These sensibilities were reflected at that time in the idiosyncrasies of utopian communities inventing new styles of communal life. Some communities were more successful, rational, and practical than others. In Shaker and Mennonite communities architecture bore a direct relationship to the practical needs of farming and to doctrinal constraints on sexual practices and child-raising. In the more loosely organized communities such as Fruitlands or Brook Farm, physical structures suffered rather comically at the hands of impractical idealists such as Bronson Alcott. Brook Farm's hybrid character was typical: it was a cross between a cooperative-operative and a joint-stock company, an effort to unite "intellectual and manual labor," and, as Hawthorne put it, "a day dream, and yet a fact."[9] The affectionate irony of his fictionalization of utopian community life in *The Blithedale Romance* is another conspicuous testimony to the ambivalences underlying American attempts to erect the structures of practical life on idealistic foundations. The architectural historian David Handlin calls the utopian communities "a direct attempt to make a physical framework for a new social order"; yet he also points out that one of the many causes of their eventual disintegration was an insufficient understanding of the technical aspects of building and maintaining the physical plant as well as naïveté about the politics of shared space.[10]

But utopian communities have always been somewhat anomalous. Since the early nineteenth century the separate, single-family dwelling has continued to be the dominant material and political objective for the upwardly mobile middle classes. Multiple-unit housing has been consigned largely to the lower classes, shelter for the "huddled masses," who presumably occupied flats rapidly degenerating into slums only as long as was necessary to build up the capital needed to acquire land to farm and build on. The "tenant houses" of urban workers in the mid-nineteenth century that gave urbanization and multiple-unit housing a bad name were notorious breeding grounds of infectious diseases, had no plumbing, and were miserable places where, as one journalist put it, "many an owner would hesitate about quartering his horse."[11]

At the same time architecture became a favorite form of conspicuous consumption for those in whose hands wealth was steadily accumulating. Henry James comments with disdain of the New Jersey suburbs in *The American Scene* on "their candid look of having cost as much as they knew how." Personifying those grotesquely opulent edifices, he writes, "We are only installments, symbols, stopgaps. . . . Expensive as we are, we have nothing to do with continuity, responsibility, transmission, and don't in the least care what becomes of us after we have served our present purpose."[12]

To avoid any association with images of communal housing while representing a radical diminishment of the late-nineteenth-century architectural aspirations of the nouveaux riches, the cookie-cutter suburbs that began to overtake the landscape after World War II with their tiny plots of land, tightly controlled spaces, and visible capitulation to the depersonalization of mass consumer culture were marketed as miniature versions of the "estates" of the landed gentry with whom home owners still aspired to be somehow identified. Bourgeois, capitalist values were built into these standardized, superficially stylized dwellings, where private space, albeit limited, was marketed as a primary desirable feature and planned in the form of a yard for each dwelling at the expense of shared public spaces like commons. Hayden describes Levittown, one of the prototypical early postwar developments, in these terms:

> Levitt's client was the returning veteran, the beribboned male war hero who wanted his wife to stay home. Women in Levittown were expected to be too busy tending their children to care about a paying job. The Cape Cod houses recalled traditional American colonial housing (although they were very awkwardly proportioned). They emphasized privacy. Large-scale plans for public space and social services were sacrificed to private acreage. . . . Levitt liked to think of the husband as a weekend do-it-yourself builder and gardener: "No man who owns his house and lot can be a Communist. He has too much to do," asserted Levitt in 1948.[13]

The focus on house-building or home ownership as a completion of the rites of passage into maturity—and, more recently, on the mortgage as a token of stability—is still with us despite the increasing percentage of the population that cannot afford housing, let alone houses. As Tom Wolfe sardonically reminds us, the old ideals, truncated now to the point of absurdity, survive in comic-pathetic form in suburban design with "cute and antiquey touches" and cheaply stylized facades that reproduce elements of colonial, Gothic, or European architecture out of context, aesthetic choices governed neither by necessity nor context nor informed taste.[14]

American architects, as well as writers, have expressed a certain "anxiety of influence" inherent in a value system that sets great store in originality as a measure of individualism. In his romantic manifesto, *The Natural House*, Frank Lloyd Wright claims, in good Emersonian fashion, to "draw inspiration from Nature herself" and to be "beholden to no man for the look of anything." Borrowing his rhetoric wholesale from the transcendentalists, he declaims, "Textbook for me? 'The book of creation.' No longer need any more to be a wanderer among the objects and traditions of the past, picking and choosing his way by the personal idiosyncrasy of taste, guided only by personal predilection. From this hell I had been saved. The world lost an eclectic and gained an interpreter. If I did not like the gods now I could make better ones."[15]

Wright's romantic approach to architectural ideas such as organicism borrows heavily from a fundamentally romantic idea of the relation between nature and culture that pretends to dismiss tradition while relying heavily on it—a posture readily recognizable to any reader of Thoreau or Emerson. Developing ideas similarly based on metaphysical notions of wholeness and integrity, Buckminster Fuller (a descendant of Margaret Fuller of the New England transcendentalists) in his later work develops a vision of the "Architect as World Planner" and calls for "total thinking," "comprehensive designing," and "fluid geography," all notions deeply grounded in a romantic cosmology that has translated directly into orthodoxies of style in the design of lives and texts as well as of buildings.[16]

The list of novelists who have concerned themselves directly with house and home is long. Cooper writes about houses in all his novels, including an 1838 novel, *Home as Found*; in it an American returns from Europe to find American houses appallingly pretentious, their ostentation signifying a fall from the democratic values of the home owners' forebears. Stowe's *Uncle Tom's Cabin* deliberately uses dwellings as tropes for social categories, and her book intensifies the debate about the nature of the American home. Later writers point out that even Uncle Tom had a decent, simple, clean dwelling, far superior to the slum dwellings in the North. W. L. G. Smith writes a subsequent novel in which Uncle Tom escapes to Buffalo and dies regretting that he left his comfortable cabin, which "never seemed half so dear before."[17]

It is with the transcendentalists that we can most easily begin to examine the symbolic appropriation of the house by American writers and its place in the Emersonian, romantic, transcendental tradition. This is where the present analysis begins, with Thoreau's *Walden*, a long meditation on building and domestic life that incorporates into those practical matters virtually the whole body of accumulated American philosophy, winnowed and honed from generations of Puritan Protestantism, the pragmatism of the early settlers, and the politics of Jacksonian democracy. Though the complications of life-style are reflected in houses of any period, I begin with *Walden* not only because that work is as explicit as any before or since in its allegorization of the house but also because Thoreau's pleas for simplicity of design and functionality have about them something profoundly, typically American: an urgent fear of vitiation by elaboration, a dread of the kinds of overdevelopment and overcomplication that would make civilized people lose touch with primal, vital, fundamental sources of experience. The puritanical impulse—the call to purification and "pruning"—is no more apparent in any Puritan document than in Thoreau's account of his sojourn at Walden Pond.

Both Thoreau's ambivalences and his practical ideals, like Emerson's metaphysics, appear again and again in American writing and most particularly in the way his successors have used the house in the same allegorical fashion—as an index not only of civilization and culture but of moral rectitude and integrity, or the failure of those virtues. Whitman, for instance, who always regretted his father's move from rural Long Island to Brooklyn, idealizes his childhood home in his poetry and less widely known fiction. His deservedly unknown 1842 novel,

Franklin Evans; Or, The Inebriate, attributes the downfall of the young hero to his leaving his country home for the wicked city. In "Song of the Broad Axe" Whitman writes nostalgically about "the shape of the planks of the family home, and home of the friendly parents and children," and he reiterates this general theme and tone in two articles entitled "Wicked Architecture" and "Decent Homes for Working Men."[18]

In numerous works by Poe, Hawthorne, and James we see a conflation of two traditions, the puritanical and the Gothic, the one essentially moral or religious, the other psychological and secular, though the latter may be seen to represent a "transposition" of the former. In both of these traditions the house is invested with far more than literal significance and in varying degrees is personified, animated, or even anthropomorphized. In a number of Poe's stories the house not only represents the labyrinthine character of the human psyche but also replicates in grotesque fashion the anatomy of the human body. Rooms as enclosures function as womb, brain, or viscera. The house can become everything from the visible hand of destiny to the self-portrait of the builder. All three of these writers represent the house as a mask and symbol of the psyche and a reflection and source of identity, and in these writers the old polarities, paradoxes, and ambivalences attaching to the tensions between material life and spiritual life are revisited.

For Hawthorne, James, and Howells, moreover, the house serves as a document of social history and source of familial and social identity, as, later, Edith Wharton's New York brownstones with their detailed interiors minutely encode the fine distinctions of class and culture among their owners. In Wharton's *The Age of Innocence* and *The House of Mirth* houses are symbols of success and status, structures that reflect and maintain a fixed social order and prescribed patterns of behavior. Cather's novels depict houses ambiguously as castle and prison, refuge and tomb; her novels reveal a variety of homes ranging from the immigrants' sod house on the Nebraska prairie to southwestern adobes to the solidly middle-class three-story clapboard home in *The Professor's House*.

Building in general can be called a "male" metaphor for the activity of writing. Wharton and Cather, among other women writers, manage to synthesize the concerns of architecture, interior decorating, and housekeeping as integral and complementary activities both in their literal sense and as applied to the activity of writing. Later women writers revisit the traditional conflicts about home ownership and freedom from a different, specifically female, point of view. Morrison's *Beloved* and Robinson's *Housekeeping* thus present old conflicts over home ownership and domestic life from startlingly different angles of vision and bring to bear on those questions shaped by postwar feminist and ethnic revisionism.

The Great Gatsby and Absalom, Absalom! both bring us back to the house as symbol of the self, but in new ways. The idea of the self-made man is both reiterated and subverted in these novels, as is the idea of the house as an essential part of that process of self-making. The houses in both books are monuments to the magnitude and persistence of ambitious dreams as well as signs of misplaced aspirations and ultimate defeat. In Steinbeck's *Cannery Row* we come to the notion of "housing," a modern word and in certain ways a modern phenomenon. In O'Neill, Cheever, and Didion, we have examples of "dream houses" in which the dream turns out to be illusion and the houses are a symbol of what Eliot called the "hope for the wrong things" that Americans are wont to recognize in their own defeats.[19]

Finally, we have evolved in recent years a literature of homelessness or rootlessness, where absence of house and home becomes the significant, defining situation of the story. The westward movement of the 1840s, the closing of the frontier in the 1880s, and the suburbanization and housing crises of the 1950s and 1960s produced images of homelessness, rootlessness, and instability in literature, wherein houses became symbols of certain classes or segments of society. Kerouac's *On the Road* perhaps most graphically depicts the endpoint of the trajectory defined by *Walden* and later by *Huckleberry Finn*: the antihero, a nouveau Puritan in his way, again finds himself marginalized and living, this time in a car, outside the houses of the civilized, stabilized, and, it is implied, anesthetized citizens of a too-comfortable and complacent society. The postwar suburbs of Cheever, Updike, Marilyn French, W. D. Weatherill, and others similarly articulate a closely defined and entrapping way of life in which the house is the public face that must be kept in repair whatever the moral disarray within. Among other things, the suburban life these writers depict embodies our profound, shared ambivalence about civilization.

The equation of civilization with loss of innocence, corruption, effeminacy, and diminishment runs like a bass note through our literature. Very quickly the houses we build around ourselves become prisons, just as do the social structures, laws, and codes by which we regulate our lives and modify our freedom. We are still struggling over our own definitions of freedom, which insofar as they emphasize Thoreauvian autonomy and separateness from social constraint involve us in moral, political, and psychological double binds.

In the following chapters I provide what I think of as a series of "house tours" through some of our most prominent houses of fiction. In examining each of these texts, I have focused on (1) the architectural environment in which the fiction was written, including, where relevant, some description of the writer's own home as a context for the domestic environments he or she creates for characters; (2) the specific development and uses of the house as a trope within the particular work; and (3) the way in which the text mirrors the house it describes. It is my hope that a look at these habitations of the imagination will reframe and reveal some of the guiding questions and creative tensions that still motivate and shape the evolution of life-styles and shared American dreams about how to live with one another.

1

WALDEN
A Manifesto in Wood and Stone

Despite its claim to the status of nonfiction, and despite the fact that it was published later than some of the works examined in the coming chapters, *Walden* is an appropriate starting place for an inquiry into the role of houses in American fiction because the little house at Walden Pond is, in a way, Thoreau's "supreme fiction"—an embodiment of an ideal and an idea, a visible text articulating and illustrating a philosophy whose roots lie deep in American Protestantism and whose branches have penetrated every area of American thought.[1] In its unorthodox form, its radical reassessment of the priorities of domestic life, and its articulation of the defining tensions of American culture with respect to material life, *Walden* has provided a model for many of Thoreau's literary descendants. No American writer could think about houses in a morally neutral way after Thoreau invested them with such profound and inclusive significance.

Under the rubric of a philosophical inquiry into the proper nature of human shelter, the book presents a rambling autobiographical chronicle of building and habitation that resembles nothing so much as an expanded sermon, complete with text, exegesis, and application. Thoreau leans heavily on a transcendental notion of the world as an endless crystalline replication of structures: elaborate analogies are drawn among the house, the life of the man within it, and the text that man writes. A house, as any architect will verify, *is* a text with its own peculiar grammar, syntax, and way of communicating and generating meaning. Thoreau's development of these simple but pregnant ideas provides a point of departure for understanding their appropriation by his literary successors.

The houses of early nineteenth-century Massachusetts that were the foils against which Thoreau measured the simplicity of his cabin at Walden Pond were by most standards neither ostentatious nor overfurnished. A tour of Concord today, which may include a number of the houses Thoreau frequented, might lead one to wonder what elicited his hue and cry against overadornment, redundancy, and loss of simplicity. It was not only in the great houses of Beacon Hill but in these humbler clapboard dwellings that Thoreau saw signs of social and moral degeneracy, love of superfluousness and show, and signs of unhealthy materialism.

A recent reading of *Walden* as a parody of the architectural "pattern books" that were very popular at the time of his writing makes a persuasive argument that one of Thoreau's multiple and complicated objectives in the book was to offer a scathing response and challenge to the claims of Andrew Jackson Downing and his followers for the morally instructive value of rightly designed domestic architecture.[2] In the years Thoreau was living at Walden and subsequently writing about it, Downing and lesser-known architects were popularizing moralistic guidebooks for the building and decoration of dwellings supposed to inculcate Christian virtues and values. Downing himself wrote an article that appeared in *Horticulturalist*, entitled "Moral Influence of Good Houses." Elsewhere he claimed, "ABSOLUTE BEAUTY lies in the expression, in material forms, of those ideas of perfection which are universal in their application. We find them in nature as well as in art"; he identified those ideas as "PROPORTION, SYMMETRY, VARIETY, HARMONY, AND UNITY."[3] These values, he believed, informed, infused, and emanated from the structures he had designed and prescribed in the pattern books Thoreau evidently found so pretentious and misleading. Much of Thoreau's rather extreme argument for a return to primitive life in *Walden* is put into more comprehensible perspective when understood as an answer to Downing's encomiums to civilized life, such as the following passage from *The Architecture of Country Houses*: "A good house . . . is a powerful means of civilization. . . . So long as men are forced to dwell in log huts and follow a hunter's life, we must not be surprised at lynch law and the use of the bowie knife. But, when smiling lawns and tasteful cottages begin to embellish a country, we know that order and culture are established" (v-vi).

Thoreau himself rarely separates aesthetic from moral issues, though his conclusions about what constitutes the good life almost diametrically oppose Downing's notions, which Thoreau regards as sentimental, effete, and dangerous. From the beginning of *Walden* it is clear that domestic architecture brings the two value dimensions together with an explicitness that serves his didactic purposes perfectly.

The first sentence of *Walden* establishes a three-point analogy among book, house, and narrator: "When I wrote the following pages, or rather the bulk of them, I lived alone, in the woods, a mile from any neighbor, in a house which I had built myself, on the shore of Walden Pond, in Concord, Massachusetts, and earned my living by the labor of my hands only" (3). Building the cabin and writing the book symbolically reiterate the simultaneous enterprise of designing and defining the author's life: "simple and sincere" statements of a "simple and sincere" man. Thoreau's biographer William Howarth views the whole body of Thoreau's work in light of the author's frequent architectural metaphors and writes of the cabin itself that "in all his days Henry Thoreau had not built a piece of writing as sound and tight as this small house. The whole process of construction—a place, a plan, a set of new uses for old materials—resembled his compositions, but here the form and function were consonant."[4] The book, like the cabin, unites a rustic style with a sophisticated and highly articulated transcendental philosophy. Like Wordsworth's, Thoreau's rustic persona is a self-conscious and indeed artful attempt to return to certain childlike simplicities, but for spiritual and political purposes not at all simple: "I wanted to live deep and suck out all the marrow of life, to live so sturdily and Spartan-like as to put to rout all that was not life, to cut a broad swath and shave close, to drive life into a corner, and reduce it to its lowest terms" (81).

The appropriateness of the cabin as an embodiment of values becomes clear the moment those values are named. Nothing but a house could more adequately and simply demonstrate the importance of economy, simplicity, and autonomy ("I built it myself"); individualism ("Wherever I sat, there I might live, and the landscape radiated from me accordingly"); integrity ("a house whose inside is as open and manifest as a bird's nest"); sincerity ("a house which you have got into when you have opened the outside door, and the ceremony is over"); closeness to nature ("The house is still but a sort of porch at the entrance of a burrow"); organicism ("What of architectural beauty I now see, I know has gradually grown from within outward, out of the necessities and character of the indweller"); or the conviction that the material is always a manifestation of the spiritual. "Most men," the writer observes, "appear never to have considered what a house is," implying that it, like all the material world, is a thing to be seen into and beyond. The building is a philosophical statement that in its medium of wood and stone sidesteps the complexities of language that "building" his book enmeshes him in.

The governing idea in *Walden* is that the material is always a manifestation of and a conduit to the spiritual—a construction of that relation that challenges old iconoclastic notions of the material world as a source of temptation and illusion. "To be a philosopher," Thoreau writes, "is not merely to have subtle thoughts, nor even to found a school, but so to love wisdom as to live according to its trust. It is to solve some of the problems of life, not only theoretically, but practically" (13). The house built with his own hands is just such a practical solution to the problems of life and a means to understand them. It is intended as a kind of sacrament—"an outward and visible sign of inward and spiritual things"—a vehicle for forming the self, and a self-portrait. Furthermore, the building of a house is a practical education—and Thoreau's house at Walden was not his first lesson in the construction of houses. As a young man he had worked as handyman for the Emersons, and in the fall of 1844 he helped his father build a new house west of the Concord railroad tracks for which Thoreau's mother had chosen the site and drawn up plans.

So in the opening pages of *Walden* the writer asks us to recognize and contemplate the house as the fulfillment of a pedagogical and spiritual agenda. Building his own house is a step in his training as a philosopher—a practical exercise in problem-solving and an attempt to integrate material and spiritual life, which are so prone to the kind of fatal disjuncture that produces the many social, political, and spiritual ills Thoreau identifies in his frequent jeremiads. Howarth takes Thoreau's own notion of his purposes a step further, pointing out that "the building of a house at Walden Pond is a positive, constructive act that liberates Thoreau from youthful solipsism. He borrows his tools, recycles old materials, builds from a foundation upward. The house is an ascending form; it . . . grows in stages that are persistently faithful to the indweller's character. His past and future selves are not contradictory, they fulfill each other: 'We belong to the community' " (94–95).

Ultimately the cabin, having served its purpose, falls away like a mollusk's shell. It is not the cabin but the kind of life engendered in such a dwelling that matters. Once achieved and fully embraced, that way of life can sustain itself in other places, having become internalized; the outer structures of daily life shape the patterns of the psyche and the grooves of habit. The house is a prop, or an aid, in a spiritual journey whose end is to rise above dependency on setting and circumstance. Thoreau's deep iconoclasm thus extends finally even to the work of his own hands. Eventually, he leaves his cabin, having taught and been taught by it, having "other lives to live."

Like the cabin, the book produces an impression of organic simplicity—almost of haphazardness at first glance—until the details of construction come under the scrutiny of an attentive reader. Characteristically, Thoreau challenges his readers to abandon conventional notions of appropriate form and to contemplate the implications of his radically unconventional textual strategies. In *Walden* temporal and spatial dimensions interpenetrate. The four seasons of the year, like the four walls of the cabin, define and encompass a private but complete universe. House and text are both microcosms, closed systems within which all of life is symbolically contained and signified. The "breathing room" that the one-room cabin is designed to create is reflected in the text as well, where themes interpenetrate and ideas are not obtrusively partitioned into discrete categories. Just as the single open room allows for interpenetration of private and public life, a blending of domesticity with intellectual and social pursuits, so the loosely structured chapters of the book allow such intermingling of various modes of discourse, and we move easily, with no thresholds to cross, from the anecdotal to the analytic to the contemplative. Our attention is drawn first to the interior and then to the exterior life, the intimate relation of the two always emphasized, thereby underscoring an ideal of absolute equilibrium, equivalence, and permeability between the outer man and the inner, between life within and life without, so that the conscious life might ultimately come full circle and attain the simplicities of the unconscious natural world.

Thoreau initially focuses his ruminations on a question of practical necessity—what does a person need to live? Anything not necessary is suspect: "Most of the luxuries, and many of the so-called comforts of life, are not only not indispensable, but positive hindrances to the elevation of mankind" (13). Here, for the first of many times in the course of his reflections, the writer encapsulates his Christian asceticism in an aphorism that points to an inflexible opposition between creature comforts and spiritual life. His rhetoric is reminiscent of Jesus' oft-reiterated, "You have heard it said . . . but I say unto you . . . ," a formula that overturned a conventional moral precept and replaced it with a paradox positing a "higher" and more complex moral standard. This is typical of Thoreau's style, in which the resolution of apparent contradictions, the reconstruction of opposites as complements, and the inversion of conventional formulas figure largely.

Whereas Thoreau the rationalist builds his house to meet the natural needs he outlines in his disquisition on necessity (a one-room, ten-by-fifteen-foot wood and brick structure with a tree as king post), Thoreau the ascetic seems to squirm even under those material necessities he allows himself, perhaps because he is not yet at the point of extreme purification of desire and possession that it took for Jesus to say, "The foxes have holes and the birds of the air have nests, but the Son of Man hath not where to lay his head" (Matthew 8:20). In the interests of "elevation" Thoreau attempts to establish a definition of necessity that is useful as a rule of life. The design of his house, the choice of his furniture, and the establishment of his daily routine are all efforts to put that standard to a test. He considers, in turn, whether food, clothing, and shelter, those things we have traditionally taken to be basic necessities, are really necessary. In doing so, he attempts to expose the moral slippage that treats luxury as necessity. "As for a Shelter," he writes, "I will not deny that this is now a necessary of life, though there are instances of men having done without it for long periods in colder countries than this. . . . Probably, man did not live long on the earth without discovering the convenience which there is in a house, the domestic comforts, which phrase may have originally signified the satisfactions of the house more than of the family" (24). The house itself, being a material thing, has to be justified as a necessity in order to be admitted as a legitimate part of the paraphernalia necessary for his experiment with life.

Having established the necessity of shelter, he traces a brief history of housing, from "roofs of palm leaves, of bark and boughs, of linen woven and stretched, of grass and straw, of boards and shingles, of stone and tiles," concluding, "at last, we know not what it is to live in the open air, and our lives are domestic in more senses than we think. . . . It would be well, perhaps, if we were to spend more of our days and nights without any obstruction between us and the celestial bodies. . . . Birds do not sing in caves, nor do doves cherish their innocence in dovecots" (25). He grudgingly acknowledges the necessity of housing, almost pronouncing it a necessary evil. The myth of progress, the notion of civilization, the value of technological advancement, are all treated here with pointed irony, as betrayed, for example, in the word *obstruction* and in the rueful observation that birds, perhaps the freest, most poetic, and spiritual of creatures, have no such obstructions between themselves and the "celestial bodies." At one point the writer fondly recalls, "I found myself suddenly neighbor to the birds; not by having imprisoned one, but having caged myself near them" (77). Thoreau's romantic fancy reaches a new poetic pitch here, which is tempered with characteristic, almost comic haste by the next passage, where poet and philosopher turn historian and craftsman: "However, if one designs to construct a dwelling-house, it behooves him to exercise a little Yankee shrewdness, lest after all he find himself in a workhouse, a labyrinth without a clue, a museum, an almshouse, a prison, or a splendid mausoleum instead. Consider first how slight a shelter is absolutely necessary" (25).

If we must build houses, he reasons, let us minimize the offense against nature. The examples that follow of what forms of shelter are "absolutely necessary" border on the ludicrous if taken to be literally prescriptive but serve to expand the spectrum on which he seeks to locate a definition of necessity: the "skin bags" of the Laplanders, the wigwams of the Penobscot Indians, Adam and Eve's bower, the caves of prehistoric men who suddenly found a handy solution to cold in the hollow of a rock. The more extreme they become, the more vividly these examples of "practical solutions" to the problem of how to live serve to measure the complexities and, ultimately, corruptions of civilized life.

The dangers of perversion increase, Thoreau suggests, in proportion to the complexities of life that come to bear on the design of our houses. Labyrinth, museum, almshouse, prison, and mausoleum constitute an inventory of grotesque caricatures that houses might resemble if their purpose is not rightly understood. Certainly the homes even of the wealthiest New England patricians of the time were hardly labyrinthine except by the severe standard of architectural simplicity Thoreau adopted when he declared that the whole of the home and the life within it ought to be apparent on crossing the threshold. In the chapter called "House-Warming" he describes such an ideal house:

> Of enduring materials, and without gingerbread work, which shall still consist of only one room, a vast, rude, substantial, primitive hall, without ceiling or plastering, with bare rafters and purlins supporting a sort of lower heaven over one's head . . . where you can see all the treasures of the house at one view, and everything hangs upon its peg that a man should use . . . a house whose inside is as open and manifest as a bird's nest. (218–219)

Such architectural ideals are borrowed directly from moral categories: the openness of a dwelling without partitions represents a kind of honesty; the absence of any unnecessary decoration, humility and simplicity; the enduring materials, moral toughness; and the relative inattention to comforts, asceticism. The "vastness" is important as well, being an attempt to approximate as closely as an enclosing structure can the open spaces of the out-of-doors. The one complaint the writer ventures to utter about his own little house is that a place so small does not lend itself to "great thoughts," which need room for expansion: "One inconvenience I sometimes experienced in so small a house, the difficulty of getting to a sufficient distance from my guest when we began to utter the big thoughts in big words. You want room for your thoughts to get into sailing trim and run a course or two before they make their port. . . . Our sentences wanted room to unfold and form their columns in the interval" (127–128).

This genuinely hospitable desire for good company and conversation runs throughout the pages of *Walden,* counterbalancing the paeans to the solitary life and the general deprecations of civilized society. While the ascetic eschews as excesses what most would deem necessities, he retains the hope that visitors will come and share his solitary and simple pleasures with him, on his terms, claiming that real contact may be enhanced, rather than inhibited, by his style of entertaining. Thus, his hospitality constitutes a challenge to his visitors: "I had three chairs in my house; one for solitude, two for friendship, three for society. When visitors came in larger and unexpected numbers there was but the third chair for them all, but they generally economized the room by standing up. It is surprising how many great men and women a small house will contain" (127).

Several times the writer wistfully observes that his challenge goes largely unmet. Visitors come infrequently: "There too, as everywhere, I sometimes expected the Visitor who never comes" (242).[5] Thoreau's ideal visitor is a seeker; Thoreau is not situated so as to be dropped in on by the casual passerby but must be sought out by one explicitly desiring what simple goods he may find there. Like Thoreau's other exercises of virtue, hospitality is as stringently held to his own terms as it is magnanimous within those terms; the visitor must come two miles out of town, thereby meeting Thoreau more than halfway.

In any case the ideal house would simply be a perching place; real living, the best living, takes place outdoors, as close to nature as it is possible to dwell. "My best room," he continues, "my withdrawing room, always ready for company, on whose carpet the sun rarely fell, was the pine wood behind my house" (128). Far from museum or mausoleum, this house would resemble more closely a kind of all-purpose outhouse designed to service bodily needs for food, rest, and shelter and to put as little obstruction between the indwellers and the ground beneath their feet as possible. For separation from nature is to be feared: it vitiates a man's powers, which Thoreau believes to be derived from direct contact with the earth and sky. As our lives grow more remote from those vital sources, they become less real, less vital. The literalness with which he espouses this notion can hardly be overstated. Even our language, he maintains, is only alive and effective by virtue of its connection with the earth:

> It would seem as if the very language of our parlors would lose all its nerve and degenerate into *palaver* wholly, our lives pass at such remoteness from its symbols, and its metaphors and tropes are necessarily so far fetched, through slides and dumb-waiters, as it were; in other words, the parlor is so far from the kitchen and workshop. . . . As if only the savage dwelt near enough to Nature and Truth to borrow a trope from them. (220)

Some of the stately Concord homes Thoreau frequented, like Channing's or Emerson's, doubtless did resemble museums, filled as they were with relics, mostly in the form of books and heirlooms. The stable old families that had lived in and around Concord for several generations had accumulated possessions in excess of those usable in daily life and had kept them for their sentimental value or as measures of status. Such useless objects, like needless ornament, were to this zealous iconoclast an offense against the virtues of reason, order, and simplicity.

Nor was the private dwelling to become, as he put it, an "almshouse." His charity was cultivated in an atmosphere of guarded solitude, a world of established boundaries and clear bargains in which hospitality was freely given but on sternly established terms. As a sacred refuge from the world of commerce and society, the walls of the home were not to be indiscriminately permeable to society; they were to be a protective barrier from the demands of social intercourse. The idiosyncratic selectivity of Thoreau's own charity and hospitality were regarded rather wryly by his contemporaries.

The ways in which a house may become a prison are manifold, and Thoreau's recognition of the imprisoning qualities of domestic life prefigure a good many women writers who find their homes to be prisons and who locate the source of their problems precisely where Thoreau does—in the perversities of a civilized life whose artificial structures are no longer grounded in the balances of nature but in an artificial hierarchy of capitalistic values. That Thoreau's list of perverse analogs for houses should end with a "mausoleum" is fitting, for the logical conclusion is that a badly designed, ill-conceived house can ultimately destroy by suffocation the life impulses of the people within it, thereby fatally impinging on their freedom of movement and discourse.

To counter these horrifying possibilities Thoreau proposes a solution that in its extremity and ludicrousness serves to establish as wide a spectrum as possible of practical solutions to his philosophical problems:

> I used to see a large box by the railroad, six feet long by three wide, in which the laborers locked up their tools at night; and it suggested to me that every man who was hard pushed might get such a one for a dollar, and, having bored a few auger holes in it, to admit the air at least, get into it when it rained and at night, and hook down the lid, and have freedom in his love, and in his soul be free. . . . You could sit up as late as you pleased, and, whenever you got up, go abroad without any landlord or house-lord dogging you for rent. Many a man is harassed to death to pay the rent of a larger and more luxurious box who would not have frozen to death in such a box as this. (26)

Characteristically, the writer constructs his argument on ludicrous juxtapositions and reductions so extreme that they caricature, lending humor to his point while sharpening it. But the equation of freedom with dispossession invites serious contemplation of the relation between the two.

The "nothing but" formula strips the idea of house down to its bare bones in exactly the fashion Thoreau has attempted to carry out in the design of his cabin. Typically, he localizes his example to bring it closer to home: "A comfortable house for a rude and hardy race, that lived mostly out of doors, was once made here almost entirely out of such materials as Nature furnished ready to their hands." He goes on to cite an early English settler's description of local Indian wigwams that concludes, "I have often lodged in their wigwams, and found them as warm as the best English houses" (26). Thoreau seems to feel obliged to apologize for any degree to which his rude dwelling exceeds the comforts of those wigwams; he is uncomfortable with his own concessions to creature comforts even to the addition of plaster to seal his walls: "My house never pleased my eye so much after it was plastered, though I was obliged to confess that it was more comfortable" (217–218).

By way of contrast to this severe standard, Thoreau goes on to consider the ordinary comforts of a middle-class American:

> An annual rent of from twenty-five to a hundred dollars . . . entitles him to the benefit of the improvements of centuries, spacious apartments, clean paint and paper, Rumford fireplace, back plastering, Venetian blinds, copper pump, spring lock, a commodious cellar, and many other things. But how happens it that he who is said to enjoy these things is so commonly a *poor* civilized man, while the savage, who has them not, is rich as a savage? If it is asserted that civilization is a real advance in the condition of man . . . it must be shown that it has produced better dwellings without making them more costly; and the cost of a thing is the amount of what I will call life which is required to be exchanged for it, immediately or in the long run. (27–28)

He deplores the exchange of so much "life" for the ownership and upkeep of houses. When the structure that enables and protects becomes a burden, a set of obligations, something that consumes rather than enhances freedom, peace of mind, and time for contemplation, it has become an evil. A person can ultimately either devote that measure of "life" to the inner dwelling place, the nurturing of soul and body, or to the house of bricks and boards "where moth and rust doth corrupt" (Matthew 6:20). In the way things have of turning from good to evil, he reasons, what is built for a good may itself become a great evil if its purposes are lost sight of:

And when the farmer has got his house, he may not be the richer but the poorer for it, and it be the house that has got him . . . and it may still be urged, for our houses are such unwieldy property that we are often imprisoned rather than housed in them. . . . I know one or two families, at least, in this town, who, for nearly a generation, have been wishing to sell their houses in the outskirts and move into the village, but have not been able to accomplish it, and only death will set them free. (30)

Once again the argument proceeds by precept, example, and application. Key ideas of freedom, true wealth, and consciousness are reasserted, as is the paradox of possession: that when it has ceased to be vigilantly purposeful, it becomes a form of dispossession. Conscious, voluntary dispossession, however, allows a man to repossess what is fundamentally his: his freedom, his time, his energy.

Thoreau's argument is deeply rooted in traditional Christian and Eastern asceticism, which reach back beyond the New England Unitarianism that formed him, and pushes to a logical extreme the transcendentalist identification with nature that was one attempt to sidestep the consequences of capitalistic Puritanism. Attention to the material world, once separated from attention to matters of the spirit, produces a dangerous imbalance that has individual as well as social and political consequences: "While civilization has been improving our houses, it has not equally improved the men who are to inhabit them. It has created palaces, but it was not so easy to create noblemen and kings" (30). The argument reiterates the body-soul dichotomy as opposition: focus on the outward material shells that house the inner life is always presumed to inhibit nurture of the life within, the soul, which is the thing of true value. Architectural ornament, therefore, is a dangerous distraction from essentials, appropriate only if it is designed and crafted by the person who is to dwell with it and can thus be "read" as an extension of that man's aesthetic impulses arising from his "true self": "Much it concerns a man, forsooth, how a few sticks are slanted over him or under him, and what colors are daubed upon his box. It would signify somewhat, if, in any earnest sense, *he* slanted them and daubed it; but the spirit having departed out of the tenant, it is of a piece with constructing his own coffin . . . and 'carpenter' is but another name for coffin-maker" (43).

This emphasis on the house as an extension of the individual soul and psyche is a grounding point for Thoreau's entire aesthetic: whatever distances or distracts a person from his essential, inner self fosters illusion and generates a false relation between self and world. Indeed, the body itself is in like fashion that part of the physical world an individual is responsible for designing and bringing into congruence with the soul: "Every man is the builder of a temple, called his body, to the god he worships, after a style purely his own, nor can he get off by hammering marble instead. We are all sculptors and painters, and our material is our own flesh and blood and bones" (199). Therefore, in order to be in right relation to the soul, the material environment we fashion around ourselves must faithfully represent and reflect the soul, so as to act as mirror and portrait: "Better paint your house your own complexion; let it turn pale or blush for you. An enterprise to improve the style of cottage architecture!" (43). (He often reiterates this relation in simple analogies: "I withdrew yet farther into my shell, and endeavored to keep a bright fire both within my house and within my breast" [223–224].) The material environment ought in all its particulars to represent an extension of the fundamental natural relation between man and nature—to reproduce faithfully the ecological economy that exists in nature. Aesthetics are therefore always tied to utility: what is unnecessary is inappropriate, and only what is appropriate is beautiful. Thoreau describes his own house as "a sort of crystallization around me" that "reacted on the builder" (77).

This belief in the formative influence of the material environment, the reciprocity of effect between man and the world he fashions around himself, binds Thoreau's aesthetics inseparably to his morality. The house that is too far removed in form and function from the lives lived in it, that has ceased to represent the conscious values and priorities of its inhabitants, and that has become an end in itself rather than a means to enhance "life" can distract a man from his true purposes.

Thoreau's reference to noblemen and kings gives his point an ironic turn as well, for nobility and kingship are designations that attach to outward and accidental attributes and have to be

stripped away to reach the "essential man." Civilization has created noblemen and kings, but not such as deserve the name.
And it has conspired to obscure the relation between a man and
his work or between work and its just rewards. Building should
be at the hand of the dweller so that the value of the act is not
lost in indirection:

> There is some of the same fitness in a man's building his own house
> that there is in a bird's building its own nest. Who knows but if men
> constructed their dwellings with their own hands, and provided
> food for themselves and families simply and honestly enough, the
> poetic faculty would be universally developed, as birds universally
> sing when they are so engaged? But alas! we do like cowbirds and
> cuckoos, which lay their eggs in nests which other birds have built,
> and cheer no traveller with their chattering and unmusical notes.
> Shall we forever resign the pleasure of construction to the carpen-
> ter? What does architecture amount to in the experience of the
> mass of men? I never in all my walks came across a man engaged in
> so simple and natural an occupation as building his house. (41)

This last observation introduces a disquisition on the evils of
division of labor as something that fragments and therefore de-
stroys human integrity. The notion that architecture and house-
building are "simple and natural" occupations falls strangely on
the ears of a modern audience, as indeed it must have even in
Thoreau's time. Specialized expertise, he implies, tends to viti-
ate initiative to the point where men do not trust themselves to
care for their own needs. Thoreau's distrust of specialists is like
his distrust of the other aspects of the civilizing process he has
mentioned: they are a manifestation of the disintegration of
human functions, so that a man is finally incapable of independence, or even of true interdependence, but is reduced to servile dependence by his own cultivated ignorance of processes
that ought simply to be extensions of ancient instinctive drives
like rooting and nesting. Thoreau waxes sarcastic on the subject, suggesting that even the best architects are not worthy
of their calling because, being specialized, their work is not
"whole" or true:

> True, there are architects so called in this country, and I have heard
> of one at least possessed with the idea of making architectural or-
> naments have a core of truth, a necessity, and hence a beauty, as if

it were a revelation to him. All very well perhaps from his point of
view, but only a little better than the common dilettantism. A sentimental reformer in architecture, he began at the cornice, not at
the foundation. It was only how to put a core of truth within the
ornaments, . . . and not how the inhabitant, the indweller, might
build truly within and without, and let the ornaments take care of
themselves. (41)

When the man who builds the house is not the man who inhabits it, a disjuncture has already occurred that militates against
integrity and initiates a system of inequity based on economic
mediation between maker and product, between work and reward. "The mason who finishes the cornice of the palace returns at night perchance to a hut not so good as a wigwam" (31).

In this last bitter observation the issue of inequity of housing
arises explicitly for the first time; houses again appear as an index of the evils and imbalances of civilized life. By a simple
technique of juxtaposition of opposites, the palace and the hut
establish a spectrum of inequities that indicts the democratic
ideal. Furthermore, such inequities generate a false sense of
relative values that deceives men into desiring what they do not
need: "Most men appear never to have considered what a house
is, and are actually though needlessly poor all their lives because they think that they must have such a one as their neighbors have" (31–32). Houses introduce competition, and competition alienates men not only from one another but from
themselves and a true relation to their own needs, so that they
can no longer distinguish what is appropriate to their character
and way of life. Competition militates against contentment, and
only retreat from the competitive economic matrix makes it
possible to restore the perspective necessary to pursue real contentment rather than continue the race toward unnecessary
and inappropriate objects of artificially generated desires.
"Shall we always study to obtain more of these things," Thoreau
asks, "and not sometimes to be content with less? . . . Why
should not our furniture be as simple as the Arab's or the Indian's?" (32).

The rhetorical question here serves as a window onto much
wider issues than furniture. To illustrate the point that "less is
more," Arab and Indian are used somewhat indiscriminately as

primitives—noble savages who have not yet been corrupted by possession, whose wisdom is presumed to lie in their nearness to the earth and to natural things. In Thoreau's zeal to articulate an ideal of simplicity, he sees material goods as bordering on positive evil because they consume precious energy, or "life": "A lady once offered me a mat, but as I had no room to spare within the house, nor time to spare within or without to shake it, I declined it, preferring to wipe my feet on the sod before my door. It is best to avoid the beginnings of evil" (60). The word *evil* once again throws so simple a thing as a doormat into the realm of universal ethical principles. No possession is neutral because possession itself is a moral issue; similarly, no structure we build for ourselves is neutral because time and space are part of the economy of the universe, the adaptation to which is our moral education; as such they are not only significant and symbolic but are commodities committed to our stewardship, by which we will be judged.

The notion of stewardship as a significant aspect of moral responsibility explains the frequent inventories of money, time, and possessions; the writer appears to be "rendering an account" to his Maker, as to his readers, for the "talents" entrusted to him:

> My furniture, part of which I made myself,—and the rest cost me nothing of which I have not rendered an account,—consisted of a bed, a table, a desk, three chairs, a looking glass three inches in diameter, a pair of tongs and andirons, a kettle, a skillet, and a frying-pan, a dipper, a wash-bowl, two knives and forks, three plates, one cup, one spoon, a jug for oil, a jug for molasses, and a japanned lamp. . . . Furniture! Thank God, I can sit and I can stand without the aid of a furniture warehouse. (59)

Unnecessary things "clutter and defile" and upset the balance between inner and outer life by consuming time, energy, and attention: "I had three pieces of limestone on my desk, but I was terrified to find that they required to be dusted daily, when the furniture of my mind was all undusted still, and I threw them out the window in disgust. How, then, could I have furnished a house?" (32). Imbalance between inner and outer life, distraction, anxiety over material things, are to be shunned as besetting sins because they upset the wider complex economy of relations between the individual and his environment. Objects tend toward evil, Thoreau reasons, because they block our vision of higher things. Comfort anesthetizes and possession blinds. The writer's positive fear of such imbalance is understandable only when we accept his belief that its implications reach far beyond personal moral life and assume social and even metaphysical proportions: "We now no longer camp as for a night, but have settled down on earth and forgotten heaven. . . . We have built for this world a family mansion, and for the next a family tomb. The best works of art are the expression of man's struggle to free himself from this condition, but the effect of our art is merely to make this low state comfortable and that higher state to be forgotten" (33).

The note of the jeremiad is sounded once again: we have become complacent in our comfort. The parallel between the mansion and the tomb presents another grim paradox reemphasizing the displacement of spiritual goods by material ones. When art, or the work of men's hands, becomes an end in itself, it becomes evil. It is only good as a means to a higher end, in the service of the ends of nature and of enlightenment. Apart from these ends, the edifices we build around ourselves are flimsy artifices that loosen our grounding in solid earth: "When I consider how our houses are built and paid for, or not paid for, and their internal economy managed and sustained, I wonder that the floor does not give way under the visitor while he is admiring the gew-gaws upon the mantelpiece, and let him through into the cellar, to some solid and honest though earthy foundation" (34).

Thoreau's stance as naive outsider lends credibility to a kind of argument that might otherwise be impalatable: the deserved moral outrage of the pure. He claims not to be involved in the outward-spiraling economy of acquisition that ultimately consumes the individual's energies and resources and leaves him in a state of impoverishment and indebtedness, a deficit economy based on multiple mediations between object and owner and between maker and consumer. Finances, like aesthetics, are inextricably connected to the moral sphere. It is a matter of pride for Thoreau to be able to tell what his house has cost him. "I give the details [of construction and cost]," he writes, "because very few are able to tell exactly what their houses cost, and fewer still, if any, the separate cost of the various materials which compose them" (43). Such practical accounting is an imitation of the spiritual accounting a person must, according to the apostle Peter, "be always ready to give" (I Peter 3: 15).

Just as the exchange between man and nature is the standard of economy, so is it the standard of aesthetic value as well, beauty being a by-product of that interaction. And as the walls of a house tend to separate us from that direct interaction, we must be wary of indoor art. Art, like money, can either preserve our connections with the natural world or, more likely, sever them. Again, however, having established the extreme, Thoreau modifies his judgments: "Not that all architectural ornament is to be neglected even in the rudest periods; but let our houses first be lined with beauty, where they come in contact with our lives, like the tenement of the shell-fish, and not overlaid with it. But alas! I have been inside one or two of them, and know what they are lined with" (35). The analogy reiterates organicism as a criterion of beauty. Elements of design superimposed from without rather than naturally evolved from within are false and hypocritical. Authenticity, and hence beauty, proceeds from the inside outward. A house, therefore, can either be a mask on or a manifestation of the life within it.

A distinct shift occurs next in the writer's approach to the subject of houses. Having established the scale of necessity, he begins to consider legitimate luxury, bringing his subject closer to home by considering what is a realistic and viable way of life in Concord:

> Though we are not so degenerate but that we might possibly live in a cave or a wigwam or wear skins to-day, it certainly is better to accept the advantages, though so dearly bought, which the invention and industry of mankind offer. In such a neighborhood as this, boards and shingles, lime and bricks, are cheaper and more easily obtained than suitable caves, or whole logs, or bark in sufficient quantities, or even well-tempered clay or flat stones. I speak understandingly on this subject, for I have made myself acquainted with it both theoretically and practically. (36)

There follows a lengthy account of the building of the cabin at Walden Pond. Thoreau's attention to the details of construction serves to exemplify the values already discussed: economy, efficiency, directness, focus, and concentration on process as spiritual activity. With a borrowed ax he hews his own timber, leaving the bark on, carefully mortising or tenoning each log by its stump with other borrowed tools. Significantly enough, the carpenter does not even own his own tools; he borrows them, the emphasis being on a simple communism of appropriation according to need. Thoreau further implies that the task is one that any man, minimally equipped, may do and that the one who makes a thing deserves to use it. Doing and thinking, in this view, are not simultaneous—the practical philosopher who digs and hews and builds is thinking with his body and thinks with his mind when his body is at rest. Writing (or thinking) and building are analogous and complementary activities, binding body to soul in imitative action.

Thoreau periodically interrupts his account of the building to reflect on its symbolic significance. Remembering the digging of the cellar in the hill, he writes, "Under the most splendid house in the city is still to be found the cellar where they store their roots as of old, and long after the superstructure has disappeared posterity remark its dent in the earth. The house is still but a sort of porch at the entrance of a burrow" (40).

This comes very close to Jung's allegory of the psyche, according to which the essential sources of knowledge are rooted in the earth, deep and hidden when we build over them; the further we build upward and outward, the more we separate ourselves from them, to our own potential detriment. They are also what survive the destruction of our edifices. Thoreau's rhetorical reductiveness here again serves his purpose in circling always back to essentials, insistently returning to the central point lest in the widening gyre of elaboration we lose it like the falcon does the voice of the falconer.

In architecture as in writing, the center is lost when elaboration loses its grounding in functional necessity. Ornamentation is conceivably good only if it is a direct, traceable, and organic extension of the idea at the center:

What of the architectural beauty I now see, I know has gradually grown from within outward, out of the necessities and character of the indweller, who is the only builder,—out of some unconscious truthfulness, and nobleness, without ever a thought for the appearance and whatever additional beauty of this kind is destined to be produced will be preceded by a like unconscious beauty of life. The most interesting dwellings in this country . . . are the most unpretending, humble log huts and cottages of the poor commonly; it is the life of the inhabitants whose shells they are, and not any peculiarity in their surfaces merely, which makes them *picturesque;* and equally interesting will be the citizen's suburban box, when his life shall be as simple and as agreeable to the imagination, and there is as little straining after effect in the style of his dwelling. (42)

Anticipating James, Stein, Hemingway, Wharton, Cather, and other literary descendants, Thoreau applies the architectural analogy directly to writing, where the same standards and cautions apply: "What if an equal ado were made about the ornaments of style in literature, and the architects of our Bibles spent as much time about their cornices as the architects of our churches do? So are made the *belles-lettres* and the *beaux-arts* and their professors" (42). Calling attention to writing as an architectural enterprise invites scrutiny of his own text in the terms he has painstakingly set out as a builder, and it meets in every particular the standards he sets for house-building: the text gives an appearance of simplicity, even rudeness, in its frontal, informal appeal to the reader but is carefully crafted of complex materials expertly joined. He "knows his material," as he claims of his house, having picked the bricks and lumber and quarried the limestone. The liberal citations from classical and biblical sources, country lore, and current news bespeak a writer well acquainted with the world he chooses to shun. The book's partitions are few and simple, each chapter serving as an "open room"—having a general topic within which a great deal of meandering conversation can take place. And the book is designed to serve the reader, and undoubtedly the writer, as a shelter from the useless erudition and frivolous gossip that fill the bookshops, making reading a dangerous and wasteful business.

The book and the house are the educational materials of a committed autodidact. Necessity has taught him at each step what he needs to know: "My bricks," he writes, "being second-hand ones, required to be cleaned with a trowel, so that I learned more than usual of the qualities of bricks and trowels" (216). He laments the money and time spent on less efficient and purposeful schooling, observing that at Cambridge College (Harvard) students pay thirty dollars a year for small, inconvenient, and noisy rooms and adding, "I cannot but think that if we had more true wisdom in these respects, not only less education would be needed, because forsooth, more would already have been acquired, but the pecuniary expense of getting an education would in a great measure vanish" (45). And, taking his reasoning a step further, Thoreau claims, "My residence was more favorable, not only to thought, but to serious reading, than a university; and though I was beyond the range of the ordinary circulating library, I had more than ever come within the influence of those books which circulate round the world, whose sentences were first written on bark, and are now merely copied from time to time on linen paper" (90).

The proper setting for an education is home, a place ideally free of distractions, the pressures of conformity, and winds of opinion and conducive to solitary contemplation. Echoing Emerson's "American Scholar" address, Thoreau sees this enhancement of solitude as a protection from the subservience to the past fostered in universities, where intellectual slavishness too often passes for thought. Dramatically he insists that the spot on which he dwells has never been dwelt on before, and he cries, "Deliver me from a city built on the site of a more ancient city, whose materials are ruins, whose gardens cemeteries" (237)—an outcry that might have served as an epigraph to Emerson's address. Moreover, a house properly built and lived in is not only a proper setting for thought but for the nourishment and free play of the imagination. "Should not every apartment in which man dwells," Thoreau asks, "be lofty enough to create some obscurity overhead, where flickering shadows may play at evening about the rafters? These forms are more agreeable to the fancy and imagination than fresco paintings or the most expensive furniture" (218).

For all his insistence on ascetic stringencies, self-discipline, and meticulous craftsmanship, however, Thoreau's final assessment of his own style of life is clearly that it is the most conducive to enjoyment. Indeed, he might well have taken for his own epigraph St. Augustine's adage that "the end of all things is delight." The profound sense of purpose that drives Thoreau's crafts as writer and carpenter rests on this foundation, and what he seeks most urgently to learn is the proper enjoyment of the things it is proper to enjoy. His house is designed as a place where he can do that. As he observes with some satisfaction on contemplating his little dwelling, "In short, I am convinced, both by faith and experience, that to maintain one's self on this earth is not a hardship but a pastime, if we will live simply and wisely; as the pursuits of the simpler nations are still the sports of the more artificial. It is not necessary that a man should earn his living by the sweat of his brow, unless he sweats easier than I do" (63).

2

"THE FALL OF THE HOUSE OF USHER"
And Who Can Tell the Teller
from the Tale?

Roderick Usher's "mansion of gloom" is one of the most memorable of Poe's dark, many-chambered Gothic mansions and one of the most richly symbolic houses in American fiction. This story, like a number of his others, explores the ambiguous interrelations of body and soul, material and spiritual reality, and the interpenetration of good and evil with a lurid fascination far exceeding even the voracity of Thoreau's audacious philosophical speculations.[1] The idea of the house as "psychological space" reaches an epitome in Poe, whose complex use of houses as animated spaces provided a model for many literary descendants. Poe's interest in houses was not, however, purely as vehicles of literary signification. In them he explored the ideas of home, comfort, and interiority as elements of psychic life, thematic issues for him perhaps particularly because, growing up in an adoptive household and being sent off to boarding schools on both sides of the Atlantic, he spent much of his childhood in places that were not, in the deepest sense, home. Like Irving, James, and other American writers with a strong European orientation, Poe played out his ambivalences about personal and national identity by developing a fascination with the predicament of dividedness itself and with the permeability of those boundaries that maintain the separateness of fundamental categories. In houses, particularly old houses with family histories, he found an ideal emblem for these concerns.

In 1840 he wrote a curiously impassioned article for Burton's *Gentleman's Magazine* that contemptuously diagnosed the epidemic of tastelessness in American interior decoration and that went on to prescribe the elements of a tastefully and comfortably decorated sitting room with all the vehemence and doctrinaire adamance of a preacher exhorting his congregation to repentance. Among the catalogue of aesthetic sins Poe regarded as peculiarly American was the indiscriminate and imitative display of wealth. He contrasted such shallow ostentation with coherent and tasteful decor that bespeaks "legitimate taste" deriving from "true nobility of blood," which "rather avoids than affects that mere costliness" that breeds petty rivalry and material envy."[2] He criticized Americans' "inartistic" arrangements of furniture in which "straight lines are too prevalent—too uninterruptedly continued—or clumsily interrupted at right angles. If curved lines occur, they are repeated into unpleasant uniformity. . . . By undue precision, the appearance of many a fine apartment is spoiled" (159). This catalog of decorative offenses continues with a critique of carpets—objects he claims should be "the soul of the apartment"—that feature "the abomination of flowers, or representations of well-known objects of any kind." Carpets, Poe claims, should have "distinct grounds, and vivid circular or cycloid figures, *of no meaning*," and should be "rigidly Arabesque" (159). And, finally, lighting should avoid the cardinal sin of "glare" and "glitter," to which he claims Americans are addicted, as they are to the mirrors and windows that increase those effects. "Flickering, unquiet lights, are sometimes pleasing—to children and idiots always so—but in the embellishment of a room they should be scrupulously avoided" (210). All these obscenities he summarily regards as evils "growing out of our republican institutions," by virtue of which "a man of large purse has usually a very little soul which he keeps in it." Poe adds, "The corruption of taste is a portion or a pendant of the dollar-manufacture" (210).

It is not surprising in light of this diagnosis that Poe chose to situate his stories in Gothic castles of indeterminate medieval origin rather than in the prosaic and literal spaces of American "apartments," where money had driven out mystery and a "soulless" environment was the result. His was the romantic project par excellence of retrieving and reclaiming the mysteries of the nether side of human nature by a retreat into the shadowy regions of myth and history and by the re-creation of environments that allowed, evoked, and even generated a dreamlike state of consciousness where darkness, shadows, and rich variations of sensual stimuli disturbed the mind into speculation. Such an environment, conversely, would seem to prohibit the rational discourse or transaction of ordinary business that Poe regarded as the pitifully limited vernacular of republican life.

By contrast with the typically "well-furnished" American apartment he finds so odious, he concludes his sermon on taste with a description of a comfortably furnished room, detailed down to the smallest matters of fabric, picture frames, and wood grain. In this room there are no "brilliant effects"; rather, "repose speaks in all." The landscapes in the pictures have an "imaginative cast," the lighting is low, the tone of the pictures is "warm but dark," and the windows and lampshade are "crimson-tinted," throwing a "tranquil but magical radiance over all" (210). Such an environment would allow, and indeed foster, a retreat to the interior chambers of the mind, with little intrusion of ordinary daylight to chase away the shadows of dreams.

This compulsive insistence on the requirements for interior repose reiterates the many characteristics of the interior spaces depicted in equally vivid detail in Poe's tales. Houses in many of his stories are depicted as places of "living entombment"—labyrinthine, claustrophobic places filled with darkness, shadows, filtered and colored light, and permeable boundaries The insistence and even urgency of the narrator's voice both in the stories and in the article on decoration suggest a disturbing unsettledness about the issue of comfort: light, mirrors, and large pictures of recognizable plants and animals seem almost intolerable; they intrude on and violate the consciousness that requires darkness in order to be at peace. Poe's stories are replete with characters who respond in the same exaggerated way to the sensory environment of interior spaces where objects, sounds, and textures threaten to overwhelm the senses and who recoil from sudden lights, reflections in mirrors, or movements of objects in the wind. Mirrors, in particular, recur as a consistent motif, betokening a blurring or slippage of boundaries between two worlds—boundaries that need to remain intact to preserve sanity.

The house of Usher has just such a disturbingly seductive interior, conducive to speculation but not investigation, full of dark corners, hidden places, mirrors and windows that suddenly cast their filtered and reflected light on faces and objects and endow them with frightening reality. The house mirrors its inhabitant, Roderick Usher, who is doubled also in his twin sister and again in the narrator, who describes himself as in certain respects a twin Roderick. Doubling effects multiply throughout the story until everything becomes an analog or image of everything else—boundaries of identity break down not only among characters but among the house, the body, nature, and the text, all of which manifest similarities of structure and behavior that bind them into claustrophobically close metaphorical relationship. The reader, having entered the text, is eventually drawn into a dark and curious labyrinth, just as the narrator is, and so becomes yet another link in this chain of doubles.

Ambiguity, one of the most pervasive devices by which this confusion of identity is accomplished, begins in the title, where both "fall" and "house" have at least one figurative meaning and a literal meaning between which the narrative oscillates until categorical distinctions between the literal and the figurative, the temporal and the spatial, begin to collapse. Throughout the story, the narrator's uncertain and ambiguous rhetoric emphasizes this blurring of boundaries. The house is situated in indefinite time and space and so could be anywhere "long ago and far away." This effect of mythic or dream time, a common Gothic device, serves Poe's epistemological purposes nicely. These purposes are, in part, to baffle the reader into questioning rational categories of experience and to blur the boundary between language and the phenomenal world, thereby forcing the reader to enter a no-man's-land where the distinction between them is uncertain. Poe seeks in effect to evoke a transcendentalist frame of mind in which the world is understood as text, subject to the devices of textual analysis, so that distinctions among moral, linguistic, aesthetic, and empirical categories tend toward the same kind of metaphorical collapse discussed previously.

The first mention of the house animates and personifies it as "the melancholy House of Usher" and later as "this mansion of gloom" (244, 246). The pathetic fallacy here confuses the subject-object relation. Again and again the narrator attributes human characteristics to the house that must, logically, be projections of his own state of mind and yet seem to him, and by extension to us, actually to inhere in the building itself. These attributions evoke whatever deep reserves of primitive animism lie in us to be reawakened, which results in confusion of the animate with the inanimate. When the narrator claims his own feelings rather than projecting them, he describes them as effects produced by some ineffable activity on the part of the inanimate world; for instance, in his further reflection on approaching the house, he remarks, "I know not how it was—but with the first glimpse of the building, a sense of insufferable gloom pervaded my spirit" (244). The house is apparently "emanating" something subtle that the narrator, sensitive soul that he is, receives. "I looked upon the scene before me—upon the mere house . . . the vacant eye-like windows . . . with an utter depression of soul" (245), he recalls, at first trying to calm his nerves by reducing the house to a "mere" neutral object and then giving way to his animistic fears before the eyelike windows, which give him an inescapable feeling of being observed. Here again there is a confusion between subject and object, viewer and viewed. Which direction energy and influence are flowing remains an unresolved question.

Another doubling occurs when the narrator looks into the tarn at the foot of the mansion and sees the house's image replicated. This simple image of the relation between dream and reality or between the world of the senses and the world of the imagination harks back to the myth of Narcissus. By means of this device the writer issues a warning and at the same time a tantalizing conundrum: that it is dangerous to take the image for the thing itself but that there are states of mind, and states of nature, in which the two are indistinguishable.

Before entering the house, the narrator pauses, "shaking off from [his] spirit what must have been a dream," to provide a detailed description of the "real aspect" of the building, a phrase intended to establish a renewed clarity about the boundaries between self and object, mood and nature (247–248). Yet as the description proceeds, these boundaries begin to blur again, and the language of the narrator is suffused with personifying metaphors that make it clear how fragile these distinctions are once the reiterative character of the phenomenal world is fully recognized. The "principal feature" of the house, he recalls, seemed to be its "excessive antiquity":

> The discoloration of ages had been great. Minute fungi overspread the whole exterior, hanging in a fine tangled web-work from the eaves. Yet all this was apart from any extraordinary dilapidation. No portion of the masonry had fallen; and there appeared to be a wild inconsistency between its still perfect adaptation of parts, and the crumbling condition of the individual stones. In this there was much that reminded me of the specious totality of old wood-work which has rotted for long years in some neglected vault, with no disturbance from the breath of external air. Beyond this indication of extensive decay, however, the fabric gave little token of instability. Perhaps the eye of a scrutinising observer might have discovered a barely perceptible fissure, which, extending from the roof of the building in front, made its way down the wall in a zigzag direction, until it became lost in the sullen waters of the tarn. (248)

The perspective of the narrator as he takes in the "real" aspect of the house is jarringly surreal: while he stands at a suffiicient distance to take in the whole discolored facade and estimate its "excessive" antiquity, he also notes "minute fungi" hanging in "fine tangled web-work" from the eaves—something it would have been impossible to see in such detail from the presumed distance. The same odd perspectival disjuncture occurs when he speculates that "the eye of a scrutinizing observer" might "perhaps" find a "barely perceptible fissure" along the front of the building, leaving it to the reader to decide whether he is in fact claiming to have seen such a thing and, if so, how such a claim is possible from his vantage point. These quick shifts of perspective, ambiguously presented, can serve either to reinforce the impression that the narrator is extraordinarily observant and sensitive, and, moreover, possessed of almost preternatural visual powers, or to undermine his credibility when added to previous proofs of his overactive and projective imagination. We might even regard them as the visual equivalent of Poe's reputed aural schizophrenia—an affliction that distorts the hearer's ability to locate the direction and distance of sound.

A further difficulty is presented by the narrator's observations about the "wild inconsistency" between the whole and the sum of the parts, adding up to what he calls a "specious totality" and introducing the old conundrum of how the whole can be greater than the sum of the parts. Somehow the "houseness" of the house manages to transcend the actual condition of the disintegrating wood and stone of which it is made. Comparing the house to woodwork in a neglected vault that no "breath of external air" can reach suggests by association that this environment, too, is somehow mysteriously hermetically sealed. By the end of the description we have again to question what degree of credibility to assign the narrator's perceptions: How many of the characteristics he attributes to the old house belong to the house before him? How much of what he is seeing is a dream image projected onto an old but unextraordinary edifice?

By the time the narrator reaches the house, the identification of his person with the house before him has been thoroughly established. As he enters it the equation of physical with psychic space becomes increasingly explicit. The butler leads the narrator down "many dark and intricate passages" on his way to Usher's studio, passing antique furnishings that he first describes as "ordinary," though they soon strike him as "phantasmagoric"— a term that grammatically refers to the furnishings but also logically describes the mental state of the narrator. Once in Usher's studio, the similarity between house and psyche broadens to include physical features that are replicated in Usher's anatomy, thus doubling the doubling effect already produced by the metaphorical relation between house and narrator. Roderick's studio is

> very large and lofty. The windows were long, narrow, and pointed and at so vast a distance from the black oaken floor as to be altogether inaccessible from within. Feeble gleams of encrimsoned light made their way through the trellised panes, and served to render sufficiently distinct the more prominent objects around; the eye, however, struggled in vain to reach the remoter angles of the

chamber, or the recesses of the vaulted and fretted ceiling. Dark draperies hung upon the walls. The general furniture was profuse, comfortless, antique, and tattered. Many books and musical instruments lay scattered about, but failed to give any vitality to the scene. (249)

Much in this description suggests that we are viewing the inside of a head, a reading already suggested by the "vacant eye-like windows" in the narrator's description of the outside of the house. If these windows are eyes, however, they allow the inhabitants to look out only on the atmosphere because they are too high to allow a view of the landscape; in fact, their "gleams of encrimsoned light" and "trellised panes" add an almost comic effect of veins infusing bleary and bloodshot eyes staring vacantly into space. When the words *the eye* appear immediately following this bizarre description, the effect resonates like sound in a hollow chamber: Whose eye? Have we not just been talking about eyes? We locate the eye, as we must, as the narrator's own, but only after a slight confusion of point of view.

The chamber itself seems to have indefinite dimensions and few distinct boundaries other than the "vaulted and fretted ceiling." Within the room are all the accoutrements of an abundant intellectual and aesthetic life, but again we encounter a puzzling disjuncture between parts and whole. The whole lacks the "vitality" suggested by the presence of all these evidences of life. As the narrator goes on to describe Roderick's own cadaverous aspect, the analogy between his person and his habitation is made even more explicit.

With the introduction of Roderick Usher, a third line is added to the fugue of ambiguities. Just as the house reflects the narrator's emotional state, it also reflects Roderick's physical state to such a degree that the building and the man seem united in a general excess of contagion and disease that has spread beyond Usher's wracked body to walls and windows; the building seems simply an outer shell, an extension of the person. The narrator remarks, innocently enough, on "the perfect keeping of the character of the premises with the accredited character of the people" (247), an observation that might betoken nothing more than mild curiosity but for the word *accred-*

ited, which reintroduces the troubling question of whether the house is a function of the inhabitants or the inhabitants a function of the house. Moreover, the contagion seems to have spread beyond the house to the surrounding countryside: the narrator "fancies" that "about the whole mansion and domain there hung an atmosphere peculiar to themselves and their immediate vicinity . . . a pestilent and mystic vapour, dull, sluggish, faintly discernible, and leaden-hued" (247)—words that precisely describe both house and inhabitant.

A brief digression into family history serves to complicate the question of identity further. The narrator pauses over the term *the house of Usher*, "an appellation which seemed to include, in the minds of the peasantry who used it, both the family and the family mansion." The house of Usher has, he informs us, "put forth at no period, any enduring branch; in other words . . . the entire family lay in the direct line of descent" (246). Like Hawthorne, Poe is fascinated with the notion of linear descent, genetic inheritance, and the ways in which genetic questions disturb the belief in individual uniqueness, free will, and originality so dear to the American romantic imagination.[3] Nothing here is itself alone; nothing is entirely self-defined or self-determining: Roderick begins to seem simply one more tarnished reiteration of an old type and, like the house, to have outlived that type's original purpose and character. Like the house, he is a withering anachronism, flawed by unbuttressed weaknesses, crumbling from within. Both Poe and Hawthorne were fascinated by the effects of inbreeding, the dangerous insularity of those notions of family so long dominant in European culture, and both suggest that the antidote to the hereditary weaknesses exacerbated by inbreeding might be precisely the cultural pluralism that adds "new blood" to old veins. The geometric equivalent of such reasoning is that a vertical must be balanced by a horizontal; a structure that is very tall or long must have proportionate width to give it strength and stability.

From Roderick's person we shift focus once again to Roderick's paintings and find ourselves in another chamber in this hall of mirrors. Claiming that "if ever mortal painted an idea," Roderick had done so, the narrator comments, "For me at least—in the circumstances then surrounding me—there arose out of the pure abstractions which the hypochondriac contrived to throw upon his canvas, an intensity of intolerable awe" (254). The label *hypochondriac* forces a reassessment of Roderick's sickly condition, which the narrator previously described as cadaverous, because the label suggests that Roderick's sickliness is an illusion. And if so, whose illusion? What is also asserted here is Roderick's power of projection (rivaled, we might observe, by the narrator's own), which seems able to duplicate on canvas an emotional state that is then recreated and possibly even magnified in the beholder. This entanglement of attribution creates in the reader a dizzying confusion as to the locus of the "special effects" being produced. Roderick's paintings add yet another term to the series of replications; the "long and rectangular vault or tunnel" recalls the long passageways of the house itself as well as an interior that in its abstraction suggests an attempt to convey something of the shape of interior mental space. Moreover, this tunnel is an image of the unresolved and the indefinite, a passageway connecting nothing with nothing. In this context the reader may recognize the tunnel as an image of the text itself.

When we get to Roderick's song, "The Haunted Palace," another displacement shifts Roderick to the position of a narrator who is telling a tale that replicates his own story and that is about a place very like his own castle, which, it seems, is very like a body whose "red-litten windows" resemble his own bloodshot eyes. We have heard this somewhere before. The story folds back on itself in what threatens to be an infinite regression and produces the effect of standing on a threshold looking across a room at a mirror, not knowing whether we are seeing an extension or a reflection. The question arises, moreover, as to whose consciousness governs here because we are getting a story within a story retailed by a narrator who is by no means reliable and indeed tends to project his own distorted frame of reference on everything he sees; Roderick's symbolic self-awareness seems to duplicate exactly the narrator's perceptions, which he has at intervals identified as quite peculiar to himself. In case we have not picked up the resemblance between Roderick's song and the other elements of the story, the narrator pauses to explain in rather simpleminded fashion that the song seems to extend the not uncommon belief in the sentience of the vegetable world to the inorganic world and, in Roderick's "disordered fancy," to the "gray stones of the home of his forefathers" (257) as well, which in their particular arrangement and their blending with the fungi and decayed trees seem to have absorbed something of the vitality that infuses objects indiscriminately. Because this is precisely the vision of the house purveyed by our own narrator earlier, his remark about Roderick's "disordered fancy" seems to boomerang, and we are left, dear reader, holding the bag, wondering whether our own fancies are not in turn being disordered to the point of paralysis given that the ability to distinguish similarity from difference and to preserve distinct categories of objects and experiences is rapidly disintegrating as boundaries are systematically extinguished. Moreover, the distinction between fancy and empirical certainty diminishes with Roderick's claim that the evidence of this sentience in the environment can be observed "in the gradual yet certain condensation of an atmosphere of their own about the waters and the walls" (257). As proof of this "atmosphere" he cites its influence on the destinies of his family, of which he himself is the end product. In language resembling a line of ratiocination about a phenomenon carefully and scientifically observed and noted, Usher makes equations that challenge both the certainties of scientific method and the definition of sanity.

To amuse themselves (and perhaps, we are tempted to think, to escape, albeit unsuccessfully, this vortex of similarities and phantasmagoric atmospherics) Usher and his friend, our unreliable narrator, undertake a program of reading. But their fare consists entirely of books that are "as might be supposed, in strict keeping with this character of phantasm" (258). These works focus largely on subterranean voyages, heaven and hell, magic, the occult, and strange creatures that belong to no clear category of life—such as satyrs. The books once again serve to duplicate the themes and impressions produced in everything the narrator looks on and so become simply one more iteration of the suffocating similarity that conflates all things under the rubric of one endlessly bifurcating design.

Into this increasingly complex miasma of mirrors enters Lady Madeline. She has appeared once, passing briefly before the narrator as he stood in Roderick's chamber and disappearing without Roderick's apparent notice, coming from darkness and returning to it with no distinct locus of entry or exit. Some days after the narrator's arrival, he finds that she has died and is to be interred for two weeks "in one of the numerous vaults within the main walls of the building" located, significantly enough, "immediately beneath that portion of the building in which was my own sleeping apartment" (258–259). By this time physical proximity and spatial relation have become so consistently significant symbolically that we cannot fail to assume that the "immediate" vertical proximity of Madeline and the narrator pairs them on a "vertical axis" as Roderick and he are paired, we might say, horizontally, making Madeline and the narrator counterparts. So we line up the ways in which we know that to be true: each is a close complement to Roderick—each in a peculiar way his other half; the narrator is Madeline's replacement as Roderick's housemate and companion—there seems to be only one position in this world of binaries to be filled as Roderick's counterpart, and the narrator and Madeline share that position in the structure, displacing each other because there is no room for a third term. Moreover, the narrator has created a similar confusion about the oppositions between each of them and Roderick: Madeline is presumed dead even though she seems a vital presence, while Roderick seems in every respect "vacant," "cadaverous," and moribund. Similarly the narrator is presumed sane (if we are still so generous or credulous as to make such a presumption,) though he has given abundant evidence of being in the grip of his own morbid "fancies," and Roderick may easily, with a slight shift of our terms of "accreditation," appear to be the more lucid, sensitive, and self-aware.

Lady Madeline's dismal quarters provide a number of clues about her role; as in our introduction to Roderick, a description of her chamber precedes information about her:

> It had been used, apparently, in remote feudal times, for the worst purposes of a donjon-keep, and, in later days, as a place of deposit for powder, or some other highly combustible substance, as a portion of its floor, and the whole interior of a long archway through which we reached it, were carefully sheathed with copper. The

door, of massive iron, had been, also, similarly protected. Its immense weight caused an unusually sharp grating sound, as it moved upon its hinges. (259)

By the logic of this description, this room is one in which, clearly, form has followed function. To have placed Lady Madeline's body in a room that was first a place of torture and imprisonment and then a storage place for high explosives resonates with sinister implications about the magnitude of her power to threaten Roderick. Why else would she be placed in a room so heavily fortified against combustion or escape? With a little "fancy"—and by this time, if Poe has had his way with us, we have become as fanciful as the narrator—we can easily imagine her as a preternatural presence whose "energy" has been released from captivity by death and so threatens to fill and dominate the house, thereby shattering what fragile and illusory claims to normalcy Roderick can still make.

Yet it is not, in fact, Roderick who appears most palpably threatened by Lady Madeline's eerie presence in the house, but the narrator, who lies above her in his own chamber, a prey to fears that he tries to attribute to the character of the place itself:

> I endeavoured to believe that much, if not all of what I felt, was due to the bewildering influence of the gloomy furniture of the room— of the dark and tattered draperies, which, tortured into motion by the breath of a rising tempest, swayed fitfully to and fro upon the walls, and rustled uneasily about the decorations of the bed. But my efforts were fruitless. An irrepressible tremour gradually pervaded my frame; and, at length, there sat upon my very heart an incubus of utterly causeless alarm. (261)

The narrator's capacity for self-delusion through projection reaches a peak here when the accoutrements of his bedroom seem to him the source of such overwhelming fears. The movement of the wind—action without visible presence—though logically perfectly explicable, becomes emotionally indistinguishable from the eerie and inexplicable activities of a poltergeist. The narrator's body imitates the involuntary and uncontrollable movement of the wind itself, as he gives way to fear that, characteristically, he describes as generated by an "incubus"—an alien presence—within his very heart. The narrator is no more master of the forces within his body than Roderick is master of the forces at work within his house; the narrator simply houses invading spirits that usurp his authority and hold him captive. Like the vaulted chamber in which Madeline lies, he seems to contain explosive forces that threaten to break out and must be carefully guarded to be held in check.

In the final scenes of the story all the fragile, vestigial boundaries between objects suffer their final collapse. Roderick enters the narrator's chamber on a dark and stormy night like the one just described. He is terrified by the strange agitation of the wind, which seems to have "collected its force" in their immediate vicinity while the clouds "flew careering . . . against each other" with "life-like velocity," and huge masses of "agitated vapour" that produced a "luminous and distinctly visible gaseous exhalation" that "hung about and enshrouded the mansion," obscuring the moon and stars. The whole place is enclosed by a thickening environment charged, it seems, with baleful intention. The house and its inhabitants seem engulfed and ingested by some hostile, vaporous being of cosmic proportions.

The narrator, who has just admitted to paralyzing fear of lesser phenomena than this, utters his hollow reassurances to Roderick, closes the curtains, and insists that "these appearances, which bewilder you, are merely electrical phenomena not uncommon—or it may be that they have their ghastly origin in the rank miasma of the tarn" (263). Of course, the terms of the latter half of the narrator's glib explanation belie the lucidity of the first half, just as his explanations of things always crack down the middle. Calming his own agitation by assuming the false role of comforter, the narrator takes up one of Roderick's "favourite romances" by proposing to pass the terrifying night reading aloud. He admits as an aside that it is a vulgar book of "uncouth and unimaginative prolixity" but is the only one immediately at hand.

Lo and behold, as it happens, the story provides a direct allegory for the situation in which the two readers find themselves: it describes a violent, drunken hero, Ethelred, entering the dwelling of a hermit by force on just such a tempestuous night, "ripping apart the door. . . . Pulling [with his gauntleted hand] sturdily, he so cracked, and ripped, and tore all asunder, that the noise of the dry and hollow-sounding wood alarumed and reverberated throughout the forest" (264). Immediately on reading this sentence, the narrator hears just such a sound in some far corner of the house—an "echo" of the noise described in the story. As Ethelred enters the dwelling and kills the dragon therein, the beast emits a shriek that is again echoed in some distant chamber of the house of Usher. Our narrator, by now in the grip of terror, suppresses his emotions to avoid exciting the "sensitive nervousness" of his companion, who, however, seems to have remained oblivious to these sinister coincidences. Roderick seems, indeed, to be in some kind of trance, his body rocking "from side to side with a gentle yet constant and uniform sway," imitating the motion of his house in the wind (265).

Pushing on with the story in a final desperate attempt at suppression, the narrator arrives at a passage where a shield falls from the wall and rings onto the silver floor at the hero's feet, apparently moved by some supernatural force. A third time, the sound described in the story is reiterated somewhere within the house, and the narrator, now "completely unnerved," rushes to Usher's side and finds him in a state of "stony rigidity," in which he gazes fixedly into space, babbling crazily about the irrepressible and inescapable presence of Madeline and ending with a shriek that she now stands without the door. As Madeline enters, the final implosion begins: she falls "inward" on her brother, united with him as one in an incestuous death throe. The narrator flees the house, which is now indistinguishable from its shadows under a "blood-red moon," and as his nerve fails and his sanity cracks, he watches the fissure in the facade of the ancient house widen under the pressure of the "fierce breath of the whirlwind." The house is rent in two, and with a "tumultuous shouting sound like the voice of a thousand waters" it sinks into the tarn and disappears completely from sight (267–268).

The elements of the story ultimately cancel each other out. All distinctions collapse under the pressure of metaphor; the structural tensions that maintain the partitions between mental categories give way, and we are left with a blurred image of a vaporous, boundless, undifferentiated atmosphere at an indefinite hour of the night somewhere on the edge of the world long ago and far away. Like the house, the story disappears, leaving us watching, like the bewildered narrator, from a bridge that presumably leads back to the "real world" we have left. The long narrative, heavy with illusory meanings, has collapsed on itself; each paragraph in some way echoes or reiterates or recalls a previous one, eventually producing a weird sense of recognition each time a new scene is introduced so that finally difference and sameness are impossibly confused and constant repetition has ended in obliteration, as an incantation deprives words of sound, leaving the one who utters them in a state of undifferentiated awareness, without form or boundary or structure, in which categories have no meaning and the fragility of logic and the speciousness of language become laughably apparent.

3

THE HOUSE OF THE SEVEN GABLES
Secrets of the Heart

The actual House of the Seven Gables stands today "halfway down a bystreet" in the old New England town of Salem, a thriving pilgrimage spot for Hawthorne's readers. On the edge of a spit of land jutting out into Salem harbor, the house was originally the home of a sea captain who, as local lore has it, did a little smuggling as a sideline. An attic room with a hidden lock and secret crannies behind camouflaged doors marks the house as a repository of secrets where any closet door may be a false front and any wall panel a door to a hidden chamber. Gloomy and Gothic as any of Poe's labyrinthine mansions, the rambling, irregular house evokes curiosity about the purposes of the architect. The "House of the Seven Gables" recast and immortalized in fiction likewise stands, we are told, "halfway down a bystreet of one of our New England towns," an ancient mansion shrouded in gloom, wrapped in mystery, and rotting with secrets.[1] Halfway between history and fable, this quaint Gothic romance looms large in the American canon as an allegory of our history that is intensely local and intensely archetypal in its representation of the divisions and self-contradictions that characterize the Puritan origins of the American mind.

Hawthorne warned readers against literal-minded comparisons between the fictional house and its prototype or between Salem and the "old New England town" of his story by insisting on the term *romance* to describe his literary objectives. Romance refuses, in a sense, what one critic has called the "social responsibilities" of the novel by shifting the ground of language and undermining its referential function in favor of enhancing its symbolic possibilities.[2] In romance, persons, places, and things become primarily symbolic vehicles; their connection with the realities of the material world is secondary. Yet the material world is as necessary to the project of romance as it is to the project of the novel: it is from our experience of actual structures that we derive a sense of structure and ultimately are able to contemplate structure and structuring as activities of the imagination necessary to the business of signification and meaning. This aspect of romance derives directly from transcendentalist cosmology in which the visible world is "charged," or impregnated, with symbolic potential and actualized by the seer, whose own idiosyncratic intelligence places it in a frame of reference made up of a unique body of experience, only part of which is shared; the other part is buried in the unconscious or kept among the "secrets of the heart," which Hawthorne believed bear on our simplest interactions with the natural and social world.

Like a stake driven into the ground, the first sentence of the story establishes the house as a focal point, moving the reader's eye inward from the lightly sketched map of a town in New England toward the "rusty wooden house, with seven acutely peaked gables, facing towards various points of the compass, and a huge, clustered chimney in the midst" (13). The sentence spirals inward toward the chimney, a vertical axis that marks the spatial center of this theater of action. Mention of the compass widens the imaginative frame beyond the parameters of a little New England town and puts the house at the center of a much larger, cosmic stage. Yet "halfway down a bystreet" also suggests marginality—something a little off center, something we would have to go out of our way to find. "Halfwayness" suggests both centrality and ambivalence; something that is neither here nor there but in between—geographically between town and countryside or (as in Salem) land and ocean, an emblem of the human situation, balanced on a point, as Pascal would say, between two infinities, where the local and the particular, understood deeply and widely enough, reveal the universal and the general.

Most critics would agree that *The House of the Seven Gables* is not Hawthorne's best novel. It is, however, remarkable in its own right as a compendium of contemporary ideas as well as a deconstruction of popular Protestant morality in which were embedded some of the most cherished, lasting, and self-serving myths of Americanness. Written in 1851, several years after Hawthorne's sojourn among the utopian experimenters at Brook Farm, the book reflects in many respects the influences of the transcendental community, whose concerns and doctrines focused heavily on the interpenetration of spirituality and material culture and specifically on the question of proper domestic environment. The novel also reflects the deeper influences of Hawthorne's New England heritage, one that he experienced very much in terms of inherited guilt. The issue of ownership looms large; who owns the land, who owns what was built with other men's hands, what money has to do with ownership, and how a sense of entitlement transcends the legal parameters of inheritance and trade are all central questions in this troubling parable of American experience.[3] Issues of morality and spirituality, psychology, health, law and justice, and national character are brought together here in a complex examination of the house as a locus of human life and an outward and visible representation of most human concerns.

Like all Hawthorne's early works, *The House of the Seven Gables* reads as a fable or allegory, appearing to offer simple equations of meaning, stark contrasts between good and evil, and symbolic characters who represent a spectrum of human qualities. The rhetoric is that of a moral tale or sermon. Yet as in his other works, these conventions soon become complicated, ironic, and ambiguous; what seem in the beginning to be simple allegorical representations open out into multivalent symbols—signposts pointing down multiple and divergent paths to possible meanings. The house, with its seven gables "facing towards various points of the compass," is a symbolic space, a theater of human action whose inhabitants, like Everyman, play out a universal human drama of greed, punishment, and redemption.

Allegory as a form appealed to the preacher in Hawthorne; the notion of world as text that so lent itself to moral object lessons and so delighted the early New England poets and divines who looked to nature to illustrate scripture served his more subversive purposes nicely. Like most well-churched New

Englanders he was familiar with texts like Edwards's "Images or Shadows of Divine Things," where every element of the visible world was assigned some moral and pedagogical significance: hills and mountains were "types of heaven" because they were "with difficulty ascended"; rivers, converging from their diverse sources to flow toward the same ocean, provided a "wonderful analogy" to humanity drawing toward God; and trees conversely an image of the church, the body of Christ with its many divergent branches nourished from the same trunk.[4] The imagery, of course, comes directly from scripture, but its insistently precise extension into metaphysical conceits was absorbed in a peculiarly dogmatic and literal-minded fashion in American usage.

This same allegorical and analogical habit of mind, overtaken and ironized, allowed Hawthorne to develop a complex semiology in the world of his novels, where objects, spaces, colors, and all aspects of the physical world are supercharged with possibilities of meaning until their emblematic significance is overdetermined to the point of confusion and each allegorical signpost seems indeed to point "towards various points of the compass." The house serves as an emblem of the psyche; a mirror of the human face and form, sharing genetic characteristics with its inhabitants; a structural replica of the social institutions that shape national character (the church, the family, the government); a text on which history is inscribed; a stage for a domestic morality play; a vaultlike repository for guilty secrets; a prison, a tomb, and a womb harboring the seeds of its own renewal. The house's appearance is deceptive; like humans whose faces belie their hearts, the evil that infests the house is concealed to the eye of the uninitiate, who may regard it with veneration rather than suspicion:

> So little faith is due to external appearance that there was really an inviting aspect over the venerable edifice, conveying an idea that its history must be a decorous and happy one, and such as would be delightful for a fireside tale. Its windows gleamed cheerfully in the slanting sunlight. The lines and tufts of green moss, here and there, seemed pledges of familiarity and sisterhood with Nature; as if this human dwelling place, being of such old date, had established its prescriptive title among primeval oaks and whatever other objects,

by virtue of their long continuance, have acquired a gracious right to be. A person of imaginative temperament, while passing by the house, would turn, once and again, and peruse it well: its many peaks, consenting together in the clustered chimneys; the deep projection over its basement story; the arched window, imparting a look, if not of grandeur, yet of antique gentility, to the broken portal over it opened; the luxuriance of gigantic burdocks, near the threshold; he would note all these characteristics, and be conscious of something deeper than he saw. He would conceive the mansion to have been the residence of the stubborn old Puritan, Integrity, who, dying in some forgotten generation, had left a blessing in all its rooms and chambers. (255)

The house, like the body that houses the soul of a sinner, is an ambiguous text, open to readers who are "conscious of something deeper" and yet are constrained to interpret these deeper things through the filters of their own innocence or guilt.

At its simplest, most parabolic level, the story of this house recalls, like a good Puritan sermon, several biblical parables and proverbs: the Pyncheons have built their house not on the rock of truth and justice but on a sandy foundation of greed, deception, and injustice. It is a house divided against itself. It is, like the house of Israel, an ancient edifice now rotting from within. Into its midst comes a stranger, who is really a rightful son, to destroy and rebuild it from its foundations, removing the curse that has been the source of its inner degeneration. The outline of Christian salvation history is reiterated in the house's story, from original sin to the moment of redemption.

The imprint of Puritan sermons is etched clearly on the novel's pages. Adopting the voice of the prophet and the rhetoric of the early Puritan jeremiads that warned the people against falling away and called them to awaken to their condition, the narrator of this tale stands above the action and outside narrative time on a moral pinnacle from which he can read signs and portents in the history of this household that bode ill for the future if the people continue in their path of greed, insularity, and enslavement to moribund traditions. He might have taken as an epigraph Edwards's warning in "Sinners in the Hands of an Angry God" that "the foolish children of men miserably delude themselves in their own schemes, and in confidence in their own strength and wisdom."[5] Like the second and third generations of settlers' children who fell away from the motivating vision that brought their fathers to the new world, the Pyncheons have "laid up for themselves treasures on earth where moth and rust corrupt." Yet their punishment remains long unrecognized because it comes in the form of gradual diminishment and decay of the family line. As the narrator points out, "There is something so massive, stable, and almost irresistibly imposing in the exterior presentment of established rank and great possessions that their very existence seems to give them a right to exist; at least, so excellent a counterfeit of right, that few poor and humble men have moral force enough to question it, even in their secret minds" (30). Over time, evil can come to be accepted as normal, but that acceptance does not right the imbalance in the spiritual economy. It is only a culpable form of blindness that delays restoration of harmony and prolongs the dissemination of evil. What is "real and present" in solid, material form can obscure things that are more profoundly real and more powerfully operative, though only recognizable by those who have not been dazzled and blinded by the light of the visible world.

But the visible world is impregnated by the spiritual and eventually and inevitably manifests the good or evil forces that govern the latter world. Thus, the "stately mansion" that seemed to the early Judge Pyncheon nothing less than a fitting tribute to his own august character, a "fair emblem," harbors in itself the seeds of its own destruction:

> Ah, but in some low and obscure nook—some narrow closet on the ground floor, shut, locked and bolted, and the key flung away; or beneath the marble pavement, in a stagnant water puddle, with the richest pattern of mosaic work above—may lie a corpse, half decayed, and still decaying, and diffusing its death scent all through the palace! The inhabitant will not be conscious of it, for it has long been his daily breath! Neither will the visitors, for they smell only the rich odors which the master sedulously scatters through the palace, that pool of stagnant water, foul with many impurities, and, perhaps, tinged with blood—that secret abomination, above which, possibly, he may say his prayers, without remembering it—is this man's miserable soul! (201–202)

Prophetically pre-Freudian in his understanding of the psychology of repression, Hawthorne details the psychological dimensions of his moral allegory with amazing clarity: the thing suppressed has more power than the thing made conscious, and that power is deeper and more dangerous than any of the forms of power by which waking life is governed. The inhabitants, like the house, are haunted and are subject to the powers that haunt them. Their minds, like their rooms, are spaces occupied by invading spirits. The narrator's description of the Judge Pyncheon now alive, Clifford and Hepzibah's cousin, reiterates this pattern of subtle and progressive degeneration: "In his youth, he had probably been considered a handsome man; at his present age, his brow was too heavy, his temples too bare, his remaining hair too gray, his eye too cold, his lips too closely compressed, to bear any relation to mere personal beauty" (56).

Into this scene of moral degeneration comes a young stranger, a Maule, descendant of the original builder, a new breed of man who, like his wizard ancestor, works his own kind of magic with the mysteries of new technology. He is a photographer, who turns light into visible forms, exposing corrupting secrets, mystifying the uninitiate, and finally embracing the daughter of his enemies in a redemptive act that promises a new covenant. The return of the laborer's descendant to claim his inheritance and exhibit his "magical" and unorthodox power leads to the verification of land stolen from the Indians in the hidden deed. Self-delusion, moral blindness, hypocrisy, and complacency all come in for the usual excoriation here, not simply as evils to which the human heart in its perennial weakness is prone but as genetic flaws in national character, bred into it by the very institutions that perpetuate culture and transmit it from generation to generation in an increasing heritage of guilt and moral impotence.

With the double edge of the social critic who draws his wisdom from the institutions he condemns, Hawthorne's narrator retails the story of original betrayal:

> Old Matthew Maule, in a word, was executed for the crime of witchcraft. He was one of the martyrs to that terrible delusion, which should teach us, among its other morals, that the influential classes, and those who take upon themselves to be leaders of

the people, are fully liable to all the passionate error that has ever characterized the maddest mob. Clergymen, judges, statesmen—the wisest, calmest, holiest persons of their day—stood in the inner circle round about the gallows, loudest to applaud the work of blood, latest to confess themselves miserably deceived. If any one part of their proceedings can be said to deserve less blame than another, it was the singular indiscrimination with which they persecuted not merely the poor and aged, as in former judicial massacres, but people of all ranks; their own equals, brethren, and wives. (15)

As Hawthorne's sermon-bred audience well knew, the proper use of the past lies in its prophetic portent for the present; application means drawing the analogy and heeding the warning. The voice of the anti-institutional Emersonian prophet rings clearly here and is made more sonorous by the heritage of guilt borne by a son of the self-righteous judges who cast the first stones at the witches in Salem in the generation of Matthew Maule. The narrator's animating vision seems to penetrate to the very heart of things and reach far beyond them to their widely rippling social and historical implications, though whether his capacity to "see" is prophetic or fanciful remains for us to judge.

An even earlier voice than those of the Puritan preachers is echoed here; the warnings of Jesus to a community whose institutions and practices have grown corrupt and whose edifices of power are rotting at the foundations are reiterated here in the dire reminders of the consequences of building on a foundation of greed and guilt a house standing over an unquiet grave haunted by restless spirits seeking restitution for injustices that time does not heal. The deep distrust of institutional religion and of civil structures with similar claims to authority makes the story of this old New England patrician family an American morality tale whose message is a secular version of the old call to repentance and renewal, abandonment of "the old man" and the old covenant, and establishment of a new order based on a new vision unclouded by archaic laws and habits of mind. And, indeed, the story ends with a promise of a "new covenant" in which familial and class antagonisms are obliterated and retribution for the sins of the past is accomplished.

As the story opens, the narrator, in his provocative way, begins by telling us how much he is not going to tell us. Though an account of the "lapse of mortal life, and accompanying vicissitudes" that have transpired within this house would "form a narrative of no small interest and instruction," he is going to "make short work" of the evidently rich and fascinating traditional lore attached to the old landmark; we shall have to settle for the comparatively paltry business of looking in on its present inhabitants. We must begin the story somewhere, and the true beginnings of things, he thus reminds us, lie buried deep in the past. The story we are about to hear is the tip of an iceberg of myth, lore, and history, informed by forces well beyond what is present and visible, though encoded in those material vestiges. If we read them carefully, they provide inklings, incitements to look further and deeper, to look again, to see more. We are not to look merely to satisfy idle curiosity of the sort that local passersby might indulge, however. Rather, we are invited to take moral stock of this place and its melancholy inhabitants; the place is to become a parable in wood and stone. Yet even as we make our judgments and read our lessons in it, we are to remember on what deceptive bases we judge the actions and appearances of men. We read always at the risk of misreading and so revealing ourselves to be bigots or fools. As we enter the story with the narrator as our guide, we embark on the slippery path of interpretation at our own moral peril.

The narrator, however, knows something of the way, though his own understanding is limited, speculative, and predicated, it seems, on much hearsay. He introduces himself as one long familiar with the household and all its curious stories. He is a seer; he has the double vision of a spiritual man who sees beyond the literal structures of the visible world to the invisible forces and spirits that animate it: "The aspect of the venerable mansion has always affected me like a human countenance" (13), he observes and thereafter induces us to regard its aspect under the same conceit. The more we do so, the more human it becomes, with its heavy "brows," its "venerable peaks," its "meditative look," and its unsightly shop door, divided horizontally, just under the brow of the front gable, looking out on the street like a half-closed and baleful eye. Here, as in "The Fall of the House of Usher," the house seems more fully alive than its inhabitants. This impression of animation is made explicit to the point of irony when the narrator, carried away with his romantic conceit, declares that "the very timbers were oozy, as with the moisture of a heart. It was itself like a great human heart, with a life of its own, and full of rich and somber reminiscences" (32).

Like the house of Usher, this house reflects and is reflected by the faces and bodies of those who dwell within it, exposing their secrets by replicating their physiognomies for the world to read, a house that embodies something so profoundly and universally human that it has come itself to participate in the humanity of its inhabitants: so much so that "you could not pass it without the idea that it had secrets to keep, and an eventful history to moralize on" (32). The windows of the house are frequently referred to as eyes, looking from their various oddly angled perspectives onto the street or garden. Its "clustered chimney" becomes, in a windstorm the day of Judge Pyncheon's death, a "sooty throat" that makes a "vociferous but somewhat unintelligible bellowing" (248).

As the narrative continues, these metaphors exceed the bounds of simple comparison and are increasingly literalized. The house indeed seems to breathe an atmosphere of brooding melancholy, and the walls creak with untold stories. The large looking glass that had hung for generations in one of the rooms "was fabled to contain within its depths all the shapes that had ever been reflected there." If he only knew how to look at it properly, the narrator seems to believe, he could "read" its contents: "Had we the secret of that mirror, we would gladly sit down before it, and transfer its revelations to our page" (26). The only obstacle that seems to stand between our ignorance and the revelations of the shrouded past is our inability to read the hieroglyphics inscribed on the material world. The answers to our riddles lie before us but are written in a language only the most discerning can decipher. Thus, the contemplation of any object becomes an effort to draw forth its stories, its lessons, the truths it has to tell us. Hawthorne's sense of the ways in which values inhere in the physical structures we erect is reminiscent of Thoreau's meditations on houses as value-bearing artifacts in *Walden*. In *Seven Gables* the home is a moral force-field where we enter into a mysteriously reciprocal relation with the inanimate objects and spaces that are the locus of daily life.

As we contemplate the old Pyncheon house, the narrator pauses to remind us in his paradoxical way of both the uniqueness and the universality of the revelations about to ensue: "Though the old edifice was surrounded by habitations of modern date, they were mostly small, built entirely of wood, and typical of the most plodding uniformity of common life. Doubtless, however, the whole story of human existence may be latent in each of them, but with no picturesqueness, externally, that can attract the imagination or sympathy to seek it there" (31). In this sardonic comparison a keynote is sounded: we must look into the past for an understanding of what is most deeply human. The present is a time of diminishment, sterility, and "plodding uniformity." But the blueprints of even our most vestigial forms can be discovered in the relics, like the hoary old house, that have survived the ravages of time, and though they recall an era of great sins and great sinners, they may serve to make us take measure of some loss of greatness that has befallen us all.

As the house reflects its human inhabitants, so they reflect back its architectural characteristics, which appear like family traits that show up transliterated in each face that bears them. Architectural terminology creeps into the descriptions of faces and human forms. The original Colonel Pyncheon, for instance, was "a gentleman noted for the square and ponderous courtesy of his demeanor" (19); Hepzibah is "black, rusty, and scowling," a woman whose "brain was impregnated with the dry rot of its timbers" (58); and Clifford is broad-faced and luminous, like the arched window of his room.

But Phoebe, who has not been molded to the rigid forms of this old structure but has been left to grow in a freer atmosphere untainted by the inherited house and all its accumulated guilt, is all sunshine and spirit and seems to move about the place with the freedom and pervasiveness of light and air. Like Holgrave, the photographer, she brings into this gloomy den of antiquity her own kind of sunshine and magic—a benevolent "witchcraft" to match his wizardry, a "natural magic" that enables her to "bring out the hidden capabilities of things." Women like Phoebe, the narrator declares, are able mysteriously "to give a look of comfort and habitableness to any place which, for however brief a period, may happen to be their home. A wild hut of underbrush, tossed together by wayfarers through the primitive forest, would acquire the home aspect by one night's lodging of such a woman, and would retain it long after her quiet figure had disappeared into the surrounding shade" (71). Thus, she transforms her room in the old house, which "had resembled nothing so much as the old maid's heart; for there was neither sunshine nor household fire in one nor the other, and, save for ghosts and ghostly reminiscences, not a guest, for many years gone by, had entered the heart or the chamber" (68–69). A few weeks after Phoebe's arrival her triumph over the dark powers invested in the house is already manifest:

> The grime and sordidness of the House of the Seven Gables seemed to have vanished since her appearance there; the gnawing tooth of the dry rot was stayed among the old timbers of its skeleton frame; the dust had ceased to settle down so densely, from the antique ceilings, upon the floors and furniture of the rooms below— or, at any rate, there was a little housewife, as light-footed as the breeze that sweeps a garden walk, gliding hither and thither to brush it all away. (123)

In pathetic contrast to this paean are the scenes of Hepzibah's domestic impotence, where the house and the forces of nature themselves seem deliberately to defeat her attempts to revive some spirit of warmth and hospitality. Thus, during a stormy afternoon, "Hepzibah attempted to enliven matters by a fire in the parlor. But the storm demon kept watch above and, whenever a flame was kindled, drove the smoke back again, choking the chimney's sooty throat with its own breath" (197).

The secret of Phoebe's power lies in her youth; her womanhood, with all the healing powers ascribed to it by the romantic imagination; her innocence of the family guilt; but perhaps more importantly, in the circumstances of her life, which have put her in normal relation to the world and spared her the deforming isolation of this inwardly turned prison-house of the soul. She is "practical"—not prey to debilitating fancies or enslaved by memory, history, or tradition. She is a woman of her own time and place whose indifference to unsolved mysteries and unpaid moral debts disarms the ghosts of the past. By contrast, the house, like its inhabitants, seems a figure of the obsessed introspective, turned always inward to feed on his own brooding imaginings, immune, after long years of isolation, to the corrective effects of social intercourse. Holgrave, himself a visitor from the world beyond the gabled walls, recognizes the character of Phoebe's healthful influence and pronounces prophetically, "Whatever health, comfort, and natural life exists in the house is embodied in your person. These blessings came along with you, and will vanish when you leave the threshold. Miss Hepzibah, by secluding herself from society, has lost all true relation with it, and is, in fact, dead; though she galvanizes herself into a semblance of life, and stands behind her counter, afflicting the world with a greatly-to-be-deprecated scowl" (190).

Miss Hepzibah's chronic scowl finds its opposite and counterpart in Clifford's childlike gaze. Both look out on the world from their framed and limited perspectives—she from her shop door and he from the arched window of his chamber. Both have lost that "true relation" with the larger world that Holgrave speaks of and see it through veils of alienation and fear. Clifford's window is of "uncommonly large dimensions, shaded by a pair of curtains," and when he goes to view the passersby in the street below he "throw[s] it open, but keeping himself in comparative obscurity by means of the curtain" (142), thus maintaining the protective but debilitating isolation that has so diminished him and his pathetic sister.

Thoreau's warning that possessions may come to possess their possessor could serve as an epigraph to this moral tale, where the dwellers seem possessed by the house and where the loss of propriety in that relation leads to the sickness of soul that seems so palpably to affect dwellers and dwelling alike. Throughout the narrative we are led thus to ponder the reciprocities of moral influence that characterize our relation to the material world. The power of those influences is reaffirmed in the final vision of the house at the story's end; after its secrets have been exposed and its guilt expiated by the marriage of a Pyncheon and a Maule, it becomes, under new occupancy, "a substantial, jolly-looking mansion, and seemed fit to be the residence of a patriarch, who might establish his own headquarters in the front gable and assign one of the remainder to each of his six children, while the great chimney in the center should symbolize the old fellow's hospitable heart, which kept them all warm, and made a great whole of the seven smaller ones" (170). Clearly the house is not evil in essence, only in usage. Having regained something of its original innocence by virtue of a redemptive act, it partakes of the vitality and health of its new inhabitants.

The tendency to regard the material world as infused and impregnated amounts to a secular version of incarnational theology just this side of animism. Hawthorne and his transcendentalist neighbors shared something very close to this worldview, which in less philosophical form was well entrenched in the popular imagination of their contemporaries. The world was, they believed, charged with moral significance and manifested in every particular the presence of the divine. Sins and secrets inhered in the objects made by men, just as redemptive grace inhered in nature. In light of this general notion Hawthorne's passages about natural beauty are more than sentimental fancies; they are reflections on the ways in which nature exerts its renewing influence on the bumbling work of human hands. Thus, the narrator pensively remarks, "It was both sad and sweet to observe how Nature adopted to herself this desolate, decaying, gusty, rusty old house of the Pyncheon family; and how the ever-returning summer did her best to gladden it with tender beauty, and grew melancholy in the effort" (33).

The one grace of this ravaged mansion is the foliage and garden that surround it. "In front, just on the edge of the unpaved sidewalk, grew the Pyncheon Elm, which, in reference to such trees as one usually meets with, might well be termed gigantic. . . . It gave beauty to the old edifice, and seemed to make it a part of nature. . . . On either side extended a ruinous wooden fence of open latticework, through which could be seen a grassy yard, and, especially in the angles of the building, an enormous fertility of burdocks" (31). The garden is a refuge for Clifford and Phoebe, gentle souls who flee the house when they can and seek solace in this place where life can flourish—where there is still some balance between the forces of nature and domestication. It is "the Eden of a thunder-smitten Adam, who had fled for refuge thither out of the same dreary and perilous wilderness into which the original Adam was expelled" (134). Here in the garden, some of the crucial scenes of the story take place because here in the garden, balance survives.

The house, however, is a dark, dank, unhealthy place. Houses seem to be necessary evils, blemishes on the face of nature. In the spirit in which Thoreau declares in his essay on civil disobedience that "that government is best which governs least," Holgrave believes with Thoreau that that house is best that separates least from nature. In both cases, manufactured structures are suspect, their utility and propriety are to be reassessed by each successive generation in light of present needs, and the entrenchment of tradition and dogma are to be resisted. Otherwise, those structures become stifling and confining and, in limiting change, growth, and "natural" development, breed sickness in the body politic.

The language of health and sickness attended much of the contemporary discussion of architecture as well as of social and political structures. Andrew Jackson Downing popularized the notion that the design of buildings had a significant impact on the health of their inhabitants, particularly in matters of heat, ventilation, and "atmosphere"—a word that was taken both literally and figuratively, as was the notion of health itself, which in popular theories combined physical and spiritual well-being. Hawthorne's treatment of the atmospherics of the Pyncheon house, where spiritual decay is made manifest in mold, rot, and dank air that slowly sicken the people within, reflects this widespread belief. The theories of William and Bronson Alcott and others about the direct influence of the domestic environment on the health of mind, soul, and body were well known, thoroughly discussed, and to some degree tested in the utopian communities at Brook Farm and Fruitlands. Nor was it only professional builders or small groups of experimental philosophers who thought of homes and houses as determinants of mental, spiritual, and physical welfare. Ministers routinely addressed the issue of the home as a formative environment whose "atmosphere" shaped the character and attitudes as well as affected the bodily health of children growing up in them; clergymen extended their exhortations beyond matters of training and discipline to prescriptions of pure air and proper ventilation.[6]

Architecture as a practical science with significant moral implications partook in the general romantic belief that manufacture must follow nature in order to promote a proper relation between public and private life. "Following nature" meant espousing some idea of organicism and a holistic approach to understanding human nature and needs. In architecture this meant building, as Downing put it, "houses with feeling." A house with feeling would provide direct access to and experience of nature by modifying the intellectual severity of classical lines and looking to forms found in nature for impetus or models. It would always be surrounded with trees, shrubbery, and other foliage; model homes depicted in popular publications of the day were surrounded by trellises and vines that gave them the general appearance of having sprung from the soil itself.[7] This aesthetic, in large part a reaction against the dogmatic abstractions of Enlightenment ideals of symmetry, proportion, and rectilinearity and against the pretensions of Federalist and Greek revival styles, is reflected in the attention to the healing influences of nature on the sickly House of the Seven Gables— most notably the protective shadow of the ancient Pyncheon elm: "It had been planted by a great-grandson of the first Pyncheon, and though now four-score years of age, or perhaps nearer a hundred, was still in its strong and broad maturity, throwing its shadow from side to side of the street, overtopping the seven gables, and sweeping the whole black roof with its pendant foliage. It gave beauty to the old edifice, and seemed to make it a part of nature" (32). The narrator goes on to describe other foliage and the garden behind the house with their softening effects on the grim mansion. Nature sustains and redeems the house and its inhabitants, providing a refuge and place of sanity to offset the deranged and unhealthy interior environment.

The notion of visible and invisible worlds as structurally analogous is reinforced in another vein by the obvious analogies between the image of the House of the Seven Gables and text of *The House of the Seven Gables*. As in *The Scarlet Letter*, the book and its central symbol bear not only the same appellation but other similarities that confuse the distinctions between the two. The house has three stories and seven gables radiating outward "towards various points of the compass." Each of the three stories is occupied principally by one of the three reclusive inhabitants: the first by Hepzibah in her kitchen and cent shop; the second by Clifford, who watches the world from behind the veil of his arched window; and the third by the mysterious boarder, Holgrave, a photographer whose art seems descended from the wizardry of his ancestors and whose fate is bound to the old house by dint of an inherited wrong that remains to be righted. The house's foundations were laid in early colonial history, and on its weathered walls are inscribed the guilty secrets of an old New England family.

The book, similarly rooted in the Puritan origins of its writer, falls rather nicely into three sections, each with seven chapters and each focused in turn on the house's three inhabitants. Including the narrator there are seven principal characters, though the narrator occupies a curious position halfway between the characters of whose world he seems so intimately a part and the audience, to whom he speaks as a familiar. The tripartite division of the text creates a symmetry that reiterates the structure and tensions of the house itself. What seems to begin as simple allegory acquires as the story proceeds a multiplicity of symbolic dimensions; simple dichotomies branch and tangle into increasingly complicated issues as the house becomes a more and more inclusive symbol of every aspect of life, history, and relationship. Conventional boundaries between the world of the text and the world outside the text dissolve as the two worlds mirror one another in an endless reiteration of signs and symbols, and the simplest objects assume archetypal dimensions. Symbolic numbers, shapes, and geometrical configurations abound; in scene after scene the architecture of the house reiterates itself in a spatial symbology that explicitly evokes comparisons with psychic and linguistic syntax, and the mind finds itself caught in a hall of mirrors where everything is mind looking at itself with the vision of Emerson's "transparent eyeball."

The equation among house, text, and human psyche, with their tripartite divisions, anatomical likenesses, and architectural congruencies, is like that established in *Walden* and "The Fall of the House of Usher," but here the analogy is taken a step further as the story of this divided house grows into an increasingly explicit allegory of American history, with its terrible heritage of guilt, oppression, expropriation, and hypocrisy. The house becomes a microcosm of the structures and conditions of American life as Hawthorne reads into it a story of stolen land, guilt, and retribution (themes that Faulkner later amplifies in a southern sequel). And indeed all the characteristic conflicts of American life: class conflict, institutionalized hypocrisy, the chronic tension between family, tradition, and orthodoxy, on the one hand, and separation, innovation, and heresy, on the other. Already in its beginnings the nation was a "house divided against itself," and those divisions are represented in this microcosm as inequities of class, race, and gender play out their consequences in this family drama.

Deeply embedded in American mythology is a belief in original integrity now lost. Until the redemptive moment is accomplished, the house is at odds with the earth on which it sits—a spot of ground the narrator calls "disputed soil." "The House of the Seven Gables, antique as it now looks," he reminds us, "was not the first habitation erected by civilized man on precisely the same spot of ground" but was erected "over [the] unquiet grave" of the earlier settler, thereby ignoring the legitimate claims of his children (12, 14). The parallel between the house and the human psyche here emerges again: the grand edifice represses—literally shoves underground—the secret that will become its curse. What is buried and what is manifest are at odds, and the house lacks integrity because the forces that divide it are built into its foundation. Though the narrator proceeds thereupon to detail the history of Matthew Maule's prior claim and settlement, underlying this story is an even earlier story of dispossession that began with the invasion of those "civilized men" into a country already in the keeping of earlier claimants. Here the theme of stolen land, which Faulkner later takes up and carries further, begins to loom large in the economy of crime, guilt, and punishment that so characterizes American mythology and fiction. With the mention of land wrested from the Indians, the story's allegorical potential begins to unfold and widen.

Like *The Scarlet Letter* and other novels of its generation, this novel conflates religious with political allegory: a story of expropriation, settlement, establishment, and building on a foundation of usurpation and injustice. The project of claiming, settling, and civilizing a continent is presented with profound ambivalence, and Hawthorne's characteristic preoccupation with guilt and expiation as a fundamental part of national heritage surfaces again. The question of what constitutes a legitimate claim to ownership is brought up explicitly not only in an ironic presentation of the complicated legalities that over time made such claims more and more ludicrously attenuated but also in the observation that over time the distance between de jure and de facto ownership tends to widen. The actual occupants of the "Pyncheon" land to which the claim is found, "if they ever heard of the Pyncheon title, would have laughed at the idea of any man's asserting a right—on the faded strength of moldy parchments, signed with the faded autographs of governors and legislators long dead and forgotten—to the lands which they or their fathers had wrested from the wild hand of nature by their own sturdy toil" (24).

Domestication and appropriation are distinguished as two entirely different enterprises, the one legitimate and noble, the other presumptuous, dangerous, and self-deluding. Those who live on and with the land, savages or settlers, are presumed to be both more intimate with nature and more properly owners of the land by virtue of their intimacy with it, regardless of the law's systems of legitimation. The representatives of the superimposed legal and social order with their "moldy parchments" operate at several removes from this primeval and archetypal relation and to legitimate their seizure of power trust to words and abstractions and indirect, oppressive forms of power derived from dead predecessors. The question of ownership is posed here not only in political and historical terms but in wider moral terms as well. What decides right of ownership? Inheritance is at least two removes from that direct claim established by those who inhabited and cultivated the land. Those who buy it have a lesser claim; those who inherit it have a very tenuous one indeed. And yet, the narrator suggests, our whole system of justice and property rights is based on just such dubious claims. Their dubiousness derives as well from the fragility of the written word. Documents are mere shadows, vestiges, or pale representations of the realities they purport to describe and control. We have mistaken, he seems to say, the insubstantial for the substantial. That confusion sounds one of the keynotes of the novel, in which the relation between the solid, substantial, and manifest and the abstract, spiritual, and hidden comes to seem increasingly problematic and reciprocal.

This line of argument culminates in a profoundly ironic self-referentiality when the very notion of textuality in a text-based culture is brought into question. What are the Constitution and the Bible, secular and sacred texts on which we predicate our whole system of communal life, but insubstantial "moldy parchments" whose claim on us is subject to the same kind of radical questioning? Hawthorne posits a similar theological conundrum in which, once again, the word made flesh throws into question the word preserved on stone or parchment.

The argument of Emerson's "American Scholar," based similarly on a distrust of institutions, books, and the recorded wisdom of past generations, is reproduced almost verbatim in some of Holgrave's impassioned speeches about the oppressive presence of the past. In that essay Emerson declares the book (and the institutions erected on the foundation of "sacred texts") a danger to freethinking men when used to blind them to and shield them from the specific needs and issues of their own generation. Book learning becomes a form of idolatry, and attentiveness to the lessons of the past degenerates easily into sterile antiquarianism that impedes originality and prevents the development of new models of action. This same view of scholarship as enslavement and history as a record of diminishment resounds in each of Hawthorne's longer tales, which end in a utopian's cry for resistance and renewal.

Holgrave, of course, is the new man described in Emerson's "Self-Reliance"—a Thoreauvian hero recast and domesticated—and a forerunner of Faulkner's Quentin Compson, with his love-hate relationship to his familial and regional past. Holgrave possesses a new, unfamiliar, and mysterious kind of power in being a photographer, using a technology that at the time was still marvelous, baffling, and even a little frightening. (He tells Phoebe, when all is revealed, "In this long drama of retribution I represent the old wizard, and am probably as much a wizard as ever he was" (275), leaving her and us to ponder the ambiguity of that claim.) He writes for magazines, places little stock in books. This vocation suits well his conviction that things are transitory, to be let go, not preserved in musty libraries and made into relics. As Phoebe gets to know him, she learns to admire precisely those qualities in him that characterize the emerging American hero of fiction and philosophy—radically individualistic, undomesticated, nomadic, and spiritually enlightened: "Homeless as he had been—continually changing his wherabout, and, therefore, responsible neither to public opinion nor to individuals; putting off one exterior, and snatching up another, to be soon shifted for a third—he had never violated the innermost man, but had carried his conscience along with him" (157). An opponent of stability and tradition, his asocial tendencies are construed as responsiveness to a higher law.

Unburdened by connections, a solitary content to be much alone with his conscience, he resembles in certain obvious ways the "Son of Man" with nowhere to lay his head. For Holgrave, the material world needs to be divested of its oppressive burden of sentimental and symbolic significance in order to be habitable. Material objects must not be invested with such power over the imagination, or they will drain the vitality from those who own them and threaten eventual collapse of the soul into a state of servile sterility. Life can be preserved and perpetuated only if equal and opposite forces come from within and without—if the quantity of a man's spiritual potency and inner vision is equal to the tendency of the material world to overwhelm those channels to truth with insistent and immediate claims for attention. Yet Holgrave, like his prototypes, is a man who knows the past more intimately than do those around him. It is not ignorance of the past but freedom from its prescriptive force that he strives to maintain. The hero that Hawthorne was helping to define, and who has survived far into the twentieth century, is the one who can bear the burden of the past without letting it crush him and can reverse the balance of forces so that the past is turned to his purposes and not vice versa. One of the primary strategies of that hero with a hundred faces is to abandon old structures and erect new ones or, if he must, to live in them under protest and insist that such settlement is a temporary expedient.

Condemning the Pyncheon house as unwholesome, antiquated, and stifling, Holgrave thus justifies his continuing presence in it to Phoebe by declaring that he is "pursuing [his] studies" there, adding, "not in books, however. . . . The house, in my view, is expressive of that odious and abominable Past, with all its bad influences, against which I have just been declaiming. I dwell in it for a while that I may know the better how to hate it" (163–164). Waxing eloquent on the virtues of escaping the past and its ossified institutions, he declares, "I doubt whether even our public edifices—our capitols, state houses, courthouses, city hall, and churches—ought to be built of such permanent materials as stone or brick. It were better that they should crumble to ruin once in twenty years, or thereabouts, as a hint to the people to examine into and reform the institutions which they symbolize" (163). The old house with its portal "broad as a church door," its gables reaching "skyward" like steeples, and its succession of judges and magistrates comes to symbolize every kind of edifice left by past generations as a vestige of their faltering social structures.

Family itself is one of the institutions that bears the seeds of its own destruction. It, in fact, exercises the most pernicious kinds of claims of the past on the present. "To plant a family! This idea is at the bottom of the wrong and mischief which men do. The truth is, that, once in every half century, at longest, a family should be merged into the great, obscure mass of humanity, and forget all about its ancestors. Human blood, in order to keep its freshness, should run in hidden streams, as the water of aqueduct is conveyed in subterranean pipes" (164).

Healthy pluralism keeps generating new heterogeneous forms, which are those most likely to flourish, withstand transplanting, and breed character fit for survival. Reconfiguration and adaptation are the keys to social longevity and are endangered by inbreeding, perpetuation of the stabilizing structures of the past, and isolation. Lest we miss the moral, the narrator adds to Holgrave's Emersonian outburst his own comment: "It seemed to Holgrave—as doubtless it has seemed to the hopeful of every century since the epoch of Adam's grandchildren—that in this age, more than ever before, the moss-grown and rotten Past is to be torn down, and lifeless institutions to be thrust out of the way, and their dead corpses buried, and everything to begin anew" (164).

Clifford joins Holgrave in this general condemnation of the misuses and misapplications of the past. Their protestations recall with comic explicitness Emerson and his younger disciples preaching the same doctrine from their different generational perspectives. Clifford's apotheosis comes in a remarkable and uncharacteristically vehement diatribe delivered to a hapless stationmaster he encounters on his flight from the old mansion to parts unknown:

> The greatest possible stumbling blocks in the path of human happiness and improvement are these heaps of bricks and stones, consolidated with mortar, or hewn timber, fastened together with spike nails, which men painfully contrive for their own torment, and call them house and home! The soul needs air; a wide sweep and frequent change of it. Morbid influences, in a thousandfold variety, gather about hearths, and pollute the life of households. There is no such unwholesome atmosphere as that of an old home, rendered poisonous by one's defunct forefathers and relatives. (228)

Clifford is also the one to articulate the vision of a future free from the weighty stabilities of house and home and all they represent:

> It is my firm belief and hope that these terms of roof and hearthstone, which have so long been held to embody something sacred, are soon to pass out of men's daily use, and be forgotten. Just imagine, for a moment, how much of human evil will crumble away, with this one change! What we call real estate—the solid ground to build

a house on—is the broad foundation on which nearly all the guilt of this world rests. A man will commit almost any wrong—he will heap up an immense pile of wickedness, as hard as granite, and which will weigh as heavily upon his soul, to eternal ages—only to build a great, gloomy, dark-chambered mansion, for himself to die in, and for his posterity to be miserable in. He lays his own dead corpse beneath the underpinning, as one may say, and hangs his frowning picture on the wall, and, after thus converting himself into an evil destiny, expects his remotest great-grandchildren to be happy there! (229–230)

Both Clifford's and Holgrave's convictions are those of victims of the evils they describe. Hepzibah, who does not have their capacity to reflect on her situation, has simply fallen prey to it and has consequently become "a kind of lunatic, by imprisoning herself so long in one place, with no other company than a single series of ideas, and but one affection, and one bitter sense of wrong" (160). Phoebe, however, though by name and heritage implicated in the family drama, has remained, by virtue of her womanly innocence and lateral kinship, unblighted by the family curse and so is able to temper this zealotry with an innate practical, sensible immediacy that the men have to strive to achieve by taking much thought. She simply brings into the old house her own modest standards of comfort and commodity and unfolds its possibilities in those terms. Thus, almost without taking thought, like the Victorian "angel of the house" that she is, she makes the house "like a home to [Holgrave], and the garden a familiar precinct" (161).

In the end it is the combination of Phoebe's unspoiled feminine influence, Holgrave's strategic revelations, and the healthy spirit of compromise that acknowledges, expiates, and dispenses with the lingering burdens of the past that provides the new beginning that is the end point of so many American stories. The resolution, though in some ways distressingly formulaic, manages to provide satisfaction on a number of philosophical questions, the main one being the question of appropriate living arrangements. Pyncheons and Maules together leave the old house for a new place in the country where they are to live an idyllic life as an extended family, steeped in nature, tranquillity, and philosophical conversation in something like the manner of the utopian communes still in fashion. Old Uncle Venner, with a last backward glance, fancies that he perceives the ghost of Alice Pyncheon, released at last by the resolution of the troubled secrets, "float[ing] heavenward from the House of the Seven Gables" (277). Houses, like souls, can be redeemed, but only by being released from the burdens of the past and claimed anew by each living generation. Fitzgerald's observation that the history of the United States is a history of beginnings provides an apt summary to the work of Hawthorne's generation, heirs of the revolution who translated its political protests and claims into metaphysical terms and sought to free themselves from an old world and its structures by abandoning them and recreating gardens in which each successive generation could rediscover innocence.

4

THE PORTRAIT OF A LADY
More Stately Mansions

Much has been written about James's houses and with good reason: of all American novels, his are the most explicitly and consistently architectural in conception and subject.[1] Understanding things "in relation," which he claims is the only way we can understand them, means understanding that all the actual structures we erect around ourselves reflect the fundamental relations we establish as parameters for living together. This includes, of course, the "houses of fiction" that dot the cultural landscape. Conversely, if fiction is like a house, so a house is a kind of fiction: a text, a story, a system of signs, a way of organizing relations into comprehensible patterns. Curtis Dahl, in a brief study of James's uses of architecture, observes about his architectural representations that they are minutely accurate as a record of actual buildings or types of buildings reflecting the architectural fashions of the time; that he regularly uses architecture, city streets, and other physical structures to reflect the attributes of individual characters and of cultures and to serve as indices of cultural differences; and that buildings become a "language through which James expresses American as opposed to British values, the New World as opposed to the Old," thus serving as a primary device for introducing the comparisons that constitute his persistent "international theme."[2]

These observations are clearly borne out in *The Portrait of a Lady*, whose houses present a study in multiple contrasts and conflicts among cultures, personalities, and styles of life.[3] They are based on actual prototypes, some with considerable specificity, such as Osmond's Florentine villa, which, according to R. W. Stallman, is an exact replica of the Villa Mercedes, which James visited in 1869; his descriptions of known houses are so accurate and at the same time so thoroughly elaborated as symbolic objects that, Stallman argues, the "illuminating point" is simply how James manages the conversion of the literal to the symbolic.[4] Each of his houses reflects the moral attitudes, political orthodoxies, structures of social intercourse, and notions of privacy and public life that most define the differences among cultures.

It is in the preface to *The Portrait of a Lady* that James first articulates the famous conceit linking houses and novels that he attributes to Turgenev but that has since become a touchstone for understanding his own theory of fiction. Ellen Eve Frank imagines James's "finely wrought prefaces" themselves as "the house that James built to house his 'houses of fiction.'" She goes on to observe:

> And what might seem to be an infinite regress of houses within houses . . . is in fact finite, ordered according to a complicated spatial and temporal scheme. The prefaces represent the outermost house enclosing the remembered houses in which James wrote his fictions; James then images these fictions as houses which enclose still smaller ones, either those real or imaginary structures which locate and set action or those house-similes which represent the minds and psychological conditions of characters.[5]

About the design of these houses, James himself observes, "The house of fiction has in short not one window, but a million" (ix). He describes Isabel Archer as a "single small cornerstone" on which is erected "the large building of *The Portrait of a Lady*." He goes on to reflect about the novel, "It came to be a square and spacious house—or has at least seemed so to me in this going over it again; but, such as it is, it had to be put up round my young woman while she stood there in perfect isolation" (xi).

Here, in perhaps its most famous American formulation, is the ubiquitous notion of the house as an extension or shell of the self that "grows up" around the inhabitant and participates in his or her attributes. In the same way, the novel is an extension of character—an unfolding of the logic of character—and all the "matter" of the novel—plot, scene, and point of view— flow ineluctably from that logic. Because Isabel cannot be understood "in perfect isolation" but only "in relation," the novelist as a student of character must put her in a variety of changing relations in order to reveal the manifold aspects of her character that are the story's raison d'être. Each house Isabel enters in this novel becomes a "frame" for a portrait of her, and within each frame new aspects of character emerge in the complex image of this girl-woman. Isabel adapts to each house in ways that change both her and our perspectives on the moral attitudes that define her. This process of adaptation may be understood, moreover, as something peculiarly female if we believe Madame Merle's rather bitter observation that "a woman . . . has no natural place anywhere" (196) and is therefore of necessity more readily adaptive than a man to the places in which she finds herself.

Here, as in so many novels about women adapting to the places in which they find themselves, Isabel's progression is toward increasing physical and social confinement and deepening moral conflict, even as her worldly vision widens and her capacity for "fine perception" is further refined. The houses she moves through on her way from Albany to Italy are all in some measure dark, imprisoning, and restricting of freedom of movement and imagination: the Albany house is closed off from the street it fronts; Gardencourt has numerous doors that close off private chambers to which she has no access and through which on several crucial occasions she "bursts" in impatience to force a direct encounter proscribed by tacit house rules; Lockleigh she perceives as a well-appointed, comfortable prison house surrounded by a moat; and Roccanera, Osmond's Roman palace, is "dungeonlike."[6] But where the darkness of the Albany house is a darkness of interiority, protection, and womblike insularity, the darkness of the Roman palace is something much more sinister. The American house, by Mrs. Touchett's assessment, is a "bad" house; the Italian house is "evil." Throughout the novel there are characters who play the parts of fairy godmothers or princes who offer to help Isabel escape these places. But not only does she refuse their aid; the escapes they offer portend their own kinds of imprisonment.[7] In the end, though she understands all too well the nature of the imprisonment to which she has condemned herself, she flees Caspar Goodwood's final attempt to lure her away from her disastrous home and marriage and flees from the garden where he has accosted her into the house, behind a locked door—a move that signifies a closure many readers regard as tragic, though certainly it is no less ambiguous than the moment when Ibsen's Nora slams her husband's door behind her.

Like Hawthorne, James always envisions and depicts human action within frames and on stages: the garden, the courtyard, the parlor, the piazza, the balcony, the bedroom, are all confined settings that generate certain kinds of social intercourse and reveal certain aspects of the manners that to him are the ground of moral understanding. Like a cameraman, he situates the reader in changing relation to the characters by locating the reader's eye at a vantage point that itself is not neutral but that forces on the reader an uncomfortable awareness of his or her own privileged perspective. The operative assumption in James's scene-setting is fairly simple: people's behavior is keyed to place, and they seek the places that allow them to express certain aspects of their character. The locus of action limits and shapes behavior because civilized people do not violate the implicit dictates of setting—civilized behavior is appropriate to context. When actions are removed from one frame of reference to another, their meaning is altered. Such removal, or "reframing," is the essential means by which change of moral perspective occurs. Reframing wrenches things out of their conventional relations and reconfigures them, opening them to reevaluation and introducing the kind of moral ambiguity that James regards as a hallmark of true consciousness.

Interested in the same fundamental questions about the reciprocal influences between individual and environment as his transcendentalist predecessors, James poses them in a different set of terms, taking them out of a large metaphysical context and focusing on the forces of social and manufactured environment rather than of nature on human character. He writes about domestic behavior among domesticated people whose civilization and morality can rightly be understood only in terms of the structures they have erected around themselves and the way they live within those structures. In the case of Americans, the very idea of structure, convention, and orthodoxy seems to produce an uncomfortable apprehension in that they signify loss of freedom and the closing off of possibility.

The Portrait of a Lady is the novel that comes closest to providing a complete catalog of James's architectural devices. Houses in this novel provide detailed semiotic keys to the primary action—the education of Isabel Archer. Each house she enters changes her outlook, her behavior, her values, her status. It may be stretching a point to call *The Portrait of a Lady* a tragedy of homelessness; certainly there is no heroine in nineteenth-century fiction to whom more palatial doors are opened than to Isabel Archer. But what Isabel most poignantly and pointedly lacks is a real home and the particular kind of social and moral formation that comes from deep and prolonged engagement with a particular house on a particular spot of ground. She has not known the intimacies of ownership and the proprietary pride that teach a person how to negotiate with the material world, that provide a sense of style, and that furnish the imagination with the forms and shapes that define cultural sensibility. Like the elder Henry James, Isabel's father was, we are told, a large-minded, restless soul whose taste for change and extravagance of vision were matched by material extravagance yet who had provided his daughters with no anchor in the world but the ability to adapt to shifting circumstances. Some "harsh critics" in the novel went so far as to claim that "he had not even brought up his daughters. They had had no regular education and no permanent home; they had been at once spoiled and neglected," though for all that, Isabel's own sense of the matter was that her "opportunities had been large" (33, 34).

Her experience of the world has been eclectic, relatively autonomous, and free-form, but freedom from conventional restraints has deprived her of a real understanding of "forms" in the Jamesian sense—social structures and rituals that give shape to human relations and make art of life. She suffers, as Elizabeth Sabiston points out, from the "Emersonian illusion" that she can "build therefore [her] own world," and her story is a tale of the disillusionment of a transcendentalist romantic.[8] The theme that dominates James's major fiction—expatriation and displacement—can be understood altogether as an exploration of the consequences of naive rejection or ignorance of civilized forms.

As an expatriated American woman, none of the houses Isabel inhabits is hers in the deep sense of being home. In all of them she lives as a guest or stranger—even, and most pointedly, in her husband's. She has charm and intelligence but little of the savoir faire that enables an individual to prevail in the Darwinian struggle for social survival. She has ideas but no developed cultural context to put them in perspective. She has money that gives her entrée into society and the "best houses" but has no standards of judgment to help her gauge the values they embody and perpetuate. And the warning note in this jeremiad is that money and ideas without grounding in material culture are dangerous abstractions.

Isabel's education lacks, in short, what James would call "manners." And without manners, as he shows in some of his most memorable characters, high moral attitudes border on the ridiculous. Many of James's Americans do, for this reason, suffer from elements of the ridiculous; they are unsubtle, uncultured, simplistic, and naive, albeit honest, high-minded, and uncorrupted by the corrosive elements of civilized life. The most stolidly un-Europeanized Americans in this novel are, in a sense, buffoons: Caspar Goodwood, Isabel's literal-minded, forthright, upstanding, American suitor, and Henrietta Stackpole, eccentric lady journalist, represent the vulgarities of American character in their purest form. Henrietta and Caspar are unable to compromise, inured to subtlety, incapable of refinement, and entrenched in a way of thinking and seeing characterized by crude, unexamined moral categories untempered by worldly experience. They are the only characters not associated directly with houses—comic, unsubtle, and lacking in cultural insight, they reveal in higher relief some of the idiosyncrasies of Isabel's own character and the consequences of some of her own parochial attitudes. The independence of which they are all so proud entrenches them in a kind of parochialism and even vulgarity that result from an inability to come to terms with the compromises refinement entails. They are restless, mobile people who have, in a sense, "nowhere to lay their heads." They live in a world of abstractions, puritanically regarding the material world as separable from the world of ideas and attitudes.

Though Isabel shares these peculiarly American shortcomings, she is, unlike them, "educable." *The Portrait of a Lady* could in fact be subtitled "The Education of Isabel Archer." Belatedly, and at great cost, she begins to learn what an individual can learn only by a fall into civilization and acclimation to its complex codes of behavior. The houses she enters become her schools. She brings into them fixed notions about life that are tempered and even undermined by the behavior enforced by the traditions and the architecture of these old homes where, as she romantically imagines, "things have happened."

The house that came closest to being a home in Isabel's childhood was her grandmother's converted duplex in Albany—a "large, square double house"—unpretentious, functional, and wholly without aesthetic distinction. It had been converted into one dwelling with a connecting "tunnel"—a place with a dark side and a light side, its shades pulled against the street it fronted, as stark, isolated, and inwardly turned as Isabel, who over the years grew accustomed to inhabiting its lowest and darkest corner, which was the library. The narrator points out that "the foundation of Isabel's knowledge" was laid in the library of this house, where she had plenty of "idleness," which she filled with wide-ranging, undirected reading in the best American autodidactic tradition. In James's universe, such random and unreferenced knowledge inevitably brings semitragic consequences.

There in the dark library Isabel's romantic fancies developed unchecked: from her nest she "had no wish to look out, for this would have interfered with her theory that there was a strange, unseen place on the other side—a place which became to the child's imagination, according to its different moods, a region of delight or of terror."[9] The image of this curious house, bicameral, androgynous, and even hermaphroditic, invites allegory in the same playful way as does Hawthorne's House of the Seven Gables. The narrator suggestively compares the converted duplex with the "Dutch House" across the street, which has been turned into a school, a fact that reinforces the impression of the neighborhood as one of odd, multipurpose structures, singular and indefinite in their character.

Mrs. Touchett, visiting Isabel in Albany some time after her parents' deaths, questions her about the value of her grandmother's house, but Isabel does not know how much it is worth—has never, in fact, considered the question. Here and

throughout the book the idealistic insularity of Isabel's upbringing is suggested by her ignorance of the commercial value
of things and even of her own person—an ignorance that, combined with an inherited fortune, turns out to be a tragic flaw.
The contrast between Mrs. Touchett's unsentimental worldli-
ness and Isabel's naïveté is evident the moment the aunt enters
the house: Isabel, not knowing her aunt, mistakenly assumes
from her manner of scrutiny that she has come to buy the
house. Mrs. Touchett compares it unfavorably to houses in Florence, some of which, her own included, are ancient palaces, rich
with history and aesthetic appeal. This one, she observes, is simply "bourgeois," and she suggests that Isabel might appropriately convert it into shops rather than sell it, a practical solution
that puts Isabel in a predicament similar to that of Hepzibah
Pyncheon: idealism, sentimentality, and family pride compete
with expediency. The tension between the commercial and the
symbolic remains thematic throughout the story, reintroduced
in a different vein as each of the characters considers the related
matters of property and propriety.

We are given our basic information about Isabel's character
in the context of this curious American house, an architectural
joke compared with the English and Italian mansions to which
Isabel and we are subsequently removed. Her own high serious-
ness is slightly ironized by it; her situation, if not her person,
has distinctly comic overtones. As Mrs. Touchett describes Isabel to Ralph, "I found her in an old house at Albany, sitting in
a dreary room on a rainy day, reading a heavy book and boring
herself to death" (42–43). Isabel's inclination to solitude and in-
trospection is conveyed by a simple account of her habits: she
habitually situates herself in a remote corner to read, or when
she is restless and agitated, she "mov[es] about the room, and
from one room to another, preferring the places where the
vague lamplight expired" (32). She acts out her inner states by
occupying a place indicative of her state of mind, generally introspective, solitary, and somewhat standoffish. (By contrast,
when her dogged suitor, Caspar Goodwood, enters, he stands
right next to the lamp, being a man who is upright, forthright,
and literal.) Isabel's aunt Varian, the only other adult involved
in her American upbringing, is introduced briefly to provide an

added bit of perspective on the cultural hodgepodge in which Isabel has been raised. Her aunt's large house, like her grandmother's, is "bourgeois" and tasteless and bespeaks an unguided, profligate affluence marked by its pointless eclecticism. It was "remarkable for its assortment of mosaic tables and decorated ceilings, was unfurnished with a library and in the way of printed volumes contained nothing but half a dozen novels in paper on a shelf in the apartment of one of the Miss Varians" (50). The "novels in paper" of course mirror the same questionable taste the house itself reflects, with, no doubt, a comparable assortment of unspecified decorations.[10]

This environment has formed Isabel and is reflected in her character with all its flaws but also with a kind of idiosyncratic charm. Like the house she loved as a child, she is two-sided, ambivalent, practical, unpretentious, introspective, and yet sociable, freestanding, and unadorned. Isabel's mind is described as a place she inhabits in the same restless way as she occupies her favorite rooms: "Her imagination was by habit ridiculously active: when the door was not open it jumped out the window. She was not accustomed to keep it behind bolts" (32). Here again, analogies between the body or the mind and the dwelling arise, opening the questions of value in a new vein because the measure of a young woman's value is also a central issue. Isabel's cousin Ralph later describes her in similarly architectural terms: " 'The key of a beautiful edifice is thrust into my hand, and I'm told to walk in and admire.' . . . He surveyed the edifice from the outside and admired it greatly; he looked in at the windows and received an impression of proportions equally fair. But he felt that he saw it only by glimpses and that he had not yet stood under the roof. The door was fastened, and though he had keys in his pocket he had a conviction that none of them would fit" (63). Ralph's observations here reflect not only his relationship to Isabel but the readers' as well and not only our relationship to her but to the "beautiful edifice" of the text—the house of fiction—into whose thousand windows we look and try by multiple perspectives to grasp a sense of the whole.[11]

The extreme contrasts between old- and new-world structures and attitudes are reiterated in the polarities that draw Ralph and Isabel into fascinated intimacy. Both uprooted children of unorthodox parents, products of American mobility, schooled to ambiguous adaptations, they represent opposite effects of deracination. Where she is an impressive edifice of fair proportions, he is a crumbling ruin—his health failing, his scope of action diminishing, his body wracked prematurely into old age. "His serenity," the narrator observes, "was but the array of wild flowers niched in his ruin" (41). For all its historic nobility and grace, the home Ralph shares with his father, Isabel's uncle, at Gardencourt is also a place of diminishment—a mere reminder of richer, livelier times. Both its inhabitants are infirm, and its mistress is gone much of the time, her marriage to Mr. Touchett a barely preserved formality. The house's long galleries, music rooms, and parlors are in minimal use. Isabel enters this house with youthful awe, the ambivalent reverence of the new world for the old, and slightly comic romantic fancies. Taking literally Ralph's ironic allusion to the "ghosts" that inhabit the old house, she asks, "You do see them then? You ought to in this romantic old house." Ralph meets her romanticism with the stark realism born of experience and disillusionment: "It's not a romantic old house. . . . You'll be disappointed if you count on that. It's a dismally prosaic one; there's no romance here but what you may have brought with you" (46–47).

Unlike his father, Ralph's acclimation to English life has been a process of steady disillusionment, chronic displacement, and deepening irony. His is the prophetic perspective of the marginalized; not only his expatriation but also his sickness places him at that margin of experience where action is replaced by observation with some claim to "objectivity." Isabel's perspective, however, is colored deeply by the desire that is the root of all idealism:

> Her uncle's house seemed a picture made real; no refinement of the agreeable was lost upon Isabel; the rich perfection of Gardencourt at once revealed a world and gratified a need. The large, low rooms, with brown ceilings and dusky corners, the deep embrasures and curious casements, the quiet light on dark, polished panels, the deep greenness outside, that seemed always peeping in, the sense of well-ordered privacy in the centre of a 'property'—a place where sounds were felicitously accidental, where the tread was muffled by the earth itself and in the thick mild air all friction dropped

out of contact and all shrillness out of talk—these things were much to the taste of our young lady, whose taste played a considerable part in her emotions. (54–55)

And, it might be added, her emotions played a considerable part in her taste—an attribute that when it is not formed by the external pressures of a highly articulated culture grows out of the mixed soil of personal fancy. So Isabel's appreciation of Gardencourt has a poignant quality of longing for the quality missing from her own milieu—the quality that James himself so missed in the United States that it caused him to regard his native country a cultural desert. The reader's perspective on Gardencourt is a triangulation of Ralph's and Isabel's vision that results in what for American readers must be a familiar ambivalence toward English culture, history, and manners.

The novel opens on the lawn of the old mansion, whose symmetries, spacious grace, and noble past suggest a host of clichés about what is best and most lasting in English culture and offer a stark contrast to the parochialism of the Albany house, subsequently introduced in flashback. The English house has a long history—the early Tudor, built under Edward the Sixth, had even, it was said, extended hospitality to Elizabeth I for a night. It was "a good deal bruised and defaced in Cromwell's wars, and then, under the Restoration, repaired and much enlarged" (6). And now, "after having been remodeled and disfigured in the eighteenth century," it has passed

> into the careful keeping of a shrewd American banker, who had bought it originally because . . . it was offered at a great bargain: bought it with much grumbling at its ugliness, its antiquity, its incommodity, and who now, at the end of twenty years, had become conscious of a real aesthetic passion for it, so that he knew all its points and would tell you just where to stand to see them in combination and just the hour when the shadows of its various protuberances—which fell so softly on the warm, weary brickwork—were of the right measure. (6)

Here, in brief, is a microcosm of English history culminating in the return of the American to English soil, able by dint of money to buy back some of the birthright he might have had on other terms. The costs of the expatriate's reassimilation are gradual compromise, humility, and the loss of vitality suggested in the image of the colonial rebel become new-world entrepreneur. Mr. Touchett's house changes him. Living in it, he develops a taste for English life, an appreciation for English style, and the kind of intimacy only ownership makes possible. The house's long galleries and private apartments bespeak a way of life in which public face and unseen interiors preserve the sorts of distinctions that arise in a culture unencumbered with egalitarian pretensions.

Once again James juxtaposes the description of the house with a detailed portrait of Mr. Touchett's "physiognomy," a parallel reiterated for each of the major characters that is similar in its allegorical explicitness to Hawthorne's elaborate anatomical analogies. Mr. Touchett's is an "American physiognomy," though tempered by thirty years of English life:

> He had a narrow, clean-shaven face, with features evenly distributed and an expression of placid acuteness. It was evidently a face in which the range of representation was not large, so that the air of contented shrewdness was all the more of a merit. It seemed to tell that he had been successful in life, yet it seemed to tell also that his success had not been exclusive and invidious, but had had much of the inoffensiveness of failure. He had certainly had a great experience of men, but there was an almost rustic simplicity in the faint smile that played upon his lean, spacious cheek and lighted up his humorous eye. (7)

The man, like the house, is a repository of a history now inscribed on his features. His face bespeaks a rich store of experience and gives the impression, like his house, of having survived eras of both prosperity and scarcity into a comfortable and commodious old age, his powers compromised but still acute.

The opening scene of the novel takes place on the lawn of Gardencourt where old Mr. Touchett, his son, and his neighbor are taking tea in the afternoon sunlight. We see first the shadows on the lawn, "straight and angular," of the three men gathered there—the younger two pacing, the old man "rest[ing] his eyes on the rich red front of his dwelling," which is, the narrator interposes, "the most characteristic object in the peculiarly English picture I have attempted to sketch." Standing on a low hill above the Thames, "some forty miles from London . . . a long gabled front of red brick, with the complexion of which time and the weather had played all sorts of pictorial tricks, only, however, to improve and refine it, presented to the lawn its patches of ivy, its clustered chimneys, its windows smothered in creepers" (6). The narrator continues with an account of the house's significant history and returns to the present with the observation that "privacy here reigned supreme, and the wide carpet of turf that covered the level hill-top seemed but the extension of a luxurious interior. The great still oaks and beeches flung down a shade as dense as that of velvet curtains; and the place was furnished, like a room, with cushioned seats, with rich-colored rugs, with the books and papers that lay upon the grass" (6–7).

As in so many romantic representations of houses and homes, the boundaries between inside and outside are blurred, but here it is manufacture, rather than nature, that seems to be the imperializing force; domestication begins to overtake the natural environment rather than succumbing to the slow, ineluctable forces of nature. This, in fact, may be that quality that is open-endedly designated as "characteristically English"—the imperial habit of mind that civilizes whatever it touches on its own sedate terms.

Into this scene of masculine domesticity enters Isabel, framed in the "ample doorway" of the house looking outwardly on its owners in another odd reversal of the logic of hospitality. It is the little dog, rather than any of the men, who sees her first—a detail that underscores the introduction of something intuitive and spontaneous into a markedly ordered and ritualized scene. She is, Ralph notices on first glance, "bareheaded, as if she were staying in the house"—a fact that perplexes him because he is unaccustomed to visitors and does not recognize his cousin anymore than she, earlier, recognized her aunt on her invasion of the Albany house. Like the aunt, Isabel in turn appears in some way already to have taken possession of the place, an entitled intruder whose scant observation of social forms seems to grant her entitlement even before it is established that she is family. In fact, she seems strangely to take possession of the whole scene by dint of her innocence of social constraints; she handles the dog with such familiarity that Ralph cedes ownership on the spot, to which Isabel responds, "Couldn't we share him?"

Her ignorance of custom and propriety continues to surface in a series of comic details: she responds to Ralph's apology for her not having been "received" with the reassurance that "we were received. . . . There were about a dozen servants in the hall. And there was an old woman curtsying at the gate" (18). Introduced to the neighbor, Lord Warburton, she cries, "Oh, I hoped there would be a lord; it's just like a novel!" And finally, looking around, she says with childlike pleasure, "I've never seen anything so beautiful as this." To which her uncle replies, "But you're very beautiful yourself," a remark that goes beyond polite rejoinder to hint at the romantic projection that infuses Isabel's vision (17, 19).

Isabel turns away from Mr. Touchett's compliment on her beauty to ask about the house. The house is an acceptable medium through which personal relations can be established and values described and discussed. Ralph compares it to others of its kind, diminishing its importance as a specimen, but Mr. Touchett defends it. Lord Warburton enters the contest, comparing it to his own Tudor: "I've got a very good one; I think in some respects it's rather better," adding, "I should like very much to show it to you" (19). There is a kind of comic chivalry in these introductory gambits in which houses become a measure of men and a kind of collateral offered in exchange for the lady's attentions. Isabel, however, refuses to play her part in the contest. "I don't know," she says,"I can't judge." And, indeed, she speaks a literal truth: she has no criteria for judging the quality of the estates offered for her consideration. In the comparisons she is asked to make lies the beginning of her cultural education. Ralph shows her his art gallery; Lord Warburton, his moat. She receives a series of impressions from her hosts that seem increasingly to call on her for some judgment—ultimately, of course, for a decision about marriage or what way of life to adopt for herself. With only the stark American home as a basis of comparison, her judgments must proceed from impression and intuition rather than cultivation, and the dangers as well as the strengths of such an approach to aesthetic discernment become more painfully apparent as the novel progresses.

One amusing measure of Isabel's heightening sensitivities to her new environment is the intrusion of her breezy American friend, Henrietta Stackpole. When this lady journalist first arrives unbidden at Gardencourt, her initial reactions are similar to Isabel's in their openmouthed naïveté and general awe of things English. But Henrietta's utterly utilitarian impulse to seize hold of these impressions and turn them to commercial profit bespeaks an Americanness distinguished from Isabel's in its crassness. What in Isabel is character appears in Henrietta as caricature. She decides on the spot to write a piece for her newspaper called "English Tudors—Glimpses of Gardencourt." Isabel forbids her to do so, pointing out that it would be a terrible breach of hospitality to subject the old place to the indiscriminate curiosities of the public. The journalist complies reluctantly, unconvinced that there is any point to such proprieties. Henrietta throws the issue of value into high relief by occupying an extreme end of the cultural spectrum James is drawing in this novel. Her vision is entirely utilitarian, parochial, and infused with the enthusiasms of the uninformed. Her insatiable curiosity is appealing in its childlikeness but counterbalanced and tainted by a tendency to pass judgment on everything she sees according to her own narrow criteria. She storms Europe as an entrepreneur of "culture," seeking ways to package and export it for easy consumption by untraveled Americans hoping to reinforce their romantic condescensions toward all things European. In every house she enters she is an intruder, albeit on most occasions an amusing one—but ironically it is the invulnerability her insensitivity affords that preserves her from a fate like Isabel's—enmeshment in a system she is not equipped to navigate. Henrietta's love affair with Europe and eventually with a European is an American comedy of adoption rather than assimilation and only serves to deepen the tragedy of Isabel's awakening.

That awakening is mediated first by her cousin, whose passionate but disinterested tutoring turns out to be the most genuine connection Isabel makes, and second by Lord Warburton, whose eagerness to initiate her is equally passionate and not at all disinterested. To accomplish this, he invites her to his local home—one of many in his possession. Another mansion that could be regarded as "characteristically English," it differs from Gardencourt in that it is inherited property, ancient, with the historical integrity of continuous family ownership, suited less to the immediate needs of its modern inhabitants than to the visible preservation of the past in its drafty halls and anachronistic moat. Lord Warburton himself, being a modern gentleman, treats this monument lightly, eventually offering to abandon it altogether and find a new dwelling more to Isabel's liking if she will marry him, but finds that such disclaiming is no more easily accomplished than giving up his seat in Parliament. The burden of the past remains with him in his title as in his property, and for all his modernized, democratized attitudes, he cannot avoid assuming it.

When Isabel visits Lord Warburton's "ancient house" with its "vast drawing room," her impressions are ambiguous. She finds that "within, it had been a good deal modernized—some of its best points had lost their purity; but as they saw it from the gardens, a stout grey pile, of the softest, deepest, most weather-fretted hue, rising from a broad, still moat, it affected the young visitor as a castle in a legend" (78). Both her nostalgia for lost purity and her taste for romance enhance the appeal of the castle and its youthful master. The latter is described as a "remarkably well-made man of five-and-thirty with a face as English as that of the old gentleman [Touchett] . . . a noticeably handsome face, fresh-coloured, fair and frank, with firm, straight features, a lively grey eye and the rich adornment of a chestnut beard." He has, we are further informed, "the air of a happy temperament fertilized by a high civilization" (7–8).

Yet when this flower of English culture comes to propose to her, something keeps Isabel from succumbing to these allurements. Though she realizes that "her situation was one which a few weeks ago she would have deemed deeply romantic: the park of an old English country house, with the foreground embellished by a 'great' (as she supposed) nobleman in the act of making love to a young lady" (104), she clings to her notion of independence unpersuaded by either property or prestige, measuring the material prosperity offered her against a rather vague ideal of independence and choosing the latter as the "higher" value. After Isabel's refusal and subsequent reluctant agreement to think it over, Lord Warburton adds, by way of inducing her further:

> "There's one thing more. . . . You know, if you don't like Lockleigh—if you think it's damp or anything of that sort—you need never go within fifty miles of it. It's not damp, by the way; I've had the house thoroughly examined; it's perfectly safe and right. But if you shouldn't fancy it you needn't dream of living in it. There's no difficulty whatever about that; there are plenty of houses. I thought I'd just mention it; some people don't like a moat, you know. Good-bye."
>
> "I adore a moat," said Isabel. "Good-bye." (110)

This touching appeal epitomizes the fundamental differences between the two; Warburton, living in a culture where money and property are neither righteously understated nor romanticized but do figure as a legitimate currency in the business of marriage, can hardly imagine Isabel's grounds for refusal. To give up what he offers on the strength of an untried ideal is beyond his reckoning. Nor does Isabel herself fully understand her hesitation, except for a feeling of resistance to the foreignness and romance of the situation she confronts. He even offers to "furbish up" England if it will suit her better to stay there, and her reply again baffles him: "Oh, don't furbish it, Lord Warburton; leave it alone. I like it this way" (108). But liking it does not suffice, and Isabel is unable to say exactly what would. His observation that her uncle would probably advise her to marry in her own country simply evokes a perverse response that the old man seems to have been happy in England.

When Isabel talks over Warburton's proposal with her uncle, he comments reservedly that England is rather crowded, though he adds that doubtless "there's room for charming young ladies everywhere." Isabel replies, " 'There seems to have been room here for you.' " Mr. Touchett answers with a "shrewd, conscious smile," " 'There's room everywhere, my dear, if you'll pay for it. I sometimes think I've paid too much for this. Perhaps you also might have to pay too much' " (114). It is a warning against the costs of expatriation and, perhaps, against the loss of what freedom might be enjoyed by a woman—certainly greater in the United States than in Europe. Both he and Ralph recognize that Isabel is ill-equipped to devise the strategies by which European women must maintain their semblance of power, and both try, in their way, to arm and empower her and protect her from the consequences of her own innocence. Ralph gives her advice and exposure to culture, training her eye and mind to habits of tasteful discrimination that might help her discern vulgarity even in its more camouflaged forms. Mr. Touchett gives her money, which, however, rather than empowering her heightens her vulnerability because it opens doors to her that begin to close behind her once she has passed through, leaving her struggling for firm footing on the slippery moral ground of polite society.

Isabel's real initiation, however, and the fatal moment in her European education, comes not from any of the suitors or protectors, or the houses that reveal so much to her about their modi vivendi, but rather from a critical conversation with Madame Merle. Another deracinated and in some senses homeless American woman, Isabel's ironic and even tragic counterpart, it is Madame Merle who imparts to her naive visitor what worldly wisdom she must have to survive. Occupying a position on the social scale that precludes her working, Madame Merle wanders about Europe from one hospitable home to another, keeping an apartment in Rome "which often stood empty," merely as a place to alight between journeys.

A centerpiece and transition point in the book and in Isabel's ill-fated European career is a conversation with Mme. Merle in which the older woman undertakes to educate Isabel in the moral and practical significance of houses in particular and material culture in general. Mme. Merle "talked of Florence, where Mr. Osmond lived and where Mrs. Touchett occupied a medieval palace; she talked of Rome, where she herself had a little pied-a-terre and some rather good old damask" (197), and they talk about suitors, which leads Isabel to give a reluctant account of the untranslatable qualities of Caspar Goodwood. If her suitor was such a paragon, Mme. Merle asks her, why did she not fly with him to his castle in the Apennines?

"He has no castle in the Apennines."

"What has he? An ugly brick house in Fortieth Street? Don't tell me that; I refuse to recognize that as an ideal."

"I don't care anything about his house," said Isabel.

"That's very crude of you. When you've lived as long as I you'll see that every human being has his shell and that you must take the shell into account. By the shell I mean the whole envelope of circumstances. There's no such thing as an isolated man or woman; we're each of us made up of some cluster of appurtenances. What shall we call our "self"? Where does it begin? where does it end? It overflows into everything that belongs to us—and then it flows back again. I know a large part of myself is in the clothes I choose to wear. I've a great respect for *things*! One's self—for other people— is one's expression of one's self; and one's house, one's furniture, one's garments, the books one reads, the company one keeps— these things are all expressive. (201)

Ironically enough, this little defense of practical materialism is sound transcendental doctrine. Thoreau himself would not dispute the point, though the rhetorical purposes to which it is put would deeply offend that puritanical champion of simplicity. And here in a clever little sermon on good taste and good manners is encapsulated the great paradox that baffles Isabel's own puritanical habit of mind. Suddenly the high-minded idealism that claims not to care about a man's house looks simply juvenile, simplistic, and self-righteous in this new light. Moreover, as one critic has pointed out, Isabel herself has been seeing and judging people in terms of their material environments ever since coming to Europe.[12] She is brought up short against her own internal contradictions; she is not above the allure and enjoyment of material culture, yet she is constrained not to admit its fundamental importance in the economy of human intercourse and particularly in the business of marriage. To acknowledge the economic factor in so intimate and spiritual a relation would be to sacrifice a basic doctrine of the metaphysical individualism on which her whole sense of herself is built. And to be called on to understand the self in so complex a web of relations—defined by the pressures of the marketplace and the shifting standards of taste—threatens the whole monolithic structure of Isabel's notions of free will and integrity. She cannot accept the implications of this short foray into social semiotics and so resorts to simple denial:

> "I don't agree with you. I think just the other way. I don't know whether I succeed in expressing myself, but I know that nothing else expresses me. Nothing that belongs to me is any measure of me; everything's on the contrary a limit, a barrier, and a perfectly arbitrary one. Certainly the clothes which, as you say, I choose to wear, don't express me; and heaven forbid they should! . . . My clothes may express the dressmaker, but they don't express me. To begin with it's not my own choice that I wear them; they're imposed upon me by society." (201–202)

Mme. Merle's rejoinder terminates the discussion without resolution: "Should you prefer to go without them?" Thoreau's admonition to beware any enterprise requiring new clothes resonates in Isabel's defiant and radical declaration of independence from the imposed structures and fashions of society, as does the far older reminder to look on the unclothed lilies of the field as models of the purest kind of life. Moreover, there is in Isabel's words a poignant recognition that the structures and designs of public life in fact have little to do with the actual lives of women. Yet her uncompromising attitude toward the world of material structures and monetary measures falls short of the heroic and borders on intellectual self-indulgence. Madame Merle has known want of a kind that is foreign to Isabel and so realizes that morality and manners both begin in recognizing what is involved in the business of survival—a business in which the material immediacies of everyday life take precedence over the luxury of ideas and ideals.

Seeming at some points to be Isabel's opposite, Mme. Merle is what Isabel might well become under the same set of influences and constraints: wily, worldly, and well schooled by necessity in the art of compromise. Her metaphysics is inseparable from social reality, and in this encounter romantic succumbs to realist with several quick turns of the Jamesian screw. Her sensitivity to the nuances of appearances, though an acquired strategy, casts a harsh light on the "honesty" of Henrietta's blunt, judgmental assessments of things ("Oh, yes; you can't tell me anything about Versailles" [219]). Like Hester Prynne before them, the women in this novel live marginally with one foot outside the social structures erected to contain them: Mrs. Touchett maintaining her costly compromise with the terms of marriage; Mme. Merle devising highly refined forms of prostitution to ensure the maintenance of herself and her daughter; Henrietta trading respect and respectability for her cherished freedom of movement; and Isabel seeking a footing in a world for which her intellectual and moral isolationism have ill-prepared her.

It is, of course, in Gilbert Osmond's labyrinthine villa (and in the duplicitous matrimonial contract that holds her there) that the innocent American becomes ensnared in a maze she cannot navigate. If the Americans in this novel suffer from a lack of refinement and civilized subtleties, the Italians (Gilbert, the complete convert to European aestheticism, among them) suffer from its opposite: mannered excesses ungrounded in moral vision, elaborate preservations of vacuous forms, effete tastes uninformed by humane values. In the marriage of Isabel and Osmond, substance without style confronts style without substance. The Florentine house in which Osmond courts Isabel and later the Roman palace into which she finds her way as bride and mistress stand at the other end of the aesthetic and moral spectrum from the large, square matriarchal house of her childhood. The former is sprawling, labyrinthine, full of hidden places and opaque fronts, its galleries and balconies dedicated to aesthetic pleasures and the sophistications of civilized pastimes. It is described as a "long, rather blank-looking structure," its front "pierced with a few windows in irregular relations" to which is attached "a stone bench lengthily adjusted to the base of the structure and useful as a lounging place to one or two persons wearing more or less of that air of undervalued merit which in Italy, for some reason or other, always gracefully invests anyone who confidently assumes a perfectly passive attitude" (226).

As with the English houses, parallels and analogies between the house and its owner are both stated and implied: words such as "lounging," "leaning," and "passive" recur with significant frequency in the descriptions of both the villa and its owner. The villa's almost absurdly spacious rooms have a diminishing and somewhat dehumanizing effect on the inhabitants; the bedroom assigned to Osmond's young daughter, for instance, is "an immense chamber with a dark, heavily-timbered ceiling," in which the child appears "but a speck of humanity" (468). And the large antechamber entered from the staircase is a space "in which even Gilbert Osmond's rich devices had not been able to correct a look of rather grand nudity" (407).

Both house and master have something snakelike, secretive, and inscrutable about them; neither is self-revealing or frank; and there is in both an alarming "blankness" or emptiness behind an opulent facade that Isabel fatally mistakes for mystery:

> This antique, solid, weather-worn, yet imposing front had a somewhat incommunicative character. It was the mask, not the face of the house. It had heavy lids, but no eyes; the house in reality looked another way—looked off behind, into splendid openness and the range of the afternoon light. . . . The parapet of the terrace was just the height to lean upon, and beneath it the ground declined into the vagueness of olive-crops and vineyards. . . . The windows of the ground floor, as you saw them from the piazza, were, in their noble proportions, extremely architectural; but their function seemed less to offer communication with the world than to defy the world to look in. They were massively crossbarred, and placed at such a height that curiosity, even on tiptoe, expired before it reached them. . . . It was . . . a seat of ease, indeed of luxury, telling of arrangements subtly studied and refinements frankly proclaimed, and containing a variety of those faded hangings of damask and tapestry, those chests and cabinets of carved and time-polished oak, those angular specimens of pictorial art in frames as pedantically primitive, those perverse-looking relics of medieval brass and pottery, of which Italy has long been the not-quite-exhausted storehouse. These things kept terms with articles of modern furniture in which large allowance had been made for a lounging generation; it was to be noticed that all the chairs were deep and well padded and that much space was occupied by a writing-table of which the ingenious perfection bore the stamp of London and the nineteenth century. There were books in profusion and magazines and newspapers, and a few small, odd, elaborate pictures, chiefly in water-colour. (226–227)

The elaborate, casual cosmopolitanism of this environment and its prohibitive privacy and ambiguous comforts are reflected in the person of Osmond, who is rendered almost as a caricature of the late-Renaissance courtier with his finely hewn face, beard "of which the only fault was just this effect of it running a trifle too much to points," and upwardly curled moustache, which "suggested that he was a gentleman who studied style." His "conscious, curious eyes, . . . eyes at once vague and penetrating, intelligent and hard, expressive of the observer as well as of the dreamer, would have assured you that he studied it [style] only within well-chosen limits, and that in so far as he sought it he found it" (228)—an observation that suggests an unsettling quality of calculation and self-preoccupation rather than the attentiveness they might be taken to connote. The narrator continues with a description that further complicates Osmond's ambiguity by belaboring the question of his origins in such a way as to suggest that cultural hybridization has denatured him and left him neither fish nor fowl—a composite social creation without the element of "soul" that derives from what Emerson would have called the "genius loci." The cumulative impression is that the whole is less than the sum of the parts:

> You would have been at a loss to determine his original clime and country; he had none of the superficial signs that usually render the answer to this question an insipidly easy one. If he had English blood in his veins it had probably received some French or Italian commixture; but he suggested, fine gold coin as he was, no stamp nor emblem of the common mintage that provides for general circulation; he was the elegant complicated medal struck off for a special occasion. He had a light, lean, rather languid-looking figure, and was apparently neither tall nor short. He was dressed as a man dresses who takes little other trouble about it than to have no vulgar things. (228–229)

There is an implied equation here between the composite and the inauthentic, particularly as contrasted with earlier descriptions of "characteristically English" or "indisputably American" characters and houses. Among other evils Osmond comes to personify, he serves to illustrate from the outset the darker aspects of cultural eclecticism, which at its extreme becomes a betrayal of the self in which the center no longer holds—a sacrifice of the roots that drive deep into native soil in the transplanting that leaves the individual only tenuously and superficially grounded in the adopted place. Like Isabel, and like the Touchetts, Osmond is a deracinated American, but his adaptations to Europe have reached a point of dubious returns in purging him altogether of national character. He has bought the forms of European life without any effort to claim or understand their moral or spiritual dimensions. Osmond raises in a far more sinister way the question Mr. Touchett ruefully pondered earlier—what are the costs of expatriation, and what are those elements of culture that cannot be acquired even with money, taste, and the will to adapt?

Osmond's Roman house is a house full of shadows, "a dark and massive structure," which Rosier, young suitor to Osmond's daughter, sees as a "domestic fortress, . . . which smelt of historic deeds, of crime and craft and violence" (364). In this house Isabel learns a whole new pattern of existence. Prepared by Madame Merle, who, like Osmond, is a cultural chameleon, to doubt her own frames of reference, Isabel enters his house primed to accept as "higher" and more sophisticated the style of life it expresses and enforces. What she finds is that Osmond's mind, like his house, is "the house of darkness, the house of dumbness, the house of suffocation" (429). Her own progress in self-betrayal begins with her first visit to the house when Mme. Merle urges him as "cicerone" of his own "museum" to show Isabel his things, having elaborately complimented him on the one talent he seems not to have allowed to atrophy—the talent for tasteful acquisition: "Your rooms at least are perfect. I'm struck with that afresh whenever I come back; I know none better anywhere. You understand this sort of thing as nobody anywhere does. You've such adorable taste" (242).

Osmond demurs at first with a cynical self-assessment that has an odd character of honesty: "I'm sick of my adorable taste" (242). But he grudgingly consents to play his part in her scheme on learning that Isabel has seventy thousand pounds. The value of his "things" is immediately recast as they become means rather than ends—props in a melodrama of intrigue and seduction, in which he is the principal actor; his former mistress and consort, the director; and Isabel, the ingenue who does not even recognize that she is on a stage, script in hand, her part assigned and her fate determined.

Vaguely aware of dangers she cannot name, Isabel visits her aunt, Mrs. Touchett, to solicit her opinion of Osmond and his entourage but finds no help in that quarter other than the blunt advice to "judge everyone and everything for yourself" (250). This is, of course, precisely what she has been trying to do, but she has lost her bearings and her standards of judgment. Mrs. Touchett, whose resistance to assimilation is as remarkable as Osmond's lack of definition, has no understanding of Isabel's susceptibility to the deceptions of her new environment. The older woman has taken Italy on her own terms. She lives in a "great house" with a "wide, monumental court," and "high, cool rooms where the carven rafters and pompous frescoes of the sixteenth century looked down on the familiar commodities of the age of advertisement." She has assessed the trade-offs involved in living in an old, cold, historic building, compensated for its darkness and inconvenience by reasonable rent and "a garden where nature itself looked as archaic as the rugged architecture of the palace and which cleared and scented the rooms for regular use." Isabel, visiting there, regards it with nothing like this practicality: for her, "to live in such a place was . . . to hold to her ear all day a shell of the sea of the past. This vague eternal rumour kept her imagination awake" (247).

This same fatal tendency to romanticize what is ancient, foreign, and grand ultimately drives her decision to marry a man and enter a house that represent what she believes she ought to value—what seems the best of European culture, so superior in its artistic variety, historicity, and complex resonance to the straightforward simplicities of American life, which now appear, like the pitiful suitor, Caspar, and the eccentric Henrietta, narrow, parochial, uninspired, and impoverished. Too late Isabel finds herself entrapped in multiple structures that surround her like the "shells" Mme. Merle spoke of and that become her identity, burying what "self" remains under layers of clothing and obscuring accoutrements. "Her light step," the narrator ominously observes, "drew a mass of drapery behind it," and her "intelligent head sustained a majesty of ornament. The free, keen girl had become quite another person." Ralph, reflecting sadly on the loss of Isabel's unspoiled youth as he sees her many months later, asks himself, "What did Isabel represent? . . . And he could only answer by saying that she represented Gilbert Osmond" (393). Osmond's house is a stage on which she finds herself condemned to play out a drama in which her role has been predetermined. The great rooms are designed for entertainment, and so she entertains. The role available to her is to be a decorative object to enhance his vast collection, and so she makes herself decorative.

Ralph's assessment of Osmond on this wistful visit is characteristically fair-minded, acute, and sharply aware of the messages embedded in the complex material environment the collector has created:

> Osmond was in his element. . . . He always had an eye to effect, and his effects were deeply calculated. They were produced by no vulgar means, but the motive was as vulgar as the art was great. To surround his interior with a sort of invidious sanctity, to tantalize society with a sense of exclusion, to make people believe his house was different from every other, to impart to the face that he presented to the world a cold originality—this was the ingenious effort of the personage to whom Isabel had attributed a superior morality. (394)

Ralph reflects with Thoreauvian scorn that far from being the master of the world he inhabits, Osmond is its "very humble servant," attentive constantly to the pose he has committed himself to maintaining, his ambition "not to please the world but to please himself by exciting the world's curiosity and then declining to maintain it" (394). The facades he erects deceive the gullible, and Isabel is the unhappiest among those deceived.

Osmond himself manages to maintain his self-respect by a combination of studied indifference and scorn for any but those under his control; after the marriage he systematically and mockingly dismisses each of Isabel's acquaintances, like old possessions no longer worth keeping, observing, "You're certainly not fortunate in your intimates; I wish you might make a new collection" (490). Ironically enough, his objections to them are quite transparent projections leveled at the very qualities he might, had he any remaining capacity for self-scrutiny, recognize in himself. Thus, he takes umbrage at Lord Warburton's pragmatic consideration of Osmond's marriageable daughter, forgetting how utterly mercenary was his own wooing:

> He comes and looks at one's daughter as if she were a suite of apartments; he tries the door-handles and looks out of the windows, raps on the walls and almost thinks he'll take the place. Will you be so good as to draw up a lease? Then, on the whole, he decides that the rooms are too small; he doesn't think he could live on a third floor; he must look out for a piano nobile. And he goes away after having got a month's lodging in the poor little apartment for nothing. (490)

The terms of Osmond's conceit comically reveal his own manner of assessing women in particular and human relations in general.

When, toward the end of the novel, Isabel returns to Gardencourt to attend Ralph in his dying hours, the house becomes for her a measure of the distance she has traveled from the state of innocence in which she began her European life. Left alone in the drawing room to await a summons by new servants to whom she is a stranger, she wanders into the gallery where Ralph had once begun her aesthetic education:

> Nothing was changed; she recognized everything she had seen years before; it might have been only yesterday she had stood there. She envied the security of valuable 'pieces' which change by no hair's breadth, only grow in value, while their owners lose inch by inch youth, happiness, beauty; and she became aware that she was walking about as her aunt had done on the day she had come to see her in Albany. She was changed enough since then—that had been the beginning. (569)

The constancy of objects restores to her a lost perspective. They force on her an appalling awareness of change and morbidity and a wistful memory of roads not taken. It occurs to her to wonder whether, had her aunt not propitiously appeared with her offer of European travel, she might have married the upright and honest Caspar Goodwood.

Fortuitously, of course, the object of this reverie soon appears, ghostlike, from her past, still in hapless pursuit, defying a marriage he considers illegitimate, to win back Isabel, now lost to him in so many senses. In the final chapter of the novel Caspar gives her one last chance to unseal her miserable fate. Finding her on the lawn of Gardencourt, he reiterates his plea with a passionate intensity that seems momentarily to redeem him from the ridiculous light in which he has consistently been cast and to ennoble him in his heroic persistence against odds he cannot possibly imagine. But his kiss—one of the most memorable moments of pure passion in all of James's writing—sends Isabel, after one brief moment of surrender, flying back to the house where, exactly reversing the historic gesture of Ibsen's Nora, she enters and closes the door behind her. As she does so, the magnitude of this rejection comes clear to her: "She had not known where to turn; but she knew now. There was a very straight path" (591). That "straight path" remains, however, unspecified. We might speculate that, like Mrs. Touchett and Madame Merle, Isabel has simply chosen a life of civilized compromise with a respectable, unsatisfying, but tolerable domesticity and that with the first light of morning she leaves England to return to Osmond's house to resume her position as its mistress, having now taken her own measure of its cost.

5

THE AWAKENING AND "THE YELLOW WALLPAPER" Ironies of Independence

The Awakening and "The Yellow Wallpaper" have by now become classic texts in feminist studies, two of the stories most often cited in discussions of women's entrapment in oppressive forms of domestic life.[1] Following many precedents in the long tradition of Western tragedy, the women in these stories, caught in social and actual structures that repress and confine them, end up enacting gestures of self-liberation that are deeply and ironically self-destructive. The tensions and paradoxes that characterize American culture assume peculiarly acute form in women's writing, where ambivalences about domestic life as a hindrance to the realization of the ideal of freedom are complicated by the inaccessibility and even irrelevancy of that ideal to women in a culture whose romantic mythology has referred so particularly to male experience. In such a culture conscious and ambitious women have had to imagine what to strive for in the relative absence of female precedents. For these women, houses, traditionally the domain of feminine activity, though designed and controlled by men, have represented either "gilded cages" (the gilding on some of which was a very thin veneer) or a medium they could turn to their otherwise frustrated purposes of creative expression and exercise of intelligence and power.

Throughout *The Awakening* Edna Pontellier, wife of a wealthy New Orleans businessman, is engaged in a restless search for a place and a way of life in which she can be comfortable and free and in which she can be in relation to, but not controlled by, the men she loves. The most definitive moment in Edna's desperate struggle for identity and autonomy besides her final swim to her death is her move into her little "pigeon house," a

121

four-room cottage to which she flees to escape the suffocating conventionalities of her overstuffed New Orleans mansion. Every setting in this story is emblematic; every room and porch and stretch of beach frame and enforce specific modes of behavior. Chopin uses houses both to define character and to serve as a graphic representation of interpersonal politics. The metaphorical and the literal merge in the structures of domestic life. Chopin's language of spatial relation is as allegorical as Hawthorne's; her characters' physical position in a room or defined space—above, below, inside, outside—always provides an important clue to the nature of the encounter taking place. Each of the three houses Edna inhabits during the nine-month span of the story generates certain kinds of action and inhibits others. Moving from one to another, she evolves from the status of captive to mistress of her environment, and, finally, finding that she cannot sustain that new role in the absence of legitimizing social supports, she dissolves into a space without boundaries as she swims to her death in the ocean.

The novel was written at the end of Chopin's ten-year writing career and met with a storm of critical outrage that put an end to her writing for the five remaining years of her life. Though by all accounts the twelve years between her marriage to Oscar Chopin and his death were "unusually fulfilling," and her relationship to her six children close and happy, there is no mistaking her profound sympathy for the plight of most women of her generation, who were confined in homes that bound them to a round of domestic and social duties that left little room for free expression of individual talents. Like her contemporary, Charlotte Perkins Gilman, Chopin subjected the norms and structures of the Victorian United States to a critical scrutiny courageous in its prophetic identification of the pathologies of Victorian family life, particularly with respect to the effective imprisonment of women.

Chopin's father died when she was five, and during most of her youth at home and in a convent school, she saw women holding and exercising authority. Reflecting on the relevance of this female-dominated upbringing in a summary of Chopin's life and writing, Peggy Skaggs suggests that "this inconsistency between training and experience [might have] contributed to the paradox between her own apparently happy marriage and her creation in fiction of female characters who feel stifled by the marriage relationship."[2] Of these characters, the most stifled and the most complex in her relation to the demands of domestic life is Edna Pontellier. Flanked on the one side by an archetypal "mother-woman," Mme. Ratignolle, whose pregnancy progresses contemporaneously with the story, and on the other by an eccentric "artist woman," Mlle. Reisz, whose unorthodox solitary life has given her an ambiguous, lonely freedom, Edna's search for a "place" for herself in the world takes on both literal and symbolic dimensions as she seeks some middle ground where she can design a life between the extremes of engulfment and isolation.[3]

The story opens at a summer resort where a group of cottages are arranged in proximity to the "House," where the families share their seasonal rituals. When we first meet Edna she is returning from a walk on the beach with Robert, her young friend and would-be lover, whose frequent presence in her household creates the first of a series of triangular relationships in the book in which Edna is in the middle position. Chopin dramatizes the relationship among the three of them, Robert, Edna, and her husband, Leonce, by the simple device of seating them on the cottage porch: "When they reached the cottage, the two seated themselves with some appearance of fatigue upon the upper step of the porch, facing each other, each leaning against a supporting post" (173). This juxtaposition, particularly when Leonce comes to join them, seating himself in a chair above and between them, alerts the reader not only to the nature of their respective relationships but to the general importance of spatial symbolism in the novel. Here Edna and Robert are equals and intimates. Their informality and their childlike playfulness differentiate them from and subordinate them to Leonce, who, emerging from the interior of the house, sits in a chair above them, literally supervising the two now at his feet. Exhilarated from their walk in the air, their freedom of spirit and their manner contrast markedly with his sober propriety.

Robert's family owns the House—the central building in the complex. His enterprising mother has developed the resort as a source of income: "Now, flanked by its dozen or more cottages, which were always filled with exclusive visitors from the 'Quartier Francais,' it enabled Madame Lebrun to maintain the easy and comfortable existence which appeared to be her birthright" (176). The woman who has taken her fate into her own hands and has made her house into a means of independence as well as a social center to support a way of life she enjoys provides a direct contrast to Edna, whose sense of entrapment is at least in part a matter of temperament and training. Three women in this novel other than Edna have achieved various kinds of independence and contentment. They complicate rather interestingly the theme of women's oppression to which discussions of the novel so often revert. It is possible, Chopin shows us, for a woman to be a mistress not only of her husband's home but of her own environment and destiny, given certain proclivities, sacrifices, and a creative imagination. In light of these examples, Edna's plight becomes considerably more problematic; she is not simply a prototypical woman but is a woman for whom the available options do not serve. The question of why then becomes a subtler problem.

Edna's marriage provides one clue. Though she spends a good deal of time apart from her husband, when he is home, his wishes are paramount, and his presence so fills the spaces they share that Edna chooses whenever possible to escape, to find breathing space. In chapter 11 Leonce comes home to find her late at night waiting for him on the porch and asks, "What are you doing out here, Edna? I thought I should find you in bed" (217). His sense of her proper place consistently differs from hers and is governed by convention rather than by recognition or understanding of her habits and needs. Time and space are carefully regulated quantities for him; her casual treatment of both troubles his sense of propriety and control. Nevertheless, he reserves to himself the right to the small irregularities that so disturb him in her. On this same occasion, after Edna has been persuaded to return indoors and to bed, Leonce remains on the porch she has vacated. She calls to him to ask whether he is coming in. " 'Yes, dear,' he answered, with a glance following a misty puff of smoke. 'Just as soon as I have finished my cigar' " (219). Leonce does not question his own right to remain outside at night, make exceptions to the regulations he imposes on his household, or claim his moments of solitude.

One Sunday morning Edna makes her escape from the cluster of cottages where shared domestic life engulfs her; she allows Robert to row her to an island where an old woman, Mme. Antoine, lives in rustic contentment. Tired in the afternoon, Edna accepts Mme. Antoine's offer of a room for a nap. Entering the house, Edna is charmed: "The whole place was immaculately clean, and the big, four-posted bed, snow-white, invited one to repose. It stood in a small side room which looked out across a narrow grass plot toward the shed, where there was a disabled boat lying keel upward" (226). This house is a refuge. The "small side room" where Edna takes a nap befits her desires: she is alone but watched over, private, accessible to the outside, away from civilizing constraints and duties. Spending a bucolic afternoon in a place apart, near the water, she allows feelings, curiosities, and desires that have no place in her life at home to begin surfacing. In this place where she has no given role a self can emerge whose contours she has yet to discover.

Shortly after this interlude we follow Edna to a third location. Whereas on the beach and at the island, both marginal places where social constraints are loosened, it has been relatively easy to lay aside the stringencies of upper-class social obligations, back in New Orleans we see her in a more confined and regulated setting—her "real life" has tightened on her like a corset, and the wistful imaginings begun in the freedom of the open-aired summer haunt her. Chopin describes the New Orleans house in some detail, guiding the reader's eye slowly around the facade and then the interior, awakening a host of assumptions about and associations with genteel southern life:

> The Pontelliers possessed a very charming home in Esplanade Street in New Orleans. It was a large, double cottage, with a broad front veranda, whose round, fluted columns supported the sloping roof. The house was painted a dazzling white; the outside shutters, or jalousies, were green. In the yard, which was kept scrupulously neat, were flowers and plants of every description which flourishes in South Louisiana. Within doors the appointments were perfect after the conventional type. The softest carpets and rugs covered

the floors; rich and tasteful draperies hung at doors and windows. There were paintings, selected with judgment and discrimination, upon the walls. The cut glass, the silver, the heavy damask which daily appeared upon the table were the envy of many women whose husbands were less generous than Mr. Pontellier. (247)

Mr. Pontellier's generosity generally takes material or monetary form; he has supplied Edna with everything a woman of her station is supposed to want—which is to say, an abundantly furnished household where she is surrounded by material comforts and both natural and artistic beauty. The possibility that this accumulation of material things might be felt to encumber rather than enhance her life would not occur to him. Well cared for and in their proper places, his possessions, like his wife, demarcate his place in the world and serve as constant and gratifying reminders of his success in securing it: "Mr. Pontellier was very fond of walking about his house examining its various appointments and details, to see that nothing was amiss. He greatly valued his possessions, chiefly because they were his, and derived genuine pleasure from contemplating a painting, a statuette, a rare lace curtain—no matter what—after he had bought it and placed it among his household goods" (247–248). His possessions are his badges, his wife among them. They are testimonies to his taste and his power as well as to his wealth— all qualities by which he seeks to distinguish himself, very much in accordance with the standards of his class and time. But his satisfaction is joyless, taken not primarily in the aesthetic and other pleasures these things might offer but in what they signify. His house is a showcase that he tours to reassure himself.

In his own terms, vividly expressed in his orderly and abundant household, Mr. Pontellier is a model husband, and his expectations of his wife are in no way excessive—certainly no greater than, though different from, what he expects of himself. Therefore, when she fails to meet these expectations, he is not only disgruntled but bewildered because her growing apathy and resistance seem to him inexplicable. When one evening he finds fault with each dish at dinner, he snaps in some disgust, "It seems to me . . . we spend money enough in this house to procure at least one meal a day which a man could eat and retain his self-respect" (251). Edna observes that he used to think the cook was a treasure, to which he responds that she, like any other sort of employee, needs supervision. Edna is not running the household up to his standards. Meals, like other commodities, are for him an index of right and successful ordering of life. Food is one element in the elaborate code by which he lives; the right kind of food eaten at the right time is one of many measures of propriety that form the foundation of his identity and self-respect. For Edna not to do her part to maintain this complex system and the values it implies is deeply troubling to him because so much of the maintenance of that system depends on her complicity. The life he has chosen is not possible without her consistent collaboration.

Edna retreats to her room after this scene. "It was a large, beautiful room," we are told, "rich and picturesque in the soft, dim light which the maid had turned low. She went and stood at the open window and looked out upon the deep tangle of the garden below" (252). Repeatedly, when she is troubled, Edna retreats to a place of solitude and space where, undisturbed, she can look both inward and outward—windows and window seats, porches, open doors, and thresholds draw her. As at her summer home she derived some peace from contemplating the limitless ocean, here she looks into the "deep tangle" of the garden below—another symbol of the wild freedom of what is natural, fluid, and unconscious. Her luxurious bedroom recalls the "gilded cage" so many women writers describe. Though from it she can look out on the lovely disorder of the tangled garden, it, too, is an enclosed space and an extension of the house—a wilderness carefully contained within walls, like Edna's own wildly blossoming inner life.

Edna's growing resistance to the material world that has become so oppressive surfaces again when Leonce wants her to help him get new fixtures for the library. She objects, "Don't let us get anything new; you are too extravagant. I don't believe you ever think of saving or putting by." Leonce's answer not only summarily dismisses Edna's concern but switches the terms of discussion to a logic formed in the marketplace, where money is the ultimate gauge of behavior: "The way to become rich is to make money, my dear Edna, not to save it" (253).

Following his pronouncement of this bit of accepted wisdom, he departs, leaving Edna in her classic posture of ambivalence, standing once again on the veranda picking bits of jessamine from a trellis as her husband leaves one domain, in which he is master, for another, in which he has a clearly defined and powerful place. Neither place is hers. The jessamine, like so many other natural things in the novel, momentarily answers Edna's hunger for simple, natural, sensual things, here opposed to the world of manufactured objects. Edna's resistance to spending and acquisition is clearly more symbolic than practical. Leonce's acquisitions are her burdens; his expenditures involve them in an increasingly complicated web of possessions and status symbols that it becomes her responsibility to maintain.

Furthermore, acquiring new things suggests an inability to enjoy the old ones—spiritual restlessness perhaps expressed in thirst for novelty. He spends very little time enjoying them; Mme. Ratignolle has observed to Edna, "It's a pity Mr. Pontellier doesn't stay home more in the evenings" (277)—and, indeed, we seem always to be seeing him poised for departure. The fact that he does not spend much time simply dwelling in and enjoying his home reflects a general incapacity to dwell in or enjoy— an ineptitude at the contemplative, the receptive, and the "feminine" capacities simply to *be* without doing or demonstrating.

Shortly after this, a visit to the Ratignolles' home presents a striking contrast to the Pontelliers', and Chopin complicates the questions she has raised about the oppressions of domestic life by presenting one that is remarkably satisfactory: "There was something which Edna thought very French, very foreign, about their whole manner of living. In the large and pleasant salon which extended across the width of the house, the Ratignolles entertained their friends once a fortnight with a soiree musicale, sometimes diversified by card-playing" (255). The wide-openness of this house contrasts significantly with the closely defined and heavily filled spaces of the Pontelliers' home. The spaces are meant and used for entertainment rather than for show—not exhibition halls but gathering places, humanized by activity rather than mummified by collections of objects. The people are the decoration and the decor, and the house is an instrument of their own radiant hospitality rather than of restraint and protection. Nevertheless, the satisfactions of this way of life seem to Edna a function of something distinctly foreign and somehow inaccessible.

This visit is the first of a series of three visits Edna makes to homes of friends before reaching her decision to move out. Each represents a style of home life that confronts her with important questions about her own. She decides in a fit of melancholy to visit Mlle. Reisz, the eccentric, crusty spinster musician who piqued her curiosity during the summer soirees at the seaside cottages and who lives, Edna knows, alone in town. On the way Edna goes to the home of the Lebruns, Robert's family, to get Mlle. Reisz's address. Arriving at the Lebruns, where she seldom visits, Edna pauses to look at the forbidding architecture: "Their home from the outside looked like a prison, with iron bars before the door and lower windows. The iron bars were a relic of the old regime, and no one had ever thought of dislodging them. At the side was a high fence enclosing the garden. A gate or door opening upon the street was locked" (262–263).

This reference to this home as both prison and "relic" underscores the sinister aspect under which Edna is coming to regard her own. The unrenovated architecture here bespeaks an anachronistic and unreflective conservatism that harks back to European roots with no adaptation to modern life, preserving outmoded aesthetic and, implicitly, social values. The connection between aesthetics and morality is, throughout, quite direct, focusing primarily on elitist preservation of privacy, social distinction, and separation from the masses as well as the containment of female sexuality or sensuality within limits strictly controlled by the master of the house.

Here, as at the Ratignolles', the European ethos is specifically mentioned, as if to establish a contrast between indigenous and imported culture, the latter paradoxically represented as both more hospitable and open and, here, as cloistered and resistant to change. Clearly one of the questions Chopin is raising about Edna's situation is how much of it is a matter of the confused, hybrid moral atmosphere bred specifically in the United States and peculiarly in the South, with its mixed vestiges of French culture. Edna's Americanness is one of the qualities that distinguishes her from several of the other women in the novel, Mme.

Ratignolle, Mlle. Reisz, Mme. Lebrun, Mme. Antoine, and Maria all having either foreign blood or strong foreign roots.

Having arrived at the Lebruns' and having contemplated the forbidding facade of their house, Edna is not eager to go inside. Instead, she takes up her usual position on the threshold: "It was very pleasant there on the side porch, where there were chairs, a wicker lounge, and a small table" (263). Here, as in other scenes, Edna not only seems to prefer to situate herself between the indoors, where it is too confining, and the outdoors, where her place is not clear, but at a side entrance to the house, a place of entry that bespeaks intimacy, indirectness, and perhaps even intrigue. Her ambivalence toward this house and her ambiguous relation to it reiterate the unclarity in her relation to Robert, who, though for her representing ease, freedom, and release from the stringencies of her marriage, also comes from this milieu, which is in its way even more complicatedly confining and repressive. She does not stay long at the Lebruns and does not go inside, but she does procure the address she needs and moves on to find Mlle. Reisz's odd little top-floor apartment. The place seems to her as refreshingly eccentric as the woman herself, provoking, as she does, curious speculation:

> Some people contended that the reason Mademoiselle Reisz always chose apartments up under the roof was to discourage the approach of beggars, peddlars and callers. There were plenty of windows in her little front room. They were for the most part dingy, but as they were nearly always open it did not make so much difference. They often admitted into the room a good deal of smoke and soot, but at the same time all the light and air that there was came through them. From her windows could be seen the crescent of the river, the masts of ships and the big chimneys of the Mississippi steamers. A magnificent piano crowded the apartment. In the next room she slept, and in the third and last she harbored a gasoline stove on which she cooked her meals when disinclined to descend to the neighboring restaurant. It was there also that she ate, keeping her belongings in a rare old buffet, dingy and battered from a hundred years of use. (266–267)

In every way Mlle. Reisz's apartment invites direct comparison with her character as we have come to know it: lofty, distant, eccentric, a little unpleasant, and yet harboring things of great beauty and value that are not kept for show but for the sort of use to which only a skilled hand can put them. The apartment is divided into three functional parts, which suggests the simplicity of a life whose public and private enjoyments are carefully circumscribed and located in a simple living plan—a life from which much has been pruned but whose simplicity seems considered and chosen, not a circumstance imposed by force of necessity. The views from her windows reflect the wideness of an imagination that dwells on broader horizons than most, has a higher and wider vantage point. And even the slight air of neglect suggests an inhabitant preoccupied with "higher" things. This strange female hermit in her hermitage provides an interesting variation on the romantic Thoreauvian solitary so common in our fiction, very like Cather's Godfrey St. Peter or James's Maria Gostrey—creatures who perch in their small, carefully furnished nests awhile to observe the world from the privileged vantage point gained there and then move on, having "other lives to lead."

In this novel Mlle. Reisz's role, viewed in its allegorical dimension, is a complicated one. She is hardly a model for Edna, who, though drawn to the woman's idiosyncratic life-style, seems, in her chronic hesitancy, incapable of the sort of decisive sacrifice required of this breed of secular saints. Mlle. Reisz serves, however, to establish a pole on the spectrum of possible choices, giving Edna some gauge by which to measure and assess the dimensions of her own existence. As she reluctantly leaves the apartment, Edna pauses on the threshold to ask rather plaintively if she may come again. Here in the freedom afforded by the simplicity and candor of the place and its inhabitant, in the presence of the music from her piano, and in the light from her high window, Edna is freed to feel what she feels at a depth she has not often allowed herself to reach.

This is the romantic side of the experience of both the woman and her home. On a later visit the darker side of Mlle. Reisz's way of life shows through—the loneliness, the dinginess, and the insufficiency:

> It was misty, with heavy, lowering atmosphere, one afternoon, when Edna climbed the stairs to the pianist's apartment under the roof. Her clothes were dripping with moisture. She felt chilled and pinched as she entered the room. Mademoiselle was poking at a

rusty stove that smoked a little and warmed the room indifferently. She was endeavoring to heat a pot of chocolate on the stove. The room looked cheerless and dingy to Edna as she entered. A bust of Beethoven, covered with a hood of dust, scowled at her from the mantelpiece.

"Ah! here comes the sunlight!" exclaimed Mademoiselle, rising from her knees before the stove. "Now it will be warm and bright enough; I can let the fire alone." (293)

This is a life easy to sentimentalize, hard to live. It is not a life Edna would be able to lead. The frequent mention of Mlle. Reisz's withered body, her quick irascibility, her ugliness, points as well to a certain imbalance in this kind of living—accepted, even raised to an art, but not ideal. At the time of this visit Edna is facing her own imminent solitude and begins here to come to terms with some of its consequences and costs. A contrast of this description of the apartment with the earlier one where the order, the view, and the fruitful simplicity were emphasized provides a measure of Edna's swiftly changing point of view.

It is Leonce's departure for an extended business trip that gives Edna her first real experience of solitude and freedom. With her children off to their grandparents, she luxuriates in her rare liberty:

When Edna was at last alone, she breathed a big, genuine sigh of relief. A feeling that was unfamiliar but very delicious came over her. She walked all through the house, from one room to another, as if inspecting it for the first time. She tried the various chairs and lounges, as if she had never sat and reclined upon them before. And she perambulated around the outside of the house, investigating, looking to see if windows and shutters were secure and in order. The flowers were like new acquaintances; she approached them in a familiar spirit, and made herself at home among them. (283)

This is Edna's first experience of a proprietorship of the sort that comes naturally to Leonce, who habitually does just such a mental inventory, though Edna's circuit of the house ends in the garden with the dogs and the flowers, where she picks up dry leaves and mucks about joyously in the mud. She brings both mud and dog into the house with her. For once she is able to see the possibilities of her home through her own eyes, rather than through the anticipated judgments of her husband. The things that before were heavy with oppressive significance now appear simply as what they are—chairs to sit in, flowers to smell, recliners to lie on. As she takes in the house's parameters, she sees it whole, as if for the first time—as something she might in fact manage quite well, left to her own devices. Even her usual domestic domain Edna surveys with different eyes: "Even the kitchen assumed a sudden interesting character which she had never before perceived" (283). In her instructions to the cook, Edna says she will be preoccupied during her husband's absence and begs the cook to "take all thought and responsibility of the larder upon her own shoulders" (284). Like a child at play among her parents' belongings, Edna is trying out a new stance in relation both to the house and to the running of the household, asserting a new authority, in small ways breaking through deadening routines and finding with gratified surprise that there is nothing to prevent her doing so.

It does not take long after this realization for Edna to make her momentous decision to move into a place of her own. With precipitous haste, she seeks out a little house not far away and arranges to take it without reference to Leonce's wishes. This domestic rebellion is characteristic in several rather amusing ways: she does not go far—lingers, in fact, almost on the doorstep of her marital home; she acts quickly so as to avoid, rather than confront, the opposition she knows will come, but the action itself is amazingly radical for a woman of her kind in her position. She is energized by a passion and urgency that strikingly contrast with the lethargy, melancholy, fatigue, and stasis in which she seemed to be sunken in so many previous scenes: "Within the precincts of her home she felt like one who has entered and lingered within the portals of some forbidden temple in which a thousand voices bade her begone" (302). Yet this passion is only partly desire for independence; that desire is complicated by her growing attraction to Alcee Arobin, who supplies at least a significant part of her incentive to leave.

Like James's Isabel Archer, Edna is a woman governed by impulses whose conflicting nature she neither understands nor even fully suspects—both a wild and a domestic creature wanting love in terms that will leave her free, not sure how to use freedom when she has it. And her situation raises an old American question in microcosm: what comes after a declaration of independence? Nevertheless, in the course of her life's events, it has become necessary to dissolve these bonds, regardless of what lies before her. In a state of radical alienation, she no longer recognizes her house as her home. Indeed, she has "awakened" to the fact that it never was, so that lingering in it seems an impropriety. Leonce has provided the norms. In his absence all that was normative has lost its raison d'être, belonging to a world and a logic of possession and identity that have nothing to do with her. He is her only connection with that world and the connection is rapidly dissolving. Her haste and anxiety have doubtless also to do with simple fear of being caught in transition—on the threshold—but more perhaps with making up for lost time: a long-unrecognized hunger is on the verge of fulfillment and grows in anticipation.

The process of moving demands that for the first time as a married woman Edna take stock of who she is and what she has apart from her husband: "Whatever was her own in the house, everything which she had acquired aside from her husband's bounty, she caused to be transported to the other house, supplying simple and meager deficiencies from her own resources" (302). Separating possessions is a way of separating on deeper levels. She is not a wealthy woman without Leonce. She has to be resourceful for the first time, careful to modify her tastes and acquisitions to available funds, to "make do."

Edna calls her little house the "pigeon house"—a name that reiterates a motif of bird imagery associated with her throughout. It is a place where she can rest between flights, a place she can escape from to try her wings and return to for safety. It is small but sufficient: the mahogany table Edna had formerly used would have almost filled the dining room. "There was a small front porch, upon which a long window and the front door opened. The door opened directly into the back parlor; there was no side entry. Back in the yard was a room for servants, in which old Celestine had been ensconced" (314). Everything Edna needs is almost literally at her fingertips: "There was but a step or two from the little table to the kitchen, to the mantel, the small buffet, and the side door that opened out on the narrow brick-paved yard" (327). Much of Edna's satisfaction with her new home seems to lie in finding how little is sufficient. Like Thoreau in his cabin, she finds relative deprivation a source of new freedom. Its simplicity is also reminiscent of Thoreau's suggestion that a dwelling be self-explanatory and open to "reading" on entering. Simple, frank, unadorned with architectural niceties and subtleties, it is still a place where certain proprieties are maintained—the servants in their quarters, the "few tasteful pictures" on the walls, the books on the table, the fresh matting and rugs on the floors, the flowers in vases— but only in their simplest form. What is there is chosen with care by a woman accustomed to just such choices. Like Thoreau, her training in a more complicated kind of life shapes her tastes and priorities even in her iconoclasm. In her carefully appointed rooms, there is a well-considered concern for comfort and beauty as well as a rejection of opulence.

In the transitional period preceding her final departure, before Leonce returns, Edna gives one last dinner party in the big house. But what is intended as a celebration becomes a strange ordeal for her; she is again on a threshold, one foot in two worlds, caught suddenly in the old uncertainty that seems to be her besetting weakness:

> There was something in her attitude, in her whole appearance when she leaned her head against the high-backed chair and spread her arms, which suggested the regal woman, the one who rules, who looks on, who stands alone. But as she sat there amid her guests, she felt the old ennui overtaking her, the hopelessness which so often assailed her, which came upon her like an obsession, like something extraneous, independent of volition. (309)

This passage encapsulates the ambiguities of Edna's transitional situation: she is exhilarated by her newly claimed authority, freedom, and self-determination, but at the same time she is plagued by apprehensions. She has not looked very far down the road, and the road beyond her gaze is dark. Like Ibsen's Nora, Edna may find herself in a cold world after slamming the door. The impulsiveness that gave her the strength to make her move will not serve to sustain her in her choice. The paucity of external supports for her choice will gradually become all too clear. All these implications are adumbrated here by a vague feeling of unrest as she luxuriates for the last time in the comforts of the home she is leaving. The trade-off is costly in ways she is only beginning to imagine.

When Leonce hears of Edna's intention, he is predictably distressed and angry and refuses to regard it as a serious decision; rather, he trivializes it as a rash and unreasoned impulse. He begs her to consider what people will say, thinking not of scandal but of his "financial integrity." After all, as he points out, "it might get noised about that the Pontelliers had met with reverses, and were forced to conduct their menage on a humbler scale than heretofore. It might do incalculable mischief to his business prospects" (316). Here the portrayal of Leonce becomes almost caricature. Incapable of responding with authentic human emotion even to such outright rejection and abandonment, he can interpret Edna's actions only in terms of their potential social and economic repercussions. The day he hears the news he sends instructions to a "well-known architect" to remodel the house, instructing the architect to proceed with "changes which he [Pontellier] had long contemplated." In short order,

> the Pontellier house was turned over to the artisans. There was to be an addition—a small snuggery; there was to be frescoing, and hardwood flooring was to be put into such rooms as had not yet been subjected to this improvement. Furthermore, in one of the daily papers appeared a brief notice to the effect that Mr. and Mrs. Pontellier were contemplating a summer sojourn abroad, and that their handsome home on Esplanade Street was undergoing sumptuous alterations, and would not be ready for occupancy until their return. (317)

Leonce's pathetic attempt to forestall the disaster Edna's move threatens to bring on him is made in the only terms he knows: by wielding the visible weapon of wealth and possessions. He can imagine only one solution to the problem because he can conceive of the problem only in one limited set of terms. Furthermore, the problem as he perceives it has more to do with appearances than with Edna's or even his own human needs. It would never occur to him that his notion of a solution might in itself represent part of the problem: the house is the stumbling block for both of them; having become the medium through which they communicate, they are unable to understand their marriage independently of it.

Edna, in the meantime, has proceeded to settle into her pigeon house and is finding there a milieu of her own making that gives her a kind of power she could never have developed in competition with Leonce's. Like his, her house is a medium of self-expression:

> It at once assumed the intimate character of a home, while she herself invested it with a charm which it reflected like a warm glow. There was with her a feeling of having descended in the social scale, with a corresponding sense of having risen to the spiritual. Every step which she took toward relieving herself from obligations added to her strength and expansion as an individual. She began to look with her own eyes; to see and to apprehend deeper undercurrents of life. No longer was she content to 'feed upon opinion' when her own soul had invited her. (317)

No passage in the novel is more reminiscent of Thoreau than this. The inverse relationship of the social or material to the spiritual, the equation of material simplicity with spiritual richness, and the notion that "things" bind and that emptiness liberates have deep roots not only in American romanticism but in ancient Eastern cultures in which the feminine is far more profoundly integrated than in our own. It is noteworthy, too, that what is described here as "filling" the house is an intangible—the atmosphere, the "warm glow" of Edna's presence—as though the relative absence of material objects had made way for something intangible that nevertheless required space to become apparent.

Edna's move into her house provides an opportunity for her to explore other kinds of liberation, first in her ill-fated love affair with Arobin and then in her attempt to pursue her more deeply felt love for Robert. The latter, however, not having descended to Arobin's level of libertinism, cannot follow Edna into her self-imposed social exile. It is interesting what a relatively minor role these love affairs play in Edna's emergence into a new consciousness of herself, however. The "love interest" in this story is quite secondary to the theme of inner awakening, a drama in which the men in her life play necessary but subordinate roles. Indeed, the most sensual scene in the book takes place in the bedroom at Mme. Antoine's, where Edna, alone, awakens from sleep, stretches, and runs her hands along the contours of her own body, as if discovering and delighting in her own sensuality in a way quite different from that experienced in the give and take of a sexual encounter with a man. Such scenes and discoveries are the more poignant because they are short-lived; she does return, and must return, to a life in which social relationships shape both behavior and consciousness.

In chapter 38, we find Edna once again alone, this time on her own little porch at the pigeon house in the evening: "Instead of entering she sat on the step of the porch. The night was quiet and soothing" (345). A number of scenes like this one in the last half of the book echo the opening scenes. Whereas her late-night meditations on the porch at the summer cottage irritated Leonce, here she is free to indulge in this little freedom with peace and pleasure, but not for long. As in so many stories about women, the road to freedom turns out to be a cul-de-sac. Edna's choices have unfit her for the society in which she has to live, and she is ill-equipped to live elsewhere. She finally returns to the beach, alone, abandoned by Robert, separated from her family, and unable to imagine a viable future. Walking there amid the reminders of those less complicated days when no bridges had been burned and her difficult awakening seemed to hold such promise of commensurate fulfillment, she comes on a young couple at the island repairing their summer house. She remarks, "I supposed it was you, mending the porch. It's a good thing. I was always tripping over those loose planks last summer" (347–348).

Edna's experiment fails. Unlike Hester Prynne, Edna would never have found a niche in society by herself, would always have lived on the margin without any sustaining community but what she was able to gather about herself by sheer strength of character. She has neither Hester's charisma nor her moral fortitude. Edna is not of heroic stature; she is simply a woman with longings and needs common to women, caught in a social web where these needs are not met, but ill-equipped to spin her own web outside it. The new house is a refuge, but it is not enough. The walls around her are only one of many structures that would need to be, as Hawthorne puts it, "torn down and built anew" for her choices to be viable. So her story ends, like that of so many women who have tried singly to resist the fate assigned to them, in a symbolic act of self-destructive self-liberation. Unable to fashion a freer life by redefining or redesigning the structures that imprison her, she makes a final journey into a realm without walls, a place of endless, undefined space, fluidity, boundlessness, in which she can lose herself completely, free in the only way she knows how to achieve freedom from the restrictions of civilized life.

Gilman's "The Yellow Wallpaper" provides a striking companion piece to *The Awakening*. The writers were contemporaries dealing with the same realities of late Victorian American life. Gilman's own married life was much less satisfying than Chopin's and ended in divorce after prolonged periods of "nervous prostration" that seemed to her later to have been directly related to the confinements of domestic life. Her abiding interest in the conditions of women's lives was grounded in her own lifelong struggle to come to terms with them. "The Yellow Wallpaper," which several medical professionals among Gilman's early readers recognized as a remarkably accurate portrayal of mental breakdown, is grounded in autobiography. Its dramatic contours are sharper and less ambiguous than those of *The Awakening*, though the two share major themes. Taken together the stories present the old, tragic double bind of female fate pushed to its extremes and ending in suicide or madness. Both tragedies are a result of the same elements: enclosure, not only physical "imprisonment" in a house but in a system that entraps women in confining roles that weaken and diminish their natural powers; trivialization by the men in authority over these women, so that their most urgent pleas for understanding go unheard; lack of a "common language" that will allow them to identify and speak their needs.

The narrator of "The Yellow Wallpaper" is a woman who remains unnamed throughout the story. The only names we hear are those she hears—her husband's diminutive endearments.

As the story begins, she presents herself as a submissive, compliant, affectionate wife who aims to please her husband and is attempting to follow her doctor's orders for recovering from a "condition" that seems to be postpartum depression. Presumably in the interests of her recuperation, the couple has moved into an old "ancestral hall" in the country for the summer. She describes it as "a colonial mansion, a hereditary estate, I would say a haunted house and reach the height of romantic felicity—but that would be asking too much of fate!" (3). She insists, however, that there is "something queer about it" for it to have been let so cheaply and have remained "so long untenanted" (3). With these mild portents, Gilman squarely situates her story in the Gothic tradition. The house and the woman are the dual focus of the story, the woman's body, like the house, imprisoning a restless spirit that has long been undernourished.

The analogy is made quite explicit on the first page of the story by the woman herself, who realizes that translating her concerns about her body into concerns about the house is the only way in which she is going to be allowed to give them expression:

> John says the very worst thing I can do is to think about my condition, and I confess it always makes me feel bad.
> So I will let it alone and talk about the house.
> The most beautiful place! It is quite alone, standing well back from the road, quite three miles from the village. It makes me think of English places that you read about, for there are hedges and walls and gates that lock, and lots of separate little houses for the gardeners and people. (4)

Like the woman, the house is isolated, complicated, confined, ensconced in a luxurious private domain but having little relation to the larger world. The difference between her perceptions of the house and her husband's provides more significant information about her psychological state and susceptibilities:

> There was some legal trouble, I believe, something about the heirs and co-heirs; anyhow, the place has been empty for years.
> That spoils my ghostliness, I am afraid, but I don't care—there is something strange about the house—I can feel it.
> I even said so to John one moonlight evening, but he said what I felt was a draught, and shut the window. (4)

John is the force of "realism" opposing her romanticism; shutting the window he summarily classifies, dismisses, and shuts out the stimuli that are awakening her fancy. The obvious and almost comic use of the Gothic motifs here—moonlight, ghosts, gusts of wind, free-floating anxiety—serves to accentuate the ambiguities of the story and to raise the questions posed by all Gothic romances: What are the boundaries between imagination and reality? What is "real"? Who can determine what is "there" if the senses cannot be entirely trusted? The radical difference between John's unimaginative rationality and his wife's feelings and fancy, attaching here to the house and its atmosphere, puts the reader in a position of choosing repeatedly between their opposed interpretations of the significance of objects and events.

When they have dwelt there a few days, the narrator begins to find other reasons to complain: she does not like their room, having wished for "one downstairs that opened onto the piazza and had roses all over the window, and such pretty old-fashioned chintz hangings! But John would not hear of it" (5). Again the house serves as a vehicle for her displaced discontentments. She wants access to the outside world and natural beauty. He chooses for her a room with barred windows designed to protect children, a "big, airy room . . . with windows that look all ways, and air and sunshine galore" that was "a nursery first, and then playroom and gymnasium. . . . For the windows are barred for little children and there are rings and things in the walls" (5). The paradox of this room is that it seems a congenial environment, open to sunlight and air, large and commodious. But the bars and the rings, the obvious intention of the design, suggest that there is something inappropriate and even sinister about the woman's assignment to this space. It is deceptive in its allowances.

The woman's mood of revolt grows stronger as she notices more and more details about the abhorrent room:

> The paint and paper look as if a boy's school had used it. It is stripped off—the paper—in great patches all around the head of my bed, about as far as I can reach, and in a great place on the other side of the room low down. I never saw a worse paper in my life. One of those sprawling, flamboyant patterns committing

every artistic sin. . . . The color is repellent, almost revolting: a smouldering unclean yellow, strangely faded by the slow-turning sunlight. It is a dull yet lurid orange in some places, a sickly sulphur tint in others. (5)

The woman's disgust continues to find expression in attacks on the house rather than on the husband. As in *The Awakening*, the house becomes a symbolic substitute for the marriage—an incarnation of the contract between wife and husband. The Gothic language she uses here to describe the sickly colors and shabby accoutrements of the room to which she is consigned takes on the "coloring" of the room: lurid, ghastly, and jarring. She uses the repugnant interior to reflect her own internal state of revulsion and rebellion, identifying more and more closely with the surroundings even as she expresses her violent distaste for them. Doubtless her distaste for her own violent feelings is equally powerful.

Her husband, however, misses all this. Oblivious as Leonce Pontellier, John blandly observes that the place is doing her good and ignores her pleas, which become increasingly frantic, to renovate the house on the reasonable ground that it would be a waste of effort just for a three-month rental period. She presses him further, "Then do let us go downstairs. . . . There are such pretty rooms there" (6). But he refuses this as well. Like Leonce Pontellier, John figures value in terms of what makes economic sense. Other modes of sense-making are alien to him. He has no way of identifying with his wife's desperation, and she is powerless to make him understand it. She wants to go "downstairs," symbolically retreating from the "higher" realms of rationality, consciousness, and intellect to a place that is closer to the ground or more "grounded" in sensuality and connected to the outside, natural world. But his answer is to take her in his arms, calling her a "blessed little goose," and exaggerate her petition to the point of absurdity in order to trivialize and dismiss it, saying, "He would go down cellar, if I wished, and have it whitewashed into the bargain" (6). The husband's joking concession both bypasses the wife's feelings and once again sidesteps her purpose; his offer to "go down cellar" is not a real concession to a real need but an exaggeration of the expressed need that makes it appear ridiculous. Moreover, his offer to "whitewash the cellar" betokens exactly the kind of repression of his own unconscious and hers that he is engaged in.

The woman, for reasons of health as judged by husband and doctor, is confined to the room with the hated wallpaper, and her hostilities toward her environment become paranoically focused on the wallpaper as the cause of her oppressed spirits. The projection becomes increasingly bizarre and explicit: "This paper looks to me as if it *knew* what a vicious influence it had! There is a recurrent spot where the pattern lolls like a broken neck and two bulbous eyes stare at you upside down" (7). This grotesque vocabulary reflects what Poe would call the "phantasmagoria" in her mind. She attributes or projects more and more onto the inanimate wallpaper, like the narrator in Poe's "The Fall of the House of Usher." The house assumes the position of the shadowy Other against which an internal conflict can be played out; ordinary facts or events assume extraordinary interpretive possibilities. As an outer shell, the house duplicates the body as enclosure or limiting wall. The sense of body as "Other" of course has its roots in the forms of Protestant Christianity that so deeply inform the American imagination, beginning back with the Puritan injunctions to escape the temptations of the body into a spiritual realm.

As time goes on, the animation of the wallpaper increases in differentiation and depth. The woman can see, "where the sun is just so," a "strange, provoking, formless sort of figure that seems to skulk about behind that silly and conspicuous front design" (8). Once she claims to herself the ability to see beyond surfaces, she is lost in a world of projective speculation. Yet her observation that this creature appears "when the sun is just so" seems a vestige of rational explanation, as though in some degree she recognizes the possibility that the phenomenon is an optical illusion.

The next stage in the woman's dementia is a perverse embracing of her confinement and the aspect of it she finds most repugnant: "I'm getting really fond of the room in spite of the wallpaper. Perhaps *because* of the wallpaper" (9). She moves from observation to involvement, accepting the wallpaper as a necessary evil in the way a person accepts an imperfect body or some impediment that may, once accepted, become a source of positive possibility.

She begins to pay more acute attention thereafter to the patterns on the wallpaper, finding in them a source of occupation in her solitary confinement; though the patterns involve her in increasingly obsessive-compulsive behavior, they do provide some stimulation in an otherwise depleted environment. The patterns, she observes, "connect diagonally, and the sprawling outlines run off in great slanting waves of optic horror, like a lot of wallowing sea-weeds in full chase. The whole thing goes horizontally, too, at least it seems to, and I exhaust myself trying to distinguish the order of its going in that direction. . . . The interminable grotesque seems to form around a common center and rush off in headlong plunges of equal distraction" (10). Jung and others have established that psychotics tend to draw open-ended figures, not to enclose space—an interesting observation here, where the center the woman establishes in the pattern is not really a center of anything but an endless web of lines. There is no closure. Furthermore, the static pattern is here perceived as animated and active.

The next stage is secrecy. The woman assures herself, "There are things in that wallpaper that nobody knows about but me, or ever will" (11). With this statement, in which she invalidates any judgment others may pass on what she sees, she closes a door on the reality that could provide a check on her construction of a separate world. The relationship between the woman and the wallpaper thereby assumes a new dimension. The closed system is complete. There is no longer any desire to appeal to outside sources for confirmation of what she sees.

Her imaginary world begins to betray her, however. The satisfaction of her secret soon slips into irritation and then torment as she begins to find irregularities in the pattern, "a lack of sequence, a defiance of law, that is a constant irritant to a normal mind" (12). She describes the pattern as aggressive—"It slaps you in the face, knocks you down, and tramples upon you"—and these metaphors literalize themselves as she decides that the wallpaper is moving, sees a woman trapped behind it, and ultimately becomes obsessed with the project of freeing the woman. In the final scene her concern for the woman behind the wallpaper has progressed from sympathy to empathy to complete identification and confusion of her self with the specter. As her husband opens the door to the locked room she turns and declares defiantly, "I've got out at last . . . in spite of you and Jane. And I've pulled off most of the paper, so you can't put me back!" (19).

This haunting story, now a standard reading in American literature and women's studies courses, encapsulates in intensely dramatic form some of the convictions Gilman elaborated at much greater length in her book *The Home*, a methodical and lucid inquiry into what she calls "domestic mythology" in the United States and its consequences.[4] Applying the principles of social Darwinism popular at the time, she claims that the home is "the least evolved of all our institutions." She poses the general questions of why it has been so resistant to progress and what is happening to women enclosed in their homes and unable to participate in the widening spheres of social action and the march of progress. Starting with chapters on "The Evolution of the Home" and "Domestic Mythology," she attempts to trace the development of the idea of home and practices of home life from their primitive beginnings in caves to their varied forms in contemporary civilized societies, the point being that with respect to the role of women they not only have not progressed toward enlightenment but have in fact been a regressive and repressive institution. "What is a home?" she asks, in much the same spirit as Thoreau's "What is a house?"

Beginning with a carefully scientific definition of the home as "the shelter of the family, of the group organised for the purposes of reproduction," likening the home to a beehive, which "is as much a home as any human dwelling place—even more, perhaps"—she claims, "we may study the evolution of the home precisely as we study that of any other form of life" (23). The study that follows courageously undertakes to identify as myths and fallacies some of the most widely held notions and practices about home, women, and family in her generation. Slaughtering one sacred cow after another, she claims that women's unspecialized work is not only demeaning but holds up the general progress of humankind; that childrearing would be more effective when carried out communally in healthy environments supervised by trained experts than when given over to the care of unskilled and often ill-adapted mothers; that cooking likewise might better be done by trained cooks and provided as a paid public service, leaving women free to follow other talents; and that "the effect of home life on women seems to be more injurious in proportion to their social development" (74). In contrast to these ideals she characterizes "normal" Victorian home life as "morbid, disproportioned, [and] overgrown" (178).

Gilman's analysis reaches a high pitch of argument in the chapter entitled "The Lady of the House," which may serve as an explicatory key to "The Yellow Wallpaper" or, conversely, to which the story provides a chillingly precise illustration. What, she inquires, has the "age-long" tradition of housebound life done to woman, "the mother and moulder of human character; what sort of lady is the product of the house?" (220). Physically, she is whiter, softer, and frailer than her ancestors, and Gilman wastes no words taking to task the fashions that glorify these conditions that betoken morbidity and weakness. But the list of mental deformities resulting from chronic domestic isolation is much more troubling: first "a sort of mental myopia" developed from "looking always at things too near"—a dangerous lack of perspective that gradually stunts a woman's ability to make any distinctions or judgments about public affairs. This small-mindedness often results in eccentricity and "a tendency to monomania" and other "pathological" conditions. Gilman looks at the profusion of fancywork and other domestic forms of expression and sees in them not a delicate craft equal in dignity to public art forms but "a senseless profusion of expression" betokening the desperate efforts of a trapped creature deprived of air and exercise and full use of her powers to put her energies to some use: "There is no pathos, but rather a repulsive horror in the mass of freakish ornament on walls, floors, chairs, and tables, on specially contrived articles of furniture, on her own body and the helpless bodies of her little ones, which marks the unhealthy riot of expression of the overfed and underworked lady of the house" (220).

She concludes her argument with a plea for the conditions that allow health and happiness in any sentient creature: legiti-

mate exercise of mental and physical powers, some public intercourse, and freedom to follow the vocational longings that demand expression. And she issues a warning: "The widespread
nervous disorders among our leisure-class women are mainly
traceable to this unchanging mould, which presses ever more
cruelly upon the growing life" (225).

In her autobiography Gilman portrays her own mother as
"the most passionately domestic of home-worshiping house-
wives" and devotes several pages to an ambivalent tribute to her
mother's homely virtues.[5] Compelled by a financially and emotionally unstable marriage to move nineteen times in eighteen
years, Mary Westcott Perkins endured disruption by clinging to
a vision of motherhood and homemaking that her children experienced as smothering. At a fairly early age, Gilman claims,
she and her brother both outgrew their mother, who, a paragon
of the womanly virtues touted in her generation, was never allowed a fully adult life. For Gilman herself that "fully adult life"
was won at a high price. This life consisted of broadening the
notions that bound women to their place; understanding these
ideas in a wide, global context; and teaching women that the vocation of motherhood could be understood as a call to serve the
"growth" of consciousness (one of her favorite concepts) and
that "home" could and should be preeminently a place where
the seeds of social reform and enlightenment were planted.

The summary chapter of her autobiography, in which she
looks back over the changes she has witnessed in nearly seventy-
five years, is entitled "Home." In it she reflects on the social and
philosophical changes of attitude that have led to what she
hopefully calls "the woman's century." She prophesies "more
and more professional women, who will marry and have families and will not be house servants, for nothing; and less and less
obtainable service, with the sacrifice of the wife and mother to
that primal altar, the cook-stove" (321). Gilman's socialist vision
remains a challenge to society to develop models of household
economy and family life that provide both loving, intelligent
nurturing and an atmosphere in which individuals can find and
fulfill their separate vocations and perform the "one predomi-
nant duty," which is "to find one's work and do it" (335).

6

THE AGE OF INNOCENCE
Tribal Rites in the Urban Village

Edith Wharton's friendship with and literary debt to Henry James have been the subject of extensive critical discussion. Certainly one of the most conspicuous preoccupations the two shared was their fascination with the semiotics of houses and the peculiar mores and ironic inconsistencies of American domestic and social life. In this respect the disciple's fiction comes close at some points to surpassing the master's in its sharp-witted irony and the acuity with which it exposes the social pretenses that passed for cultural aspiration among the American upper class, whose dogged provincialities were comically apparent to the truly cosmopolitan. The pretentious elaboration of class structures and rituals in America's Gilded Age were mirrored in the heavy and overelaborated late-Victorian architecture that Wharton knew intimately and heartily despised. In *The Age of Innocence*, one of the most graphic examinations of social structures in American fiction, she exploits the potential of the architectural metaphors with a merciless irony that puts its own sharp twist on the old theme of American ambivalence.[1]

It is hardly surprising that Wharton's vision of American life focuses on the politics of space—how people (and which people) appropriate and occupy space, build buildings, design homes, and decorate them; her youth in the New York of the Gilded Age and her European travels furnished her with a wide exposure to architectural styles, both imitative and innovative, as well as to changing fashions in interior decoration and a life among people who lived sumptuously and expended much time and attention on material comforts. William Coles writes of the United States of Wharton's generation, "During this period the scale of American life and artistic ambitions was transformed. It was perhaps the most crucial period of our cultural evolution, and much that we take for granted in libraries, galleries, shops, and universities—in the sophisticated tone of our society—was either founded at this time or was given its essentially modern form."[2] Hers was a generation whose architects, artists, and writers thought of themselves as participating in a cultural renaissance, as signified by ambition, grand scale, and unprecedented technological progress.[3]

In Wharton's New York the structures of indoor life were fraught with symbolic significance. Women of her class expended a good part of their time and energy decorating their houses, and that decoration became, especially for the wealthy, who had a range of choice in interior design and materials, an elaborate code invested not only with aesthetic but also with moral significance. With so few acceptable avenues of expression open to them, American Victorian middle- and upper-class women poured their creative energies into their houses, as indeed they were enjoined to do by their advisers in the pulpits and by the pages of magazines, among which household management was an increasingly popular topic. Mrs. E. F. Ellet, for example, wrote in her *New Cyclopedia of Domestic Economy* in 1873, "The daughter of the millionaire is seldom taught to consider how great are the social responsibilities her wealth and position impose upon her,—to regard herself as a steward of the Almighty."[4] Among those responsibilities proper care and beautification of the home were, of course, paramount, and the same authorities that took it on themselves to form women's consciences in this area offered abundant prescriptions on matters of taste and style and of how to find and use appropriate help, be it a staff of servants or an expanding repertoire of mechanical aids to housekeeping.

With the advent of mass production, women in Wharton's position also began to define themselves as preservers of a culture threatened by a general lowering of standards of taste. Wharton herself is quite explicit about this sense of mission in *The Decoration of Houses*, the manual on interior decoration she co-authored with Ogden Codman.[5] The prescriptions in that book have, like Poe's on the matter of furnishings, a quality of moral fervor that stops just this side of evangelism. Wharton recognized that her recommendations could be applied only by those who could afford the luxury of designing and decorating their own homes in the first place, and so she addressed her plea to the wealthy to follow a principle of noblesse oblige in setting exemplary aesthetic standards, which could "in time, find [their] way to the carpenter-built cottage." "Once the right precedent is established," she reasoned, "it costs less to follow than to oppose it" (introduction).

Having spent many of her formative years in Europe, Wharton was sensitive to the heaviness and stodginess of the architecture and interior decoration of her native New York. She learned early to love the acknowledged best in European art and culture and attempted to Europeanize her own homes as explicitly and tastefully as possible. Like James, she valued cosmopolitanism as that which gave comparative perspective, and therefore greater validity, to an individual's judgments and taste. Like him, she deplored the thinness of indigenous culture in the United States and lamented that for artists and architects "no amount of travel abroad and study at home can compensate for the lack of daily familiarity" with monuments of style available in Europe (1). Those elements of style designated specifically as American are, throughout the book, characterized as borrowed, inherited, and adapted, often in terms of the diminishment and loss implicit in those processes. The same attitude is reflected in her late novel, *The Custom of the Country*, where she writes, "What people called society was really just like the houses it lived in: a muddle of misapplied ornament over a thin steel shell of utility."[6]

Wharton's predisposition to criticize what is native to her own culture extends to a generally damaging comparison between "Anglo-Saxon" and "Latin" sensibilities; she claims that beauty comes more naturally to the latter. "English taste," she writes,

> has never been so sure as that of the Latin races; and it has, moreover, been perpetually modified by a passion for contriving all kinds of supposed "conveniences," which instead of simplifying life not unfrequently tend to complicate it. Americans have inherited this trait, and in both countries the architect or upholsterer who can present a new and more intricate way of planning a house or of making a piece of furniture, is more sure of a hearing than he who follows the accepted lines. (49)

The Thoreauvian call to simplicity is sounded once again, though in a context and by a woman whose notions of simplicity were certainly more liberal and far more complicated than those of the hermit at the side of his pond and had more to do with classic ideals of harmony and coherence than with spirituality or asceticism.

As a young married couple the Whartons traveled to Europe annually and fostered several formative friendships with artists, sculptors, and architects. One of these was Ogden Codman, Wharton's eventual collaborator on *The Decoration of Houses*, her first book, which enunciates stylistic and aesthetic principles that illuminate not only her own decorative practices but her writing as well. Wharton rewrote the book extensively after it had been accepted by Scribners', under the tutelage of Walter Berry, a lifelong friend, whom she credited with tightening and shaping her style. In that sense, this prose work on architectural and interior style became for her an exercise in prose stylistics as well. Numerous critics have noted the direct relationship between this early aesthetic manifesto and the architectonics of her novels, with their characteristic focus on the social and political significance of interior spaces. Throughout Wharton's adult life the two interests went hand in hand: her career as a writer began simultaneously with her first independent ventures into home ownership and decoration. In 1889, the year she received her first acceptance from Scribners' for a poem, she also received a sizable legacy from her father that enabled her to take her first independent house in New York, on Madison Avenue. In 1893, a "landmark year in American architecture," she bought Land's End, her property at Newport, and began to remodel and decorate it.[7]

The Decoration of Houses is not a particularly innovative work; rather, it is characterized by the same informed conservatism that makes her fiction, ironic as it is toward the superficialities of the upper classes, so deeply ambivalent. The book is an attempt to "explain, order, and correct" existing tastes; to relate the best of current trends in architecture and decor to a historical tradition; and to make that tradition intellectually and practically available to "laymen of cultivated taste."[8] Wharton's project, then, in her writing on decoration as well as in her fiction, is to articulate and emulate a great tradition rather than to innovate. In this her stance recalls T. S. Eliot's in "Tradition and the Individual Talent," where he claims that the only authentic originality is that which is deeply rooted in an understanding and appropriation of tradition and in an application of its wisdom to the issues of contemporary civilization. Certainly her literary enterprises echo this general reverence for what is, as her Newland Archer puts it, "good in the old ways."

Wharton and Codman regarded *The Decoration of Houses* as a study of "house decoration as a branch of architecture" (xxxix). In light of Catharine Beecher and Harriet Beecher Stowe's earlier pleas to architects to recognize the proportionate importance of house interiors, particularly to women, this notion of aesthetic and philosophical unification of the two enterprises is understandable as a continuation of a long-standing debate among those who concerned themselves with the value systems implied in the design of living space. Moreover, the tension the book attempts to resolve accounts for the emphasis placed on organicism—the notion that the outside and the inside of a house need to be consistent in style, proportion, color, and appeal. The opening sentence of the manual reads, "Rooms may be decorated in two ways: by a superficial application of ornament totally independent of structure, or by means of those architectural features which are part of the organism of every house, inside as well as out" (196). They go on to point out that in the Middle Ages, "the architecture of the room became its decoration . . . but since then various influences have combined to sever the natural connection between the outside of the modern house and its interior. . . . As a result of this division of labor, house decoration has ceased to be a branch of architecture." In the modern world, they lament, "we have passed from the golden age of architecture to the gilded age of decoration" (196).

Closely related to organicism is Wharton's notion of "sincerity," which in architecture means "simply obedience to certain visual requirements, one of which demands that what are at once seen to be the main lines of a room or house shall be acknowledged as such in the application of ornament" (62). The idea of truth in architecture is an old one; the expression of that idea as sincerity gives it a romantic cast that recalls Downing's tendency to couch architectural principles in the language of personal ethics, though she scoffs both at Downing's sentimentality and at the "sincere furniture" of Charles Locke Eastlake, whose *Hints on Household Taste* was enormously popular among Americans from its first publication here in 1878 until the end of the century. Judith Fryer points out that Newland Archer's taste for "sincere Eastlake furniture," given Wharton's condemnation of his superficiality, is one of a number of clues we are given that Newland is "a man of 'taste' rather than a man of principle—or at least, he is a man whose principles are determined externally, according to taste."[9]

Another ideal enunciated in *The Decoration of Houses* is "suitability," meaning accommodation of style to function and visible differentiation of purpose. "When suitability departs," the authors write, "every room tends to become a living room" (xvii). Proportion, another central value, they define as "the good breeding of architecture . . . in its effects as intangible as that all-pervading essence which the ancients called a soul" (31). They speak of "the tendency of many modern decorators to sacrifice composition to detail, and to neglect the observance of proportion between ornament and structure" (98). "If the fundamental lines are right, very little decorative detail is needed to complete the effect; whereas, when the lines are wrong, no overlaying of ornamental odds and ends, in the way of pictures, bric-a-brac and other improvised expedients, will conceal the structural deficiencies" (47). It was recognition of this principle that "kept the work of the old architect-decorators (for the two were one) free from the superfluous, free from the intemperate accumulation that marks so many modern rooms" (197). Finally, simplicity is declared "the supreme excellence," a virtue related to "moderation, fitness, and relevance." "There is a sense," Wharton and Codman write, "in which works of art may be said to endure by virtue of that which is left out of them," and it is this "tact of omission that characterizes the master hand" (198).

Other key principles are propriety, privacy, symmetry ("the sanity of decoration"), reason, and order. Like Thoreau, Codman and Wharton see themselves in this manual to be addressing a culture that has lost its grounding and to be recalling a people to its first principles. The book, written "after a period of eclecticism that has lasted long enough to make architects and decorators lose their traditional habits of design" (xxxvii), compares the contemporary decorator to "a person who is called on to write a letter in the English language, but is ordered, in so doing, to conform to the Chinese or Egyptian rules of grammar, or possibly to both together" (16).

Wharton's own home at Lenox, built around the turn of the century, which she played a master role in designing and decorating, embodies all the values she articulates in *The Decoration of Houses* and applies in her fiction. Designed with obvious allusions both to the Italian Renaissance palazzo and to the English country house, it was praised by her most notable guest, Henry James, for its "penetralia," by which he meant "some part . . . sufficiently within some other part, sufficiently withdrawn and consecrated, not to constitute a thoroughfare."[10] The house is ingeniously designed to keep private spaces from violation by incidental traffic and to enhance the distinct and separate character of each of the spaces accessible to company. A large open foyer on the ground floor makes the transition from outside to inside both ceremonial and gradual. Wharton's sense of the syntax of domestic space entails dynamic notions of progression, flow, pace, and climax, which she describes in expressly literary terms: "Every house should be decorated according to a carefully graduated scale of ornamentation culminating in the most important room of the house; but this plan must be carried out with such due sense of the relation of the rooms to each other that there shall be no violent break in the continuity of treatment" (24).

Wharton may have been one of the earliest to use the now popular term *life-style*. All her New York books tell about people's lives in terms of the houses they live in; it is difficult to remember any character of hers without situating him or her in a doorway or by a window or next to a mantel or framed by an opera box. Their settings are as essential to their character as are their clothing and speech. Characters are introduced and developed with reference to their houses and furnishings: they choose them, use them, or escape from them with a deliberation that constantly foregrounds the role of material environment in shaping behavior. We know the floor plans of the main houses and gradually develop a sense of propriety, of knowing what can and cannot take place in any given room. Descriptions of movement from one room to the next convey the degree to which manners and mores are determined by architectural conveniences—or the lack of them.

William Coles points out that "the concern shown in *The Decoration of Houses* for the relationship between art and life is also manifested in Mrs. Wharton's later books, especially those on art and travel. She is always looking for larger organic relationships, whether they be between house and garden; between garden and region, climate, and way of life; between house, street and city; or between city and national values."[11] That concern pervades *The Age of Innocence*, a masterpiece of American satire in which the role of architecture in American life is ruthlessly examined as an index of values and behavior.

When Wharton's narrator first introduces us to Newland Archer, the memorable "hero" of *The Age of Innocence*, he is arriving late to his "club box" at the Metropolitan Opera. As he enters, the narrator observes, by way of introduction, "There was no reason why the young man should not have come earlier, for he had dined at seven, alone with his mother and sister, and had lingered over a cigar in the Gothic library with glazed black-walnut bookcases and finial-topped chairs which was the only room in the house where Mrs. Archer allowed smoking" (4). Most of Wharton's characters live, like Newland, in an indoor world of carefully placed furniture, closed doors, and tastefully decorated rooms. Descriptions of those rooms serve again and again as introductions to the characters and as indices of their tastes, values, and habits as well as of their place in a complex network of social relations that unfolds for us as the novel progresses. Wharton consistently characterizes by context, situating her characters in a setting that provides essential information about them—Newland in his Gothic library, May hovering statuesquely and expectantly on a threshold, Ellen swathed in red velvet in her softly lit Italianate drawing room and ensconced in a sofa before a glowing fireplace.

Wharton teaches us in this novel to read architecture and interior decoration, and indeed the entire environment of fabricated objects, as an intricate network of symbolic systems that make visible and reinforce the behavioral mores and severe social stratification whose implications are so consistent an issue in her work. Living space is always significant space, never free of moral resonance from the moment the colors are chosen for the curtains.

Houses provide an index not only of social position but of individual psychology. The stately old mansions inhabited by Wharton's little clan of patrician New Yorkers—the Mingotts, the Archers, the van der Luydens, the Beauforts—are not only measures of their wealth and taste but also, in a more subtle fashion, of their priorities, their authority, their recognition of consensually decreed standards of taste and behavior, and their various degrees of hesitancy to depart from these standards. The acute aesthetic sensitivity of the narrator's often ironic descriptions of furniture, fabrics, and facades reminds us that every house and every object within it reflect a choice, if only a choice to conform to prevailing fashion, and that these choices have moral and psychological as well as aesthetic consequences. The relationship of character to environment is emphatically reciprocal, and the houses the characters inhabit influence them as surely as these houses reflect the characters' influence.

Mrs. Manson Mingott's house, the first to be fully depicted, is described in terms of its idiosyncratic departures from architectural and social proprieties. It is "cream-colored" rather than the more conservative and more fashionable brown. It sits in lonely splendor, as defiantly distinctive as the spirited old matriarch who sits "enthroned" within it, "waiting calmly for life and fashion to flow northward to her solitary doors" (28). She seems oddly oblivious to the binding imperatives of tribal conformity and behaves "as if there were nothing peculiar in living above Thirty-fourth Street, or in having French windows that opened like doors instead of sashes that pushed up" (14). Hers is an earned impunity. Her eccentricities are tolerated by dint of long service to convention and an unquestioned seniority as matriarch of a large and devoted clan and are excused as well because she belongs to the tightly knit inner circle only by marriage: her mother was a Spicer of Staten Island, not one of the first families of Manhattan.

Newland, through whose eyes we see and judge this architectural oddity, interprets its eccentricities of style with a skilled and critical, yet admiring, eye, only too aware of the stringencies of the codes Mrs. Manson Mingott has so blatantly defied:

> A visit to Mrs. Manson Mingott was always an amusing episode to the young man. The house in itself was already an historic document, though not, of course, as venerable as certain other old family houses in University Place and lower Fifth Avenue. Those were of the purest 1830, with a grim harmony of cabbage-rose-garlanded carpets, rosewood consoles, round-arched fireplaces with black marble mantels, and immense glazed bookcases of mahogany; whereas old Mrs. Mingott, who had built her house later, had bodily cast out the massive furniture of her prime, and mingled with the Mingott heirlooms the frivolous upholstery of the Second Empire. (28)

The ironic phrase *grim harmony* suggests Newland's own discomfort with prevailing taste but is offset by the condemnation of Mrs. Manson Mingott's Second Empire furniture as "frivolous." His observations are as detailed as his tastes are decided at this early stage in the story; if he is capable of regarding the old woman's oddities with indulgence, he is equally capable of issuing judgments as opinionated as those of Lawrence Lefferts, the "foremost authority on 'form' in New York" (8), until Newland's complacencies are shaken by the aesthetic and moral awakening he experiences when he enters Ellen Olenska's home and life.

In contrast to the Mingott mansion, Julius Beaufort's palatial residence, into which the reader is ushered in the third chapter, so far fulfills and exceeds prevailing architectural and decorative fashions as to border on ostentation:

> The house had been boldly planned with a ballroom, so that, instead of squeezing through a narrow passage to get to it (as at the Chiverses'), one marched solemnly down a vista of enfiladed drawing rooms (the sea-green, the crimson and the *bouton d'or*), seeing from afar the many-candled lusters reflected in the polished parquetry, and beyond that the depths of a conservatory where camellias and tree ferns arched their costly foliage over seats of black and gold bamboo. (22)

Perhaps, it is hinted later, there is in this lavish style too much of a good thing. The lines of good taste are drawn very finely. The narrator is conspicuously ambivalent about the magnificence of the house, as measured in part by the amount of space the Beauforts can afford to waste and the lavishness of entertainment proffered there, and is uncertain whether it sufficiently compensates for Beaufort's questionable social status:

> The Beauforts' house was one of the few in New York that possessed a ballroom (it antedated even Mrs. Manson Mingott's and the Headly Chiverses); and at a time when it was beginning to be thought 'provincial' to put a 'crash' over the drawing-room floor and move the furniture upstairs, the possession of a ballroom that was used for no other purpose, and left for three-hundred-and-sixty-four days of the year to shuttered darkness, with its gilt chairs stacked in a corner and its chandelier in a bag; this undoubted superiority was felt to compensate for whatever was regrettable in the Beaufort past. (19)

"Whatever was regrettable" is left decorously unspecified until later, increasingly explicit references to a kept woman and shady financial dealings establish Beaufort as a marginal figure tolerated principally for the status his wealth has bought. Beaufort and his mansion personify the social problem posed by the nouveaux riches in a society that by its own vociferous denial of class distinctions condemns itself to recognizing wealth in any hands as entitlement.

By even more subtle innuendoes Wharton alludes through Beaufort to the disquieting undercurrents of anti-Semitism among the very Anglo-Saxon upper classes. Though she nowhere explicitly identifies him as a Jew, he, like Rosedale in *The House of Mirth*, plays out a role recognizable in accounts of the actual lives of upper-class Jewish New York families such as the Belmonts and the Loebs. Beaufort is a European immigrant who "passed for an Englishman" and entered New York with references from the English son-in-law of Mrs. Manson Mingott. Wharton insinuates here and elsewhere that Americans, precisely because they cannot comfortably admit to their system of fine race and class distinctions, preserve them all the more anxiously for their denial. In any case, conspicuous possession, a residence of distinction, and marriage to a "respectable" family are badges of membership in a club that would otherwise decidedly be refused him. The Beauforts' "brownstone palace" is acknowledged to be "the most distinguished house in New York," in which the coddled but hapless Mrs. Beaufort, a cousin of Medora Manson and therefore Beaufort's most secure claim to membership, sits "throned" and, like Mrs. Manson Mingott, draws "all the world there without lifting her jewelled little finger" (20).

Both Mrs. Manson Mingott and Julius Beaufort are marginal in certain ways while in other ways are central and essential characters to this tight little clan. Their irregularities of behavior and status are duly noted but tolerated because both characters serve an indispensable social function. They provide the necessary exceptions that prove the rules by which their more conventional compatriots govern their own lives. They establish the peripheral boundaries of acceptability and thereby help to define social territory. Furthermore, the two houses provide stable points of reference, each occupied by an "enthroned" social power to whom the loyal, the dutiful, and the aspiring gravitate like bees to their queen. The houses are showpieces that in their respective ways proclaim the power both people exert. Beaufort's house, for instance, is "the one that New Yorkers [are] proud to show to foreigners," and the proprieties of behavior observed there acquire prescriptive force: "They had . . . inaugurated the custom of letting the ladies take their cloaks off in the hall, instead of shuffling up to the hostess's bedroom and recurling their hair with the aid of the gas-burner; Beaufort was understood to have said that he supposed all his wife's friends had maids who saw to it that they were properly *coiffeed* when they left home" (22).

If in the description of the Mingott and Beaufort houses Wharton provides us with an architectural key to the social conventions that govern this small society, her description of the van der Luydens' large, cold, seldom opened mansion completes the spectrum of standards. This aloof but gracious old couple, so it is believed, embody the traditions, the proprieties, and the social dogmas against which the other members of this exclusive circle measure themselves. The van der Luydens occupy the pinnacle of the social pyramid. Here Wharton gives her irony free rein. Gracious and sensitive as they are, the van der Luydens are as bloodless and static in their complacent serenity as figures on a tomb—and their house is a veritable house of the dead. Their social graces are perfect executions of ritual gestures so thoroughly adopted as to have obliterated individualizing foibles altogether. Newland's awe of the van der Luydens and their august home, before Ellen has broken the spell of their pervasive influence, is tinged with a discomfort he is reluctant to identify:

> It was all very well to tell yourself in advance that Mrs. van der Luyden was always silent, and that, though noncommittal by nature and training, she was very kind to the people she really liked. Even personal experience of these facts was not always a protection from the chill that descended on one in the high-ceilinged white-walled Madison Avenue drawing room, with the pale brocaded armchairs so obviously uncovered for the occasion, and the gauze still veiling the ormolu mantel ornaments and the beautiful old carved frame of Gainsborough's "Lady Angelica du Lac." (52)

The pale, icy colors of the house are reflected perfectly in the persons of Mr. and Mrs. van der Luyden, eerily doubling one another and their setting, perfectly designed to complement its pale halls. As Newland waits in the chill parlor, Mr. van der Luyden appears from behind imposing double doors, "tall, spare and frock-coated, with faded fair hair, a straight nose like his wife's and the same look of frozen gentleness in eyes that were merely pale grey instead of pale blue" (54).

In this almost caricatured couple Wharton embodies, moreover, her deep ambivalence about the social structures and legalities she uses the van der Luydens to parody. For they are not simply figureheads, as they seem at first to be, nor is their aloofness simple inhospitality: they, along with Mrs. Manson Mingott and Julius Beaufort, are the only members of the New York circle with sufficient flexibility or tolerance to welcome Ellen, overlook her innocent improprieties, and make a place for her in the rigid social structure. In Mrs. Manson Mingott's case, it is affection that prompts such acceptance of Ellen's differences, and the older woman's tolerance goes unquestioned by dint of her matriarchal authority. Beaufort's charity is perhaps less purely motivated but is made possible by the customary tolerance of his own irregularities won by virtue of wealth. In the van der Luydens' case, it is sheer right of position that allows them to extend a charity and hospitality that come from precisely the same code of behavior that makes Ellen's loose, European ways a problem: family solidarity, discretion, and a desire to preserve a genteel serenity and to avoid scandal.

Within the spectrum defined by these three powerful houses, the reader, too, as he or she continues through the novel, begins to master the code. Every description of a facade, a street, a living room, a boudoir, or a library provides information about character that we learn to understand from context and to which we learn to attribute precisely the kind of significance it conveys to visitors like Lawrence Lefferts, who glance around critically as they cross the threshold and follow the butler through the inevitable double doors to be ushered into the next scene. These three houses provide measuring devices against which the other significant houses in the novel—Newland's, Ellen's, and May's—can be compared and judged.

The house in which Newland lives with his mother and sister is less fully described than are the larger homes of the pacesetters. What the description does tell us is something of the relationship of space to gender. Household decoration and decorum may be controlled by the woman who can forbid smoking except in the library, but the allocation of private space favors the man. If the library is a retreat from feminine control, it is also a place of privilege with no analogous place for the women. Their house on West Twenty-eighth Street is succinctly but pointedly described in these terms: "An upper floor was dedicated to Newland, and the two women squeezed themselves into narrower quarters below. In an unclouded harmony of tastes and interests they cultivated ferns in Wardian cases, made macrame lace and wool embroidery on linen, collected American revolutionary glazed ware, subscribed to 'Good Words,' and read Ouida's novels for the sake of the Italian atmosphere" (34). Even to readers unfamiliar with the class connotations of the objects described, the material environment betokens a certain unexamined mediocrity of taste, conventionality, and unsophisticated concern with niceties.

Newland's library is by far the most distinctive room in the house—the only one that reflects aspirations to refinement and learning—and here the feminine touch is evident only in the care with which order and comfort are preserved so that Newland may enjoy his solitary retreat in the fashion to which he is accustomed: "A vigilant hand had, as usual, kept the fire alive and the lamp trimmed; and the room, with its rows and rows of books, its bronze and steel statuettes of 'the Fencers' on the mantelpiece and its many photographs of famous pictures, looked singularly homelike and welcoming" (43). This description of Newland's room, while perhaps revealing certain unfulfilled cultural aspirations in the photographs of famous paintings, also makes abundantly clear just how ensconced he is in the comforts of his way of life and how much he would have to lose by deciding to leave it. And it is increasingly questionable whether Newland is a hero of sufficient moral fiber to resist the seductions of comfort and predictability for romance and a wider vision of the world.

The symbolic dimensions of Ellen's house are also more understandable against the backdrop of the van der Luyden, Beaufort, and Mingott mansions. As one of the notable features of the great brownstones is a certain sacrifice of comfort to propriety, the apparent coziness and comfort of Ellen's small house not only reveal its owner's innocence of proprieties but compared with an aesthetic of carefully guarded privacy seem suspiciously and even suggestively intimate. Ellen's casually tasteful and artistic decor contrasts significantly with the self-conscious collection of artifacts that symbolizes Newland's acquired taste for the artistic and the European. Her "peeling stucco house," with its "giant wisteria throttling its feeble cast-iron balcony," dubiously situated "far down West Twenty-third Street," challenges Newland's insular notions of propriety and comfort at first sight and leads him to more of the sort of baffled assumptions about Ellen he has been making since her first appearance at the opera in an unfashionably plain dress:

> It was certainly a strange quarter to have settled in. Small dressmakers, bird-stuffers and 'people who wrote' were her nearest neighbors; and further down the disheveled street Archer recognized a dilapidated wooden house, at the end of a paved path, in which a writer and journalist called Winsett, whom he used to come

across now and then, had mentioned that he lived. Winsett did not invite people to his house; but he had once pointed it out to Archer in the course of a nocturnal stroll, and the latter had asked himself, with a little shiver, if the humanities were so meanly housed in other capitals.

Madame Olenska's own dwelling was redeemed from the same appearance only by a little more paint about the window frame; and as Archer mustered its modest front he said to himself that the Polish Count must have robbed her of her fortune as well as of her illusions. (68)

The discomfort suggested in Newland's passing ironic observation about the poverty to which the United States condemns its artists and writers is as yet the only sign of an incipient revolt at the provincialities of his crowd, which Ellen, in her unabashed Europeanness, will bring gradually to a climax of ambivalence. In that ambivalence Wharton embodies a generations-old American problem of patronage of the arts. The bitterness with which Melville and Hawthorne and others like them confronted the sad fact that a writer could not expect a living from the American public is here alluded to from the perspective of that public—vaguely appreciative, even reverent, but unwilling to recognize the economic and social realities that surround the creation and production of art and literature.

Newland's uncomfortable survey of Ellen's neighborhood betokens as well his difficulty in establishing in his own mind whether Ellen is "one of us" or "one of them." Hardly so crude as to present the question to himself in such bald terms, he rationalizes what he regards as the pitiable irony of her surroundings by assuming she would not live there if she did not have to—that her house is a measure of her victimization. And yet when he enters her "low firelit drawing room" he is forced to retract his pity and retreat into the bafflement to which Ellen has several times brought him; its charm and character are as unexpected as they are inexplicable—as unclassifiable as Ellen herself:

The atmosphere of the room was so different from any he had ever breathed that self-consciousness vanished in the sense of adventure. He had been before in drawing rooms hung with red damask, with pictures 'of the Italian school'; what struck him was the way in which Medora Manson's shabby hired house, with its blighted background of pampas grass and Rogers statuettes, had, by a turn of the hand and the skilful use of a few properties, been transformed into something intimate, 'foreign,' subtly suggestive of old romantic scenes and sentiments. He tried to analyze the trick, to find a clue to it in the way the chairs and tables were grouped, in the fact that only two Jacqueminot roses (of which nobody ever bought less than a dozen) had been placed in the slender vase at his elbow, and in the vague pervading perfume that was not what one put on handkerchiefs, but rather like the scent of some far-off bazaar, a smell made up of Turkish coffee and ambergris and dried roses. (71–72)

Newland immediately senses in the palpable difference of this exotic environment an implicit indictment of the stiff and unimaginative homes to which he is so thoroughly accustomed and the corresponding narrowness of sensibility in their inhabitants. His aesthetic sensibility is awakened by something dangerously sensual to his carefully schooled decorum. The artistry in Ellen's drawing room seems to have blossomed out of a combination of spareness, eclecticism, and indulgence of whim, all of which make the predictable abundance and restraint of homes like his own and the Wellands' seem suddenly drab.

Before Ellen even enters the room Newland is seduced by the atmosphere—the perfume, the roses, the draped damask—which seems so clearly a manifestation of the qualities in her that he likewise cannot quite name. He seems suddenly to remember something he never had and to long for it. It is a short progress from the moment of awakening he experiences on crossing her threshold to a sudden wistfulness when he contrasts this home to the one he will soon establish with May in a newly built house on Thirty-ninth Street decorated to conform to the latest architectural trends:

The house was built in a ghastly greenish-yellow stone that the younger architects were beginning to employ as a protest against the brownstone of which the uniform hue coated New York like a cold chocolate sauce; but the plumbing was perfect. . . . The young man felt that his fate was sealed: for the rest of his life he would go up every evening between the cast-iron railings of that greenish-yellow doorstep, and pass through a Pompeian vestibule into a hall with a wainscoting of varnished yellow wood. But beyond that his imagination could not travel. He knew the drawing room above had a bay window, but he could not fancy how May would deal with it. She submitted cheerfully to the purple satin and yellow tuftings of the Welland drawing room, to its sham buhl tables and gilt vitrines full of modern Saxe. He saw no reason to suppose that she would want anything different in her own house; and his only comfort was to reflect that she would probably let him arrange his library as he pleased—which would be, of course, with 'sincere' Eastlake furniture, and the plain new bookcases without glass doors. (72–73)

Whatever distaste he has been suppressing at the ponderous and garish decorations characteristic of the familiar New York mansions suddenly reaches consciousness. As it does so, the image of May as distressingly and inextricably a part of that environment fails for the first time to awaken tenderness. Rather, it becomes the target of a barely acknowledged impatience he is to feel increasingly with the imprisoning stone edifices and the more imprisoning social and mental structures that make up his world.

When Ellen enters the room, therefore, unconsciously stepping into the magnetic field of Newland's ruminations, she has already become a symbol, a foil to May, a measure of all that May lacks. Even the way Ellen moves about in her room, the way she drapes her brightly clothed body like the damask on her wall, with the same easy artistry and careless beauty, heightens the polarities he is beginning to conceive. In contrast to May, who unconsciously assumes static and statuesque poses, usually standing, often hesitant, often on a threshold, Ellen moves easily about any room she enters, seats herself comfortably and informally, and seems to possess the space she occupies. Her frequent protestations of uncertainty about the "rules" are ironically belied by the worldly ease with which she inhabits her home, her clothes, and her expressive body. Ellen's body and May's in fact mirror the buildings they inhabit, and their clothing, like their interior decorating, is described and judged by its conformity to or departure from complicated standards of taste and propriety that seem to be at odds with the simple needs of flesh and spirit. This dichotomy, while posing a pregnant contrast between the two woman and all they represent, is not, however, as simple as it might appear. May's frequent appearance in white gowns, with bouquets of lilies of the valley and cuts of maidenly modesty and simplicity against Ellen's dark blue and red velvet robes, seductively revealing bosom and forearm, certainly presents a contrast so stark as to be almost comic in its archetypal extremity, as do the bodies of the two women—the tall, striking Diana-like blonde and the shorter, curly-headed, lively brunette. But the traditional counterpoint of "dark woman/ light woman" is here subverted in numerous ways.

One of the most interesting phenomena of characterization in the novel is May. There is more to her than we may think at the outset, when descriptions of her extreme maidenly innocence and unimaginative conventionality tempt the reader to categorize and dismiss her as a mere cardboard figure placed in the scenery as a foil to Ellen's multidimensionality. In the second half of the novel we come to realize what surprising quarries of worldly wisdom underlie May's smooth surface and to understand her conventionality in less conventional terms. Having inspired us to virtually despise the great houses and their docile and superficial inhabitants, Wharton sets out to undermine that too-easy judgment by changing lenses on the scene. Her ironies are suddenly focused on those who too easily reject the elaborate protective structures that people like May represent and reflect with such schooled finesse. Newland's romantic rebellion suddenly shows up May's acquiescence to the demands of her social situation as a kind of maturity—the kind he eventually reaches when in old age he reflects that "after all, there was good in the old ways" (347).

Never entirely redeemed from the aspersions cast on them in the opening chapters, the grand old houses and the lives of the people in them nevertheless become more comprehensible as the novel proceeds to examine the limited alternatives. And so May as well, a character who utterly fulfills type, serves to remind us that typicality is not necessarily shallowness or absence of character. Her loyal maintenance of the conventions, the traditions, the rituals, the customs, seems a more conscious stance than is at first apparent, and her conservatism seems a keeping of the flame—a careful preservation of values that, even though ambiguous, are worth preserving. One of those values is the careful distinction between private and public life that the houses enforce with their carefully distinct private and public spaces. May's extreme discretion, doubtless the less sympathetic to modern readers by the very public and confessional nature of American life now, is one of many qualities that becomes in the end comprehensible as a virtue, though, like all virtues in Wharton's moral scale, ambiguous and vulnerable to perversion.

Ellen's jarring candidness, a quality Newland comes to cherish in her, completes and complicates the contrast between the two women and the two ideological poles of the novel. Like all the personal qualities of the characters, the contrast is reiterated in both dress and decor. Whereas May lives in the houses and within the parameters provided for her, an art object that decorates the rooms she stands in, Ellen is clearly the designer and maker of her own environment; her idiosyncrasies and personal tastes, expressed in her house and her possessions, are as "readable" (and suspect) as the books on her drawing room table. Even though her opening deprecation of her own "funny little house" seems predictable enough, and draws from Newland a gracious, "You've arranged it delightfully," her next words give him "an electric shock": "Oh, it's a poor little place. My relations despise it. But at any rate it's less gloomy than the van der Luydens'." Newland is completely taken aback at her casual irreverence: "For few were the rebellious spirits who would have dared to call the stately home of the van der Luydens gloomy. Those privileged to enter it shivered there, and spoke of it as 'handsome.' But suddenly he was glad that she had given voice to the general shiver" (73, 74).

Ellen goes on to explain her bewilderment at the subtle distinctions and seemingly arbitrary prohibitions to which she has been subjected in her search for a place to live decently on her return to New York: "I've never been in a city where there seems to be such a feeling against living in *des quartiers excentriques*. What does it matter where one lives? I'm told this street is respectable" (73). Newland's reply that "it is not fashionable" is greeted with an outcry of baffled impatience that Newland eventually adopts and reiterates with the zeal of a convert: "Fashionable! Do you all think so much of that? Why not make one's own fashions?" (74). Here we witness the first step in a dance of awakening between Newland and Ellen—a long process of adaptation, compromise, and retreat on her part; of rebellion, compromise, and ironic acquiescence on his. In the course of the novel they undergo a complicated exchange of points of view as each respectively comes to question and qualify the point of view from which he or she started and comes to terms with the necessity of compromise. In these two characters Wharton demonstrates with unforgettable poignancy the double bind of civilized life: that we inevitably generate for our protection structures that eventually imprison us, that they become imprisoning precisely because we need them, and that altering those structures, stepping outside them, or moving from one set of social structures to another is a heroically difficult task.

And Ellen and Newland are not heroes. They are only individuals slightly more conscious than those around them and hence more ironically aware of the limitations of the protocols and values they are forced to accept. The almost adolescent romanticism of Newland's rebellious fancy of "finding a place" where he and Ellen might live outside the thick brownstone walls of New York society is perfectly balanced by Ellen's growing resignation to the costs of social acceptance and the protection it affords. Their capitulation, however, acquires stature in contrast to characters such as Newland's mother, who never questions the "givens" of fashion, custom, and social hierarchy. Wharton's comic irony is at its best in her narrator's sardonic descriptions of such insularity as Mrs. Archer's: "Beyond the small and slippery pyramid which composed Mrs. Archer's world lay the almost unmapped quarter inhabited by artists, musicians and 'people who wrote.' These scattered fragments of humanity had never shown any desire to be amalgamated with the social structure" (102). The disquieting "Bohemianness" of Ellen's life among these marginal types seems to result from two factors: poverty, which embarrasses her wealthy relatives, and the social eclecticism of her neighborhood, particularly the distressing evidence it offers that "art" and "literature" emanate from such dubious and unpedigreed sources.

The place of paintings and books in Wharton's houses is always significant. In the hands of the dutifully "cultivated" but

uncultured upper-class matrons and devoted but uncritical pa-
trons of "the arts," books and paintings become, like all other
objects, a part of the decor, designed to enhance a general impression of tastefulness without actually betokening real capacity to judge and discriminate. Books and artworks themselves
may be subject to appropriation by the fashionable in a manner
that Wharton patently regards as quasi-blasphemous, though
their misuse may be due to a genteel ignorance that is perhaps
the less culpable in those to whom the arts have always been
presented as a means rather than an end.

One more sign of the difference of Ellen's house, therefore, is
the unconventional selection and prominence of pictures and
books, which are obviously to be enjoyed and read rather than
to serve as totems or tokens. The narrator observes that Ellen
has already discerned the family's suspicion of "literature" but
that she nevertheless "had no fears of it, and the books scattered about her drawing room (a part of the house in which
books were usually supposed to be 'out of place')" (104) were
chiefly works of fiction. Both the presence and the nature of
the books "whet Archer's interest" and touch him at a point of
vulnerability because his own authentic intellectual and literary
interests are something he pursues in isolation, finding very few
among the "respectable" who share them.

In its broadest terms the contrast between Ellen's house and
the Mingott and Welland mansions provides a scale by which to
measure both the characters and the material setting of the
novel in terms of "simplicity" or "complexity." Both words are
qualified and complicated in the course of the book, and here
Wharton betrays a pointed and poignant antiromanticism in
endowing her most conscious characters with a longing for a
kind of Thoreauvian simplicity and with the recognition that
such simplicities are also forms of artifice and are ultimately
impracticable. The tension between simplicity and complexity—even prolixity—is brought to a head in the abortive love
scene between Ellen and Newland in the little "patroon house"
on the van der Luyden estate at Skuytercliff. This little four-
room retreat, reminiscent of Edna's pigeon house in *The Awakening*, contrasts dramatically with the great house to which it is

attached. That house the narrator describes with typical irony as a masterpiece of imitation and acquired taste:

> People had always been told that the house at Skuytercliff was an Italian villa. Those who had never been to Italy believed it; so did some who had. . . . It was a large square wooden structure, with tongued and grooved walls painted pale green and white, a Corinthian portico, and fluted pilasters between the windows. From the high ground on which it stood a series of terraces bordered by balustrades and urns descended in the steel-engraving style to a small irregular lake with an asphalt edge overhung by rare weeping conifers. To the right and left, the famous weedless lawns studded with 'specimen' trees (each of a different variety) rolled away to long ranges of grass crested with elaborate cast-iron ornaments; and below, in a hollow, lay the four-roomed stone house which the first Patroon had built on the land granted him in 1612.
>
> Against the uniform sheet of snow and grayish winter sky the Italian villa loomed up rather grimly; even in summer it kept its distance, and the boldest coleus bed had never ventured nearer than thirty feet from its awful front. (130–131)

Like the van der Luydens' icy Manhattan mansion, the estate partakes of the innocent pretensions time and tradition have rendered venerable and of the aloofness of its august and silent owners. The weather itself (in broadly romantic fashion) reiterates the manufactured environment.

The house on the hill clearly represents an ascent to power and prestige made visible by the enduring presence of the little patroon house in the hollow. Here again the central ironies of the book are reinforced as the ascent to civilized conditions and comforts is implicitly presented as a loss of something vital and essential. That loss is signified here in the little firelit house with its "squat walls and small square windows compactly grouped about a central chimney" (134) where Ellen and Newland have their unexpected tryst.

The patroon house is a place set apart from the complicated world of society and fashion, suitable for honeymoons and quiet weekends, quaintly rustic, a place to soothe the spirit fatigued by multiple worldly obligations. As Ellen enters it, she laments the oddly paradoxical exposure of a tenant in a mansion full of servants and riddled with daily rituals: "One can't be alone for a minute in that great seminary of a house, with all the doors wide open, and always a servant bringing tea, or a log for the fire, or the newspaper: Is there nowhere in an American house where one may be by one's self? You're so shy, and yet you're so public. I always feel as if I were in the convent again—or on the stage, before a dreadfully polite audience that never applauds" (133–134).

Newland, too, finds himself powerfully affected by the relieving simplicity of the little retreat. As he follows Ellen in, we are told, "his spirits . . . rose with an irrational leap." He looks around with sudden joy at the simple room purged of all but a few necessities: "The homely little house stood there, its panels and brasses shining in the firelight, as if magically created to receive them. A big bed of embers still gleamed in the kitchen chimney, under an iron pot hung from an ancient crane. Rush-bottomed armchairs faced each other across the tiled hearth, and rows of Delft plates stood on shelves against the walls" (134).

The accoutrements of this room bespeak an older time and a simpler way of life. Like so many romantic heroes before him, Newland experiences a longing for something mythic, past, un-recapturable, and as he enters this anachronistic little structure he finds himself in a timeless moment that comes on him like a spell, sweeping away the complexities of his situation. But the simplicity of the patroon house is not of the "real" world. The freedom Newland and Ellen find in that tiny firelit room for "one brief shining moment" vanishes with the appearance of Julius Beaufort and can be remembered only as a tantalizing but illusory promise or reminder of something lost. With Beaufort's untimely appearance Wharton modulates back into comic irony: "The ostensible reason of his appearance was the discovery, the very night before, of a 'perfect little house,' not in the market, which was really just the thing for [Ellen], but would be snapped up instantly if she didn't take it" (136). The spell is broken and Beaufort's words serve only as a reminder that the "perfect little house" in which they came close to a moment of consequential truth is a mythic place uninhabitable by mortals in a world of competition and commercial real estate.

But the patroon house and the memory of Ellen and the childlike simplicities of that afternoon haunt Newland—and the reader—for the rest of the novel. They awaken him to a standard so unlike the standards he is schooled to that it seems to bear no relation to them and so presents him with a radical, if illusory, choice. The patroon house suggests a way of life infinitely seductive to a man burdened with increasing social obligations and yet aware enough to fear the loss of his soul in the immediacies of daily navigation through the complicated straits of family and social ritual. The house calls to the Thoreau in him and assumes an attractiveness not wholly a matter of taste but of a moral order. The little house stands in Newland's imagination as an indictment of the burgeoning complexities and ritualized deceptions of city life. Something old, romantic, and as deeply American in its iconoclasm as Huck Finn's rejection of "sivilization" is being suggested here. But Wharton is no Thoreau, and Newland is not Huck Finn. As surely as she evokes in her characters and perhaps in her readers a longing for the simplicities of the frontier cabin, she also insists on the impossibility of that return to romantic simplicity as a way of life. She distrusts the romantic idealism even as she seems so powerfully able to share it. It is a mark of Ellen's greater maturity that she accepts the conditions of life and rejects Newland's romantic fervor. She realizes that one cannot live apart from the world. One can escape from one world into another, but one cannot deny or reject the conditions imposed by a society that one cannot escape. One must return to the great house and open the cottage only for an occasional vacation. If these conditions are "unreal," so is the attempt to deny them.

On his return to New York after the deeply disturbing moment in the little house at Skuytercliff, Newland finds a shipment of books awaiting him. Unpacking it he comes on "a small volume of verse which he had ordered because the name had attracted him: *The House of Life*." His passion deepens as he reads, far into the night, allowing himself once more to weave a fantasy around "the vision of a woman who had the face of Ellen Olenska," thereby prolonging the feelings of the previous day. But awakening the next morning he is brought back to the inescapable: he "looked out at the brownstone houses across the street, and thought of his desk in Mr. Letterblair's office, and the family pew in Grace Church" (139–140), and the encounter at Skuytercliff recedes into dream. Shortly thereafter he abruptly departs for Florida to ask May to set forward the date of their marriage.

Ellen, to whom our attention is turned after these lyrical interludes, decides suddenly to take the family's advice and Beaufort's aid and prepares to abandon her "funny little house," which has been the subject of so much interfamilial controversy. Newland's last interview with her in the warm half-light of her drawing room begins as an ostensible business call and concludes with one of the most poignant love scenes in the modern novel, a moment in which Newland breaks through his lifelong habits of prudence and offers to throw over his carefully planned future for Ellen, only to encounter in her an unexpected retreat into ethical propriety. Her loyalty to the family and what it stands for has grown, over time, out of a need that she recognizes as born of defeat. His newfound disgust with the constrictions of social and familial responsibility turns him into a tragicomic Romeo swearing by the moon. Wharton dramatizes this moment of the two passing in their odysseys like two ships in the night as in the course of their stormy interview they exchange places on the hearth, first Newland, then Ellen, looking down at the other. Here, as always, spatial relationship tells the story symbolically. Never in this scene are the two so situated as to look one another levelly in the eye; one is always looking down at the other, in pity, in anger, in mute resignation.

The second half of the novel opens with an apparent resolution of these romantic quandaries. Much of it consists of a meticulously symmetrical restatement and variation of the themes raised in the first half but shifted into a new key. A new depth of irony is achieved in the first pages when after their lavish and eminently proper wedding in Grace Church May surprises Newland with the news that they are to honeymoon in the very cottage where his fall into the disillusionments of adulthood was so poignantly completed. May, pleased with her quaint surprise, which represents a last-minute solution to thwarted plans for grander lodging, enthuses, "Only fancy, I've never been inside it—have you? The van der Luydens show it to so few people.

But they opened it for Ellen, it seems, and she told me what a darling little place it was: she says it's the only house she's seen in America that she could imagine being perfectly happy in" (190). With this innocent report we are made aware of the secret irony that is to color the rest of Newland's life: the haunting of the unmade choice, the burden of the untold secret desire, the more painful because unrequited, the regret of a joy voluntarily foregone. And the little house remains in his imagination as a symbol of these simple joys, a measure of the increasing complexities of his domestic existence.

Typically, however, Wharton does not allow Newland the luxury of tragic heroism: the life he has chosen has its pleasures and its many comforts, and we are made to wonder if, after all, Newland's renunciation was not in some measure simply a characteristic choice against a life whose hardships and anomalies he could not have tolerated. Indeed, we are provided with a few scenes of domestic tranquillity so pleasant as to belie the tragic dimensions of the renunciations that preceded this settling:

> In New York, during the previous winter, after he and May had settled down in the new greenish-yellow house with the bow-window and the Pompeian vestibule, he had dropped back with relief into the old routine of the office, and the renewal of this daily activity had served as a link with his former self. Then there had been the pleasurable excitement of choosing a showy gray stepper for May's brougham . . . and the abiding occupation and interest of arranging his new library, which, in spite of family doubts and disapprovals, had been carried out as he had dreamed, with a dark embossed paper, Eastlake bookcases and 'sincere' armchairs and tables. (205)

So Newland's rebellion is reduced to an unpopular choice of unfashionable furnishings, as the harness of domestic life begins to settle on his shoulders. He begins once again to assume the habits proper to his class and to emulate the in-laws he once so high-mindedly despised. The seductions of comfort become, in fact, a prominent theme in this second half of the story. Newland's moment of illumination begins to fade with the pressure of habit, which he vaguely realizes one day on entering the now familiar Welland house:

> There was something about the luxury of the Welland house and the density of the Welland atmosphere, so charged with minute

observances and exactions, that always stole into his system like a narcotic. The heavy carpets, the watchful servants, the perpetually reminding tick of disciplined clocks, the perpetually renewed stack of cards and invitations on the hall table, the whole chain of tyrannical trifles binding one hour to the next, and each member of the household to all the others, made any less systematized and effortless existence seem unreal and precarious. (217)

Only Ellen's reappearance disrupts this process of slow settling. The mere knowledge that Ellen is visiting her grandmother takes him out to the Mingott summer estate, as odd and idiosyncratic as the cream-colored mansion above Fortieth Street.

Wharton's description of this peculiar summer house, the scene of yet another abortive attempt on Newland's part to make connection with Ellen, waxes ironic in its abundance of detail, the effect of which is to portray the house as an architectural hodgepodge, albeit a fairly faithful depiction of certain decorating fads of the period:

> In this unfashionable region Catherine the Great, always indifferent to precedent and thrifty of purse, had built herself in her youth a many-peaked and cross-beamed *cottage orne* on a bit of cheap land overlooking the bay. Here, in a thicket of stunted oaks, her verandahs spread themselves above the island-dotted waters. A winding drive led up between iron stags and blue glass balls embedded in mounds of geraniums to a front door of highly-varnished walnut under a striped verandah-roof; and behind it ran a narrow hall with a black and yellow star-patterned parquet floor, upon which opened four small square rooms with heavy flock-papers under ceilings on which an Italian house-painter had lavished all the divinities of Olympus. One of these rooms had been turned into a bedroom by Mrs. Mingott when the burden of flesh descended on her, and in the adjoining one she spent her days, enthroned in a large armchair between the open door and window, and perpetually waving a palm-leaf fan which the prodigious projection of her bosom kept so far from the rest of her person that the air it set in motion stirred only the fringe of the antimacassars on the chair-arms. (212)

The emphasis here on thrift, tasteless eclecticism, and disharmonious lavishness, along with the almost slapstick reminder of the matriarch's obesity, displays a tendency echoed throughout the characterizations in the second half of the novel: each character is painted in slightly darker colors; the humor is heavier, and the depictions of architecture, like those of characters, tend toward caricature. Book Two is very much about the consequences and costs of the choices that were made and portrayed in a lighter vein in Book One. The narrator's editorials acquire an unmistakably bitter edge.

Newland makes one more attempt to escape the structures of life that enclose him when he travels to Boston to seek Ellen out where she is staying in the Parker House hotel. They meet in a park and spend an afternoon on a boat, condemned to outdoor and semipublic spaces, literally unable to find shelter for their touchingly proper rendezvous. Thereafter, when Newland meets Ellen, it is most often in marginal or outdoor spaces. Just as he no longer has any hope of escaping the rectilinear maze in which his fate will play itself out, so she has admitted the impossibility of finding a niche in a structure whose partitions and boundaries simply will not accommodate her sense of the shape of things. They meet in a hotel lobby, in a brougham, on a ferry, always looking at one another across an unbridgeable chasm of difference, literally unable to find a place to live out the reality of their acknowledged relation of the heart.

There is no place for them in this world. That fact lies at the heart of Wharton's irony. This new world with its vast wilderness has succumbed to civilization, but tragically with less time, less understanding, and far less grace than Europe, where human contradictions are absorbed and accommodated without the burden of moral justification added to every stone the builders lay. There the aesthetic and the moral orders seem capable of separation.

So Newland returns to his club and his library, retreating increasingly from the exigencies of domestic life to those two male bastions. Once when May spends an evening in his library, he is overcome with nameless restlessness and opens a window explaining, "The room is stifling: I want a little air." As he moves toward the window, the narrator provides this commentary:

> He had insisted that the library curtains should draw backward and forward on a rod, so that they might be closed in the evening,

instead of remaining nailed to a gilt cornice and immovably looped
up over layers of lace, as in the drawing room; and he pulled them
back and pushed up the sash, leaning out into the icy night. The
mere fact of not looking at May, seated beside his table, under his
lamp, the fact of seeing other houses, roofs, chimneys, of getting
the sense of other lives outside his own, other cities beyond New
York, and a whole world beyond his world, cleared his brain and
made it easier to breathe. (295)

May objects as he opens the window that he will "catch his
death," to which Newland inwardly responds, "I *am* dead—I've
been dead for months and months." The claustrophobia in this
passage is palpable. It is, furthermore, an interesting variation
on a theme of entrapment feminist critics have recognized as
recurrent and dominant in women's stories of domestic life,
here assigned to a male character. It would be hard to accuse
Wharton, however, of partiality to the plight of one sex over the
other, as some have tried to do. Her complaint is always with
structures and systems, institutions and customs—products of
human desire and human politics, entrapping all in them, even
those who most assiduously work for their preservation. Moreover, that entrapment is only the dark side of something so indisputably necessary that simple rebellion against it seems just
as misguided as enslavement to it.

Newland's solution is one many a female character has taken:
retreat to the interior. He carves out an imaginary space within
the privacy of his own mind to which he retreats when the pressures of quotidian life become too great, and there he keeps
Ellen, now returned to Europe, as ever-available mistress to
his fantasies:

> He had built up within himself a kind of sanctuary in which she
> throned among his secret thoughts and longings. Little by little it
> became the scene of his real life, of his only rational activities;
> thither he brought the books he read, the ideas and feelings which
> nourished him, his judgments and his visions. Outside it, in the
> scene of his actual life, he moved with a growing sense of unreality
> and insufficiency, blundering against familiar prejudices and tradi-
> tional points of view as an absent-minded man goes bumping into
> the furniture of his own room. (262)

Finally, the structures of the social order seem to demand of the conscious and the sensitive this schism between inner and outer life. The delicate balance Newland manages to preserve until and beyond May's death is in the end a measure either of his heroism or of his capitulation. It is up to the reader to determine which. Certainly the final scene gives no help in passing judgment on Newland's compromises. When Newland finally arrives in Paris with his son, marriage and career behind him, May a memory and a picture in a frame enshrined on his desk, and finds his way to the building where Ellen's apartment is marked by an inconspicuous green awning, he faces another choice, not so radical as before but deeply reminiscent of that original choice when he found himself at a moral crossroads. He gazes up at the "modern building, without distinctive character, but many-windowed, and pleasantly balconied up its wide cream-colored front" (359). Apparently Ellen, too, has made her compromises. The disproportion between the color and vitality of the character we remember and the bland facade that Newland gazes at so fixedly is a final ironic addition to the catalog of significant structures commensurate with the characters within them. In a single description of a building Wharton takes her parting shot at the diminishments of modern life.

Newland remains seated before this unremarkable building in inscrutable contemplation until a servant comes and closes the shutters. "At that," the narrator reports, "as if it had been the signal he waited for, Newland Archer got up slowly and walked back alone to his hotel" (361). At the moment of long-awaited opportunity, Newland finds that he cannot "enter Ellen's space" any more than years before she could find a place in his. His location in the world has been defined by his place in a vast and complicated structure. Outside of that he has no real identity or purpose. He might have found one once, but that choice is not available indefinitely. We are, Wharton seems to suggest, increasingly dependent on the environments we create around ourselves, so that finally they form us, and what we are becomes inseparably a function of where and how we live.

7

THE PROFESSOR'S HOUSE
Escape to the Interior

The scenes of Willa Cather's novels alternate between large open spaces—the plains of Nebraska, the New Mexican mesas, the wide fields of the Midwest—and the minutely detailed interiors of the houses erected on them. Each of her major novels is constructed on a series of social and moral polarities embodied in the houses her characters inhabit. In *My Antonia* the Burdens' great white Nebraska farmhouse contrasts starkly with the sod dugout of the immigrant Shimerdas. What neater way is there than in the image of these dwellings to encapsulate the inequities of immigration, expansion, and land acquisition and the desperation born of the failed hopes and shattered visions of many settlers for whom the great undomesticated land proved too strong a beast to tame? Or the ironies and hard trade-offs of romantic ambition that plagued family life on the American frontier? In *A Lost Lady* Captain Forrester's house on the hill, focal point and center of the action of the story, is like a castle in a fairy tale—a place to which a man of heroic proportions has brought his bride as a fitting prize to enhance his later years and crown his achievements. The fulfillment of his dream becomes for his bride a form of nightmarish entrapment; she finds herself restless in the proverbial "gilded cage" but unsuited to live outside it, her plight a commentary on the institution of marriage itself. In *The Professor's House* the protagonist is caught between old and new homes, loath to leave the old, with all its defects and inconveniences, for the new, which is comfortable, commodious, and sterile.[1] In this novel, as in the others, two houses represent conflicting values and competing ways of life that establish a field of tension within which the story is played out.

As in most of her novels, Cather describes the rooms in the houses and the objects within them with the meticulous detail of the Dutch painters she admired and to whom she has often been compared. In the character of the professor, who is almost obsessive about maintaining the complicated private order of his study and garden, she raises questions that come up in most of her novels and are centrally important in this one: What is the right relation between the life of the mind or spirit and the material life? How do the objects and structures with which we surround ourselves reflect and shape the interior life? The title of one of her best-known essays, "The Novel Démeublé," suggests how central to Cather's conception of interior life are the ideas of architecture, space, and furnishing. "How wonderful it would be," she writes,

> if we could throw all the furniture out of the window; and along with it, all the meaningless reiterations concerning physical sensations, all the tiresome old patterns, and leave the room as bare as the stage of a Greek theatre or as that house into which the glory of Pentecost descended, leave the scene bare for the play of emotions, great and little. . . . The elder Dumas enunciated a great principle when he said that to make a drama, a man needed one passion, and four walls.[2]

Her emblematic treatment of spaces, furnishings, and material objects suggests how inescapable are the terms of the material world and how profoundly environment shapes and limits the life of the mind.

The Professor's House is a study in the multiple structures that confine and define Professor Godfrey St. Peter's existence. The old house and the new house reflect dichotomies that characterize both his family life and his own ambivalent nature. His inclination to insularity competes with his affection for his family and his sense of social obligation; his intellectual masculinity resists feminization, though, paradoxically, his sensibilities are in a deeper sense profoundly feminine and as such opposed to his wife's practical, commercial bent; his asceticism vies with an appetite for certain conveniences and comforts; and his youthful dreams of adventure give way to recognition of the demands of encroaching age as he finishes his life work and faces the diminishments of retirement. He is surrounded by family members who exert various pressures on him, creating a field of tension that he inhabits uncomfortably and from which he retreats into solitude at every opportunity. The three women in his family represent both what he most loves and what he most anxiously resists: feminization (in its most negative sense), compromise, sexuality, and distraction from the single-mindedness he believes his work demands.

The three young men who extend his family define a spectrum of attitudes that reflect something of the professor's own complicated choices: Tom, his student and protégé, is all the professor has wished for in the son he never had. Tom has lived out fantasies the professor entertained but never fulfilled and has embraced values that the professor secretly harbors but that do not accord with the choices he has made. One son-in-law, Louie, is a model of upward mobility, fashion consciousness, and cosmopolitan taste. The other, Scott, is a careful middle-class conservative living in a modest home on a modest income and pursuing modest goals. Neither of the sons-in-law seems ever to have cherished the intellectual and spiritual ideals the professor senses are dying with himself and his generation. Only Tom would have carried on his dream, and Tom is dead— Tom who successfully escaped the confining structures of small-town family life and found a way into a world with wider boundaries in space and time and into a consciousness that encompassed a broad sweep of history and ideas fostered in open spaces and solitude.

Augusta, the faithful family seamstress, aging, androgynous, and independent, represents a female counterpart to Tom. She is a woman who has made her own separate peace with the world, has managed to sidestep the ambiguous entanglements of family, and has preserved her integrity and innocence in a way perhaps accorded only to the solitary and the celibate.

Like so many American novels, this is a tragedy of confinement and compromise. The four main characters in *The Professor's House* represent four different ways of coming to terms with the tension between the abstract and the material, or between the demands of the inner life and those of the world of social intercourse, necessarily involved with the getting and spending that threaten to "lay waste our powers." Each character has made a different kind of compromise between the "world" and the "self"—a relation, in Cather's worldview, necessarily predicated on compromise. Domestic life is generally presented in terms of uncomfortable accommodation, diminishment, and loss of something grand and true—an inevitable disappointment of romantic aspirations and a betrayal of deeply rooted Thoreauvian values. Solitude, self-reliance, autonomy, and transcendental spirituality sit uncomfortably in heavily upholstered pastel living rooms. The three-part story chronicles a series of losses, roads not taken, and adjustments by means of which the professor acquiesces to the realities of his life, his entrapment in place, time, and the social web that has paradoxically been both an impediment and an enabling structure in shaping his successful career. The cost of his successes has been a chronic ambivalence that he only now begins to recognize as an elaborate habit of evasion. The new house and the more integrated family life it seems to presage threaten his strategies of escape.

Here, as in her other books, Cather frames character and conflict in archetypal terms, counterbalancing a complicated and ambiguous vision with the radical simplicity of her conceptual framework, simple and stark as that of a fable or fairy tale. The novel is full of polarities (old/new, convenient/inconvenient, his/hers, place of retreat/place of social activity) and triads (the three-storied house mirrors the three-part novel, as well as the three parts of the Freudian psyche; the professor's family consists of three women, complemented by three "sons"). So carefully balanced are the elements in this domestic tableau, they seem almost allegorical, like figures in a morality play. Throughout the novel the reader's vision of the characters alternates between apprehension of their realistic, even idiosyncratic particularity and their studied representativeness as figures situated like pillars around the temple of family.

As in a number of her novels, Cather chooses to view the problems of domestic life from the perspective of a male character, recasting some of the same kinds of questions Chopin, Gilman, and other late-Victorian feminists raised about the pathological effects of home life on women. Like Wharton's Newland Archer, Godfrey St. Peter personifies the husband and father for whom home and family represent enmeshment in a web of relations and responsibilities that is both a support structure and a prison from which he continually seeks avenues of symbolic escape. Cather's own pastoral Virginia childhood was spent in a large, comfortable, three-story brick farmhouse with fireplaces, portico, and box hedge, a setting she revived in loving detail in *Sapphira and the Slave Girl* and later in the open spaces of the Nebraska plains to which her family moved when she was nine, subjecting her to one of the most formative traumas of her childhood and perhaps endowing her with her abiding fascination with topography, landscape, and space. Sharon O'Brien points out that in this move, "Cather left behind the intimate, domestic space of Willow Shade [Virginia]," where the large kitchen was the center of her world, for the land of the open sky, where the dimensions of her imagination were permanently widened.[3]

Her sensitivity to the politics and poetics of space, both interior and exterior, was developed in the context of people who still worked the land, staked out boundaries, and assigned places and tasks to men and women still functioning under the basic terms of an agrarian economy; this sensitivity was complicated by the travels of her adult life to the places recorded in her fiction with such remarkable geometric precision: the New Mexican mesas, the coastal cliffs of the Northeast, the Colorado foothills. All her life she pondered and reworked questions of categories, territory, and boundaries, transgressing and trespassing even as she reaffirmed the necessity of definition and limitation in the drama of human action as the stage that, framing human activity, gives it meaning.[4] Her early work as a journalist for two women's magazines, the *Ladies' Home Journal* and later *Home*, was openly iconoclastic; she characterized the philosophy and literary output of *Home* as "just great rot: home and fireside stuff, all babies and mince pies."[5] Nevertheless, the structures of social life, and preeminently of family life, are a central focus in Cather's work, and though she spurns conventional sentimentality, her portrayals of homes and families are imbued with nostalgia for a lost ideal. The family and the house it inhabits provide a center and structural model or blueprint for the wide web of social relations radiating out from them.

In the opening chapters of the novel Professor St. Peter is doggedly pursuing his academic work in the drafty attic, loath to leave the environment in which he has for twenty years pursued his academic enterprises. A great deal of description is devoted to the professor's attic room, a place characterized by eclectic disarray, in quiet rebellion against the niceties of the bourgeois household below. The story begins with the declaration of a fait accompli: "The moving was over and done" (1). Professor Godfrey St. Peter is alone in a "dismantled house" that seems in some ways a scene of desolation—a personal wasteland. It is the scene of his "best years," his active professional and intellectual life. Now he is a survivor in a state of depletion rather than triumph, having served his term, raised his children, written his great work. His attic study is the only place where that life persists in its vestigial forms. The rest is the shell of an absent past. So the story opens with a scene of death: the impending slow demise of a man who feels he has lost his vital, sexual, creative life and is faced with changes that signal his descent toward age and death. He is passively resisting the final, painful throes of moving by ensconcing himself in his remaining academic work.

The physical description of the house the professor is so loath to leave draws a clear dichotomy between practical and sentimental value. "It was almost as ugly as it is possible for a house to be; square, three stories in height, painted the colour of ashes—the front porch just too narrow for comfort, with a slanting floor and sagging steps." This is a house loved, despite its many flaws, by a man for whom fashion, convenience, and even beauty are subordinate to the security, continuity, and stability that physical reminders of the past offer him. The house is an assurance that some things do not change. It is ridden with "needless inconveniences," which the professor is capable of fixing but has not because "there was not enough time to go around" (11). To win time and space for his inner life, the professor economizes on his outer life. He seems actively to shun convenience, as though it were a form of temptation. Moreover, undone household tasks testify in their perverse way to the fact that he has chosen "the better part"—a higher life.

Like those before him who have chosen an unworldly way, he finds himself misunderstood. Mrs. St. Peter objects to his stubborn retreats to a cold study with a dangerously leaking stove that threatens asphyxiation. "And don't you think," she asks, "it's a foolish extravagance to go on paying the rent of an entire house, in order to spend a few hours a day in one very uncomfortable room of it?" The professor replies resentfully and somewhat self-righteously, "It's almost my only extravagance" (97). The house's ugliness and inconvenience simply enhance his affection for it as something others do not value as he does because he sees beyond surfaces. It puts him in a position of slight moral superiority to be "above" mundane concerns. But the house and its demands also epitomize the demands of family life—always too multiple to be fully met. Objects degenerate slowly, like his marriage, while he skirts around them, decides not to see them, though he trips over them daily, as he does the crooked stairs.

The professor's study, which doubles as the sewing room, reveals numerous idiosyncrasies that betray his moral biases. The room is singularly unattractive and uncomfortable, the walls and ceiling are covered with yellow paper "which had once been very ugly but had faded into inoffensive neutrality," and the floor has scratchy matting. "Fairly considered," we read, "the sewing room was the most inconvenient study a man could possibly have, but it was the one place in the house where he could get isolation, insulation from the engaging drama of domestic life. No one was tramping over him, and only a vague sense, generally pleasant, of what went on below came up the narrow stairway" (26). The description of domestic life as an "engaging drama" suggests the degree of the professor's disengagement. He has a role to play in that drama, but it is not "real life." He participates in domestic life primarily as a benevolent but cautious spectator, keeping it deliberately at the level of drama, insulating himself from it by walls and floorboards, as by so many other devices, staying a little "above it all."

St. Peter does not recognize the sentimentality implicit in his self-imposed disciplines or the hint of self-righteousness in his engagement with "loftier" things that prevents real emotional and physical engagement with marriage and family life. Cather's own ambivalence toward social life and sexuality is surely being expressed here; she tends here and in her other work to represent them as a giving way to the "world and the flesh" and a diminishment of the intensity of inner life that only chosen solitude can produce.

The fact that his retreat and vantage point are up on the top floor so that no one can "tramp over" him suggests as well his desire to be "out from under" the demands of family life that threaten to stifle and smother him. Paradoxically, he comes to a stuffy room with a tiny window and bad ventilation to get air, escaping the spiritual suffocation of the inhabited space beneath. In this "dark den," lit by a kerosene lamp or a single bare light bulb hung awkwardly over the professor's desk, the only source of natural light and air is a "single square window" facing east, held ajar by a hook in the sill. The room is so poorly ventilated that heat becomes a dangerous problem:

> The furnace heat did not reach the third floor. There was no way to warm the sewing room, except by a rusty, round gas stove with no flue—a stove which consumed gas imperfectly and contaminated the air. To remedy this, the window must be left open—otherwise, with the ceiling so low, the air would speedily become unfit to breathe. If the stove were turned down, and the window left open a little way, a sudden gust of wind would blow the wretched thing out altogether, and a deeply absorbed man might be asphyxiated before he knew it. The Professor had found that the best method, in winter, was to turn the gas on full and keep the window wide on the hook, even if he had to put on a leather jacket over his working coat. By that arrangement he had somehow managed to get air enough to work by. (26)

This passage is both ominous and ludicrous. Deliberately contriving ways to overcome his self-imposed inconveniences involves the professor in an odd paradox of self-deception. The room designed to be a testimony to his ascetic virtues also bespeaks a certain indulgence to the demands of a finicky and idiosyncratic taste. Things must be as he wants them, and he is as demanding in his insistence on the drab, incommodious setting as his wife is in her desire for a home commensurate with their means and station. The deliberate negligence of safety suggests, moreover, an unconscious death wish or at least a passive toying with danger that betrays the professor as a man not wholly committed to living fully who breathes only enough air to sustain the energy he needs to work, inhabits only the space he needs for that work, and narrows his needs and his movements to a confined space in order to widen correspondingly the inner spaces he frequents. An economy of mutual exclusivity between outer and inner life is presumed.

The description of the study as a "dark den" and the wallpaper faded to "inoffensive neutrality" can easily be extended to apply metaphorically to the tone of his writing—militantly different at first, fading into respectable neutrality. The den is both a protected place and a place where wild things hide. His more public study downstairs, however, is a "sham." In it he has a "proper desk at which he wrote letters" (16). The letters, however, are not "real" writing. His "real" life goes on outside the public view.

The professor's own lack of warmth corresponds to that of his study; he is afraid to descend into the sensual realm of the body as he is "afraid" to leave his attic to descend through the house for more supplies, as he would on the way "almost surely become interested in what the children were doing, or in what his wife was doing—or he would notice that the kitchen linoleum was breaking under the sink where the maid kicked it up, and he would stop to tack it down. On that perilous journey down through the human house he might lose his mood, his enthusiasm, even his temper" (27). The degree to which the professor reins in his natural, social impulses for the sake of his single-minded pursuits is nowhere more poignantly or clearly expressed than here. He is quite susceptible to the ordinary pleasures and distractions of family life but denies himself those pleasures with monastic severity. The "perilous journey" through the house in fact recalls Christian's perilous journey through Vanity Fair on the way to the Celestial City. But the professor's puritanical single-mindedness is driven by fear as much as by inspiration, its virtue tainted by the ambivalence that characterizes nearly all his pursuits outside his study. His austerities are undertaken not simply for their own sake but also in order to sustain an image of himself as a man set apart. A certain distrust of any passion but the "passions of the mind" keeps him working—as though the fragile spell might be broken with terrible ease. Here Cather seems drawn into reflection on the delicacy of the writing process, which requires, as Virginia Woolf insists, a "room of one's own," isolation, and leisure as preconditions for the flowering of creativity, while at the same time implying how great is the cost of creating these conditions.

One of the particularly rankling points of controversy between the professor and his daughters is the bathroom. They insist that the bath should be "the most attractive room in the house," while he counters that he has known "many charming people" with houses that can claim no bathroom at all. Here the issue of comfort and beauty as indices of moral softness is raised in a comic vein. Doing without luxurious amenities is a point of honor. He takes the bathroom as a measure of the difference between old-world and new-world values: what is taken for civilized life in the United States is really the life that progressive self-indulgence, technology, and affluence make possible, but unaccompanied by a corresponding refinement of taste or sensitivity to matters of the mind.

Moreover, the professor tends to equate "civilized" comforts with emasculating effeminacy. This equation arises repeatedly in Cather's novels. Her women, when they are not the strong, self-reliant, outdoor women of *My Antonia* or *O, Pioneers!* are often morally inferior to their husbands—consumers who do not produce, people who do not feel deeply, women whose values are gross rather than subtle and tend toward the sensual and the materialistic. So with particularly biting irony, Cather makes the bathroom the point of contention in the sexual politics of the family and the women's measure of civilized living. It is the place where a person attends to the needs and adornment of the body, in contrast to the study, the professor's most valued space, where all things, except those that serve the life of the mind, are neglected.

For the same reasons the commodious new house makes Professor St. Peter uncomfortable. It represents a departure from the asceticism he has been able to cultivate in the solitude of his attic and the austerity represented in the benignly neglected inconveniences of the old house. It is a concession to the women, primarily his wife, whose values seem so different from his own, a capitulation to female desires and tastes. The idea of the house as a concession to a woman reiterates an old American theme that domestication amounts to emasculation. The professor does not dare to acknowledge to himself the degree of his own dependence on the domesticity he shuns. So he becomes involved in a vicious circle of denial and dependence; he calls the new house his wife's even while he lives in it and depends on it to support his own semidetached way of life.

Seeing the professor smiling by the fire one evening after dinner, his wife asks him what he is thinking. He replies, "I was thinking . . . about Euripides; how, when he was an old man, he went and lived in a cave by the sea, and it was thought queer, at the time. It seems that houses had become insupportable to him. I wonder whether it was because he had observed women so closely all his life" (156). Here once again houses and women, domesticity, and femininity are linked. It seems that a house and a woman represent a phase in a man's life that the professor thinks he is nearing the end of. Both finally become spiritually confining. Typically he finds a classic precedent to lend stature to his impulse to retreat. (And it is typical of Cather to lend his point of view a certain sympathy by means of the same device.)

Ironically enough the professor has over his years of writing his histories been "building" this house for his wife. It is the money from these histories that has made the move possible: "The two last volumes brought him a certain international reputation and what were called rewards—among them, the Oxford prize for history, with its five thousand pounds, which had built him the new house into which he did not want to move" (33). To his wife's inquiry whether there is something he would rather have done with the money, he replies, "Nothing, my dear, nothing. If with that cheque I could have bought back the fun I had writing my history, you'd never have got your house" (33). A number of ironies are implied in this little exchange. Metaphorically and literally he was building a house as he wrote his books. Just as the manuscripts were blueprints or "patterns," so the finished volumes were the stones of the edifice in which he now finds himself about to be imprisoned. The thing that had set him free has transformed itself into a frightening enclosure.

In Cather's metaphysics originating energy always loses something in the process of articulation, as heat is lost in physical transformations. So the transformation of St. Peter's ardor, vision, and creative energy into books, then into money, then into a building (and later the money from Tom's discoveries is transformed in the same way), represents a tragic debasement of the original impulse. The "word made flesh"—or the idea made product—is a descent from the spiritual into the material realm that results in disillusionment and loss. He thought he was doing one thing while doing another. In a discussion between Kathleen and her father, he reminisces about Tom, "You children used to live in his stories. You cared more about them than about all your adventure books" (131). Kathleen replies, "Yes, and now he's all turned out chemicals and dollars and cents, hasn't he? But not for you and me! Our Tom is much nicer than theirs" (132). They used to "live in his stories." Now one lives in the house his money built, but the stories and the man and his work have all been lost in translation. Later, alone in the study, gazing out at the university and the sky beyond, he contemplates the irony of Tom Outland's money, left to Rosamund and now financing her house, and the pain it has brought.

In the study the professor can be "above" the petty jealousies of his family and the university. The physics building and beyond it the open sky are the mosques of his devotion. They symbolize for him two modes of escape: escape into research and escape into a "world of speculation." Both the professor and his protégé worked without thought of the indirect ends of their labor; the left hand did not know what the right hand was doing. The professor's present plight—having to live with the unanticipated and largely unwelcome fruits of his labors—suggests that one may always be working toward ends out of one's control and not entirely of one's own choosing.

The professor's refusal to take pleasure in the comforts of the new house seems in one light almost childish—a refusal to come to terms with the change that represents the end of an era in his life and a loss of power and control. When his wife tries to cajole him into admitting that he likes the new house, he does go so far as to concede that he is glad of more closet space. This concession is appropriate enough because the closet is a place where secrets can be kept, where things can be stored and preserved, hidden away. It is private space, something he feels he has too little of in his new home. Annoyed with his resistance to enjoyment, his wife asks him one morning, "Just when did it begin, Godfrey, in the history of manners—that convention that if a man were pleased with his wife or his house or his success he shouldn't say so, frankly?" (48). She senses with some accuracy that he is suppressing whatever pleasure he may feel about the new house because it would not be in keeping with his enforced austerity or the private mythology that defines him as an outsider. This house threatens to integrate (or implicate) him more deeply into conjugal life. His wife manages, with her conventional logic, to expose his pretenses, though without understanding their complicated motives.

The description of the three-story house is paralleled by a description of the professor's body, which in several particulars seems to resemble his dwelling.[6] It is aging but sound, something he has taken great care of in certain respects, though not in others; as with his house, cosmetic considerations are quite secondary: "The fewer clothes he had on, the better. Anything that clung to his body showed it to be built upon extremely good bones, with the slender hips and springy shoulders of a tireless swimmer" (12). As with the house, the essence exceeds the appearance; what others see belies the youth and strength and beauty of the body that remains hidden behind indifferent attire.

Close focus on the professor's head and eyes as his outstanding and noteworthy features reflects another parallel with the spaces he creates around himself and how he occupies them. His eyes are "set in ample cavities, with plenty of room to move about." They have "lost none of their fire, though just now the man behind them was feeling a diminution of ardour." And his daughter observes, "The thing that really makes Papa handsome is the modelling of his head between the top of his ear and his crown; it is quite the best thing about him." Subsequently the narrator adds that his is "more like a statue's head than a man's" (13). The professor is a man who lives largely in his head, has furnished it meticulously and elegantly but privately, and only inhabits the rest of his body on occasion, as a relief from incessant mental activity. When his daughter looks at him she sees his head; it is the part of himself he presents most conspicuously to the world.

Dichotomies like this are in fact the most consistent feature of St. Peter's character. In almost every respect he is described in terms of splitness: "Though he was born on Lake Michigan, of mixed stock (Canadian French on one side, and American farmers on the other), St. Peter was commonly said to look like a Spaniard. That was possibly because he had been in Spain a good deal, and was an authority on certain phases of Spanish history" (12). His split identity derives not only from hybrid origins but also from his divided loyalties; straddling two homes, drawn to two cultures, a cosmopolitan sensibility living in the provincial Midwest, torn between living in the present and dwelling in the past, between family and solitude, the professor is afflicted with a pervasive ambivalence that colors all that he loves with a certain melancholy sense of loss. He is a hybrid in every sense. Bringing disparate things together is his vocation and his very being.

The information that the professor's preferred form of recreation is swimming gives us another clue to his paradoxical character. Both his small, stuffy attic study and Lake Michigan are places of escape—the one to the wide world of the mind, the other to a natural place without boundaries, both solitary retreats. On land he surrounds himself with boundaries, even barriers; in his house and walled French garden he demarcates and protects his own space clearly and uncompromisingly. But the water gives him a needed escape from his own defenses. The lake was "the always possible escape from dullness. . . . The sun rose out of it, the day began there; it was like an open door that nobody could shut. The land and all its dreariness could never close in on you. . . . The sight of it from his study window these many years had been of more assistance than all the convenient things he had done without would have been" (30–31). The lake, like his window, is that door to the unbounded, to the freedom that he longs for but can attain only symbolically. He can escape upward to his attic or downward to his garden or the lake.

The house itself is a place to escape from, just as the study is a place that draws all things unto itself.[7] Like the body-mind dichotomy suggested in his character, the house has been split vertically, and the two halves work against each other. It is a house divided against itself, and the peril of that division is now clear as the division has been magnified by the move and consequent effort to maintain two houses.

The walled-in French garden, which the professor began "soon after the birth of his first daughter, when his wife began to be unreasonable about his spending so much time at the lake and on the tennis court," is the other space claimed, designed, and defended as his own inviolable territory. The walled-in garden is an extension of the house—and another extension of the professor's work. "It is the one thing the neighbours held against him" (14).

The professor speaks of his having "got the upper hand" of his plot of ground—a contentiousness mirrored in his relationship to his work as well. "In the spring, when home-sickness for other lands and the fret of things unaccomplished awoke, he worked off his discontent here" (15). Like Thoreau, who "travelled a great deal in Concord," the professor has invested heavily in his one plot of ground, devising ways to content his adventurous spirit there. The garden is "the comfort of his life—and it [is] the one thing his friends h[o]ld against him," representing as it does, perhaps, a certain visible rejection of the casual company to which porches and lawns are congenial as well as a preference for the European, the decorative, the exclusive, and the secluded over the more frank, sociable American use of outdoor domestic space. The garden is a French garden—an imported idea, a transplant. The professor is cosmopolitan in almost every respect—and in an unlikely place. Highbrow culture in a middlebrow setting again reflects the relationship of the professor's inner world to his environment: uncomfortable, slightly out of context.

His retreat to the garden is a compromise: he has consented to spend free time at home but in return claims a space there that can be private and separate and designs it in a way that suggests an antagonistic, asocial, and somewhat arrogant attitude. The garden has "not a blade of grass." It is "a tidy half-acre of glistening gravel and glistening shrubs and bright flowers" (14). There is no grass to be mowed, trampled on, weeded. The design of the garden suggests a deep need for control and reflects exactly and schematically the designs of the gardener—nothing wild or rampant, everything ordered according to an idea. The landlord objects to "dem trees that don't bear nothing" (51). Their value is lost on the practical old European who senses a certain sterility implied in the professor's choices. The hard surface of gravel and the severity of the design also suggest something dry and life denying in the professor's stance toward the rest of the world. Life is messy. He does not want to cope with its messiness except on his own terms. His deliberately ordered existence is fashioned according to an internal logic—the same logic that insists on leaving the old, irrelevant sewing forms in his study after the seamstress has gone—a logic of association and sentimental attachment; a dependence on elaborate private rituals and artifacts that create a symbolic world for him, link him to the past, and suggest a continuity that is in fact very fragile.

Just as the professor shares his attic with only one sympathetic and unthreatening companion, Augusta, the seamstress (about whom more will be said), so he shares his garden with his protégé, the son he never had, Tom Outland. During a period of solitude while his women are traveling, the professor brings his work to the garden, eating his meals there and talking long into the night with Tom. Like the attic study, the garden is a sacred spot. It is apart from the rest of the house, as it is apart from the rest of the world—a protected and private space that he shares only with the privileged initiate, holding court or office hours like the professor he is. It is a place to escape to so as to live his "real" life. The antagonism of the neighbors suggests how clearly the language of landscaping has communicated the message to them that they are not welcome except on carefully defined terms and that he insists on preserving signs of difference to assure himself that he is not like other men.

His "real" life has consisted of both solitude and the select intellectual companionship of a confidant who is himself a solitary. Every Saturday during one summer when the family is in France, the professor turned his house over to the cleaning woman, and he and Tom went to the lake and spent the day in his sailboat (176). He remembers also domestic dinners, cooking and talking with Tom in the evenings. This memory parallels Tom's account of the idyllic life of the three men at the New Mexican mesa, housekeeping for themselves in the absence of women while exploring the ruins of an ancient cliff city. It raises the question Cather often implicitly broaches: is contentment possible only without sexual politics? In this scenario space is a thing shared, not contended over. The house is a refuge rather than a trap because he is keeping it. Is it perhaps that he cannot have that role while sharing his space with women who control it in ways he is not free to dispute?

The two women who most intimately and immediately share the professor's life and space, Mrs. St. Peter and Augusta, represent another polarity between which the professor is located in an uncomfortable middle ground. Mrs. St. Peter's logic represents a combination of fashion consciousness and utilitarian practicality: midwestern thrift tempering the ambition of the upwardly mobile to measure achievement by conspicuous consumption. She has never been able to understand the professor's quirky preference for an attic alternately drafty and stuffy, where the danger of asphyxiation in the winter from the gas heater gives way to the discomforts of prostrating heat in the summer. She has no understanding of the significance the professor assigns to his chosen spaces and the ritual importance of the apparent disarray of the books, papers, and artifacts that surround him. She offers him a larger, airier, lighter room in the new house where he can work at the spacious new desk he has heretofore relegated to the status of showpiece in the unused ground-floor library of the old home. He does not want this room. He is uncomfortable with comforts. They represent a capitulation to what is feminine, weak, undisciplined, indulgent. The building of the new house is a sign of too easily achieved prosperity, a shallow sense of beauty, consumerism rather than the work of "homo faber." The house is a thing bought, not made, a sign of wealth rather than of life and work. The things in it have a surface beauty but no personal, human significance. It betrays a tragic loss of a sense of real value, real beauty, the connection between quality and beauty.

Mrs. St. Peter's ambivalences about the new house are of a different order from her husband's. Over dinner in the new dining room she chats sociably with her daughters and son-in-law about the "trials of building" when the buzzer under the table will not work to call the maid. The process that to her is a trial has been to him a joy and an end in itself. The process is his; the product, hers. Picking up on Mrs. St. Peter's complaints about the trials of building, Louie, the ambitious son-in-law, rejoins with an account of his own enmeshment in home-building:

> My wife and I are in the throes of it. . . . We have a magnificent site; primeval forest behind us and the lake in front, with our own beach—my father-in-law, you must know, is a formidable swimmer. We've been singularly fortunate in our architect,—a young Norwegian, trained in Paris. He's doing us a Norwegian manor house, very harmonious with its setting, just the right thing for rugged pine woods and high headlands." (38–39)

Louie's self-conscious pretensions make a mockery of the implied ideals of organicism, harmony, and cosmopolitanism. He imports without understanding, owns without reverencing, and is not building his own house, nor even doing it with his own money, but is having it built by a non-native architect, consuming without producing, thus clearly offending an ethic that the author explicitly, and the professor implicitly, holds dear. Louie goes on, "We found just the right sort of hinge and latch . . . and had all the others copied from it. None of your colonial glass knobs for us!" (39). The other daughter and her husband have just put glass knobs in their bungalow; houses and interior decoration are a means of designating class distinctions even within the family.

Knowing how to consume is a talent for which Louie is praised and envied. Louie is not a sentimentalist but a pragmatist. He later announces that he and his wife will give up the house when they go abroad, wondering if the professor could make use of it, thinking Scott and Kitty might make use of their things. He does not understand why any of them should refuse such an offer. In Louie's insensitivity to the significances, sentimental and otherwise, of ownership and borrowing, Cather revisits the issue of the abiding tension between practical and sentimental value from a new angle. For Louie, a house is wealth to be shared, and in his manner he is broadly generous in sharing it. His generosity, however, lacks an essential sensitivity to the symbolic dimensions of things.

Even Kathleen and Scott, who have the humble bungalow presumably more in keeping with the ideal of simplicity the professor cherishes, do not value their own home in the way he does his but regard it as a stage on the way up. Austerity seems a lost ideal—something only comprehensible as an ideal by someone like the professor, who, being a scholar and so having a wider view of the world, is presumably less bound to the terms of his contemporary culture than the others are. Kathleen and Scott's "spick-and-span bungalow" is contrasted with the vision of Louie and Rosamund's ambitious and extravagant home. Houses and money are a source of jealousy between the two daughters, a fact that reinforces the professor's jaundiced view of the ambitions these two commodities represent.

Rosamund, Louie's wife, shares her husband's and mother's interest in building, design, and decoration of homes as forms of consumption. Accompanying her on an expedition to Chicago to buy things for her country house, the professor comments, "I should say she had a faultless purchasing manner. Wonder where a girl who grew up in that old house of ours ever got it. She was like Napoleon looting the Italian palaces" (154). She has acquired her husband's consumerism, though it may well be seen as an inherited taste for fine things that has become vulgarized and superficial, no longer rooted in an educated sensibility. To the professor, "that old house of ours" symbolizes unpretentiousness, austerity, simplicity. Yet he does go along with her, participating while at the same time preserving the stance of critic. Half-hearted participation, reflecting both his real ambivalences and his efforts to protect a particular vision of himself, puts him always slightly at odds with both his family and himself.

For the professor does take an interest in decoration, albeit in a more reflective way. He is no American primitive romantic, proclaiming the superiority of unadorned nature. Looking through French windows to the drawing room one afternoon where he sees bouquets of seasonal flowers, "it struck him that the seasons sometimes gain by being brought into the house, just as they gain by being brought into painting, and into poetry. The hand, fastidious and bold, which selected and placed—it was that which made the difference. In Nature there is no selection" (75). His own French garden testifies to the fact that the professor is an artist, not a naturalist. His world is artificial. He is an admirer of nature but does not sink his feet and fingers into it except to arrange, to weed, to design.

The fairly stereotypical male-female polarities represented in the contrast between the professor and his wife, and by extension, his daughters, are complicated by another pair of characters, Augusta and Tom, who raise the issue of the tensions between the material life and the spiritual life in different terms. Augusta, the long-term family servant and seamstress, is an immigrant whose stolid German Catholicism, simple loyalty to the professor and his family, and sturdy, conventional morality make her a representative of a traditional order in which both interior and exterior life is governed by the established hierarchies and categories of European Catholic culture. Augusta knows what is expected of her, does her work, goes to Mass, tells the truth, and understands her place in the order of things. She is a maker, a craftswoman, whose purpose and fulfillment lie in responsible service. What makes her interesting in the context of the novel is the analogous and ironic relation Cather sets up between her and the professor. They share the attic room; when he is away, Augusta uses his study for sewing, having the distinction of being the one person with whom the professor will share his sacred space. Her dress forms and patterns mingle companionably with his books and papers, patterns and manuscripts occupying the same box. The juxtaposition of their "working papers" establishes a parallel between the professor and the seamstress.

The interpenetration of their working materials signifies profound similarities between them that transcend their class differences: both work with designs; both work in solitude to produce something beautiful for others' benefit. Both manuscripts and patterns are forms of history and structural designs. The professor and the seamstress have had a sort of Cox and Box arrangement, Augusta working there by day, the professor mostly by night, each observing little courtesies that have protected the other's privacy and work space. Augusta is described as "devout, Catholic, and reliable" and, we might add, thoroughly asexual. She is a partner to the professor in a way that his wife cannot possibly be, a person with her own life pattern, her own solitude, whose relationship with him is one of mutually respectful independence. She represents an ideal of congenial separateness apparently impossible among family members. She accepts without understanding, is present without demanding, and cohabits without invading his privacy. Her Catholicism and her European origins surround her with a set of moral structures and strictures that he respects without completely understanding them, just as she does his academic disciplines. The measure of the extraordinary quality of the professor's relationship with her is his willingness to share his space with her. In fact, the paraphernalia of her work has become so fixed a part of his own working environment that he refuses to allow it to be taken away when the time comes to move.

Augusta's dress forms, which for years have been a "subject of much banter" between them, become a resonantly symbolic point of contention when she attempts to move them. There are two of them. The first looked "ample and billowy (as if you might lay your head upon its deep-breathing softness and rest safe forever)," but "if you touched it you suffered a severe shock, no matter how many times you had touched it before. It presented the most unsympathetic surface imaginable. Its hardness was not that of wood, which responds to concussion with living vibration and is stimulating to the hand, nor that of felt, which drinks something from the fingers"; rather, the dress form possessed an unresilient, cold, metallic hardness that seemed to repel contact (17–18). Clearly this form represents disappointments associated with the professor's wife, a woman who has not met his expectations, perhaps in part because his expectations are based on unconsciously conflicting desires. Where he seeks softness he finds hardness, unaware that his own ungiving attitudes may have contributed to it. The same hardness he has created in his austerely uncomfortable study, reeking faintly of self-righteousness, and in a glistening rock garden where little grass grows to cushion the feet, he has instilled in his wife, who has developed her own protective shell against the hurt of his neglect.

The second dress form, "light and springy," seems correspondingly to evoke opposite associations: "At times the wire lady was most convincing in her pose as a woman of light behavior, but she never fooled St. Peter. He had his blind spots, but he had never been taken in by one of her kind!" (19). Together the two forms represent what he finds most deceptive and disillusioning in femininity. He does not trust women. Augusta seems to be the only woman he wholly trusts and respects, and it is perhaps precisely her asexual quality that allows him to do that. The professor needs his "ladies" in his study to be empty forms. He clings to the forms of feminine life while rejecting the realities, as in so many other ways he clings to forms and formalities that preserve a sense of order and structure and act as protections against impinging chaos. In these forms both the beauty and the treachery of the feminine are displayed, thereby confirming the professor's ambivalence about the opposite sex on whom he unwillingly depends for so much. He explains to Augusta, for instance, that he is staying on in the old house to finish a piece of work but admonishes her that this arrangement is "confidential" because "if it were noised about, people might begin to say that Mrs. St. Peter and I had—how do they put it, parted, separated?" (19–20). The maintenance of appearances is continued here, as well as the dividedness, now not so easily camouflaged from the public eye and public opinion. The professor is being forced to declare his loyalties and tries here to rationalize them, to preserve those same appearances, but the device is fragile and unconvincing. The separation has effectively taken place; the distance between his private life and his family life has stretched his pretenses to a point of extreme tension.

Augusta's dress forms stand like statues in the corner; the professor calls them his "ladies," and, indeed, they serve as ludicrous ironic replacements, safe in their headless, wiry anonymity, for his real "ladies," who inhabit the house beneath him. Augusta's dress patterns are mingled with the professor's manuscripts in the space beneath the window seat. The two activities that take place in this room are not conflicting but complementary, unlike the contrasting concerns of the professor and his wife. Augusta is his spiritual companion and complement. She is, in an odd way, the "mistress" appropriate to the professor's peculiar appetites: with her he has forged a separate alliance based on a kinship between makers and doers that contrasts poignantly with the antagonism he feels for his wife as a passive consumer. Augusta's sewing, with its forms and patterns and routines, is an exact counterpart to the professor's writing. She is his analog, her simplicity and devotion to her work as serious as his. Her forms change as the family grows, however. His do not. His work is to excavate, preserve, solidify; hers to adapt, remake, accommodate to change.

Both of them are engaged in ongoing creative activity in the service of others, and both derive their pleasure from the work itself: the professor, from his writing; Augusta, from her dressmaking. Both are highly regulated creatures—she, by her faith and imported cultural traditions; he, by his self-generated and self-protective rules of life. Augusta is content, virtuous by the standards of her own notions of virtue, fulfilled in the limited terms of her own ambitions, and strong and clear in the simplicity of her convictions. She values beauty and prides herself on making beautiful things. Her values are uncomplicated by either puritanical ambivalences about material life or sexual competition. Like many of Cather's significant characters, she is androgynous and asexual and hence free of—and even somehow above—the conflicts and confusions of sexual politics. Yet precisely because of this she is capable of a quality of intimacy with the professor he never achieves with his wife or daughters. Augusta and the professor are both creating work and living spaces for themselves in a domestic world in which they are, or perceive themselves to be, marginalized. Their separateness from the material details of the domestic life of the household is the precondition of their work and, through it, of their respective identities.

Augusta attempts to help the professor bridge the difficult distance between the old house and the new by a tactful pretense that in her turn preserves the forms through denial: she reminds him that in the new house they will have separate spaces—he, a "beautiful new study downstairs" and she, "a light, airy room on the third floor" (20). The irony of this maneuver is that the professor has always had a nicely appointed study within the precincts of the house and has chosen not to use it. It was a "show study," off the back parlor, with a collection of his less-used books and a desk at which he wrote letters, "but it was a sham." The downstairs study has been a concession, like so many others, to the preservation of forms and appearances, but a concession belied by the passive defiance of disuse. Augusta puts the proposed rearrangement in the new house in the most positive terms possible, knowing, however, as she must, what a loss it will represent to him. The fact that she has been given the third floor suggests a total inversion of the order of things that has made it possible for the professor to preserve his separateness and the illusions that accompany it. The arrangement is, of course, a restoration of a conventional household order; the servants and help have usually occupied the third floor of upper-middle-class homes large enough to house them at all. Augusta therefore on several counts can make a "natural" claim to the space he wants because she has no family, does not need to integrate herself beyond the closely defined demands of her position, and has her solitude as (in his eyes) a reward.

Occupying a special place in this family structure and representing a fourth, and more comprehensive, approach to the economics of material and spiritual life is Tom Outland, an outsider who, having found his way into the professor's home, comes to play a key role in the development of the family. Similarly, Tom's story occupies a central place in the structure of the book, a "window" inserted into the story, like the window through which the professor gazes toward the world beyond. Tom's story represents that wide world where dimensions expand and possibilities to feed the imagination abound. Significantly enough, in this section Cather's style slips into high lyricism, as though she participates in the professor's own idealization of Tom and all he represents: youth, adventurousness, innocence, high ideals, and love of the kind of beauty available only to those who pay a high price to see.

When we first meet Tom, he slips on the stairs on his way to the bathroom and comments, "I'm not much used to stairs, living mostly in 'dobe houses" (117). In response to Mrs. St. Peter's inquiries, he begins to expand on the subject of "Indian housewifery." Tom's awkwardness in the house characterizes him as a man of nature, uncivilized, akin to the mythic noble savage, an American type. His aura of mystery is underscored by the information that Tom's mother had died in a covered wagon, leaving no information about Tom's birth date. He seems to come from a simpler time and place—and that element of mystery and mythic simplicity is exactly what the professor loves in Tom and strives to reconstitute in himself. An important distinction between the two of them, however, is that Tom is attracted to those aspects of domestic life the professor feels so compelled to resist and deny: "There was evidently something enchanting about the atmosphere of the house to a boy who had always lived a rough life. He enjoyed the prettiness and freshness and gaiety of the little girls as if they were flowers" (124). He is not afraid of domestic life; his solitude and simplicity are not born of fear but of a combination of necessity, habit, affinity, and circumstance—they are a calling in a different way from the professor's idealized notions of them.

Tom in many ways represents the ideal response to the question posed about the right relation of the inner life to the material world. Like Augusta, Tom, before his untimely death, arrives at a kind of fulfillment and balance the restless professor has managed only on uneasy terms. Unlike Augusta's, Tom's is not a simple compromise with the terms of life but a deeply examined and tried worldview. Like Mrs. St. Peter, Tom values family life, courts the professor's daughter, and takes a genuine interest in the home, its inhabitants, and its comforts. Unlike her, his interest is entirely detached and innocent of vain ambition. He maintains a Thoreauvian distance from middle-class civilized life and escapes to the mesas of New Mexico for a spiritual renewal that the bourgeois professor's wife would neither desire nor understand. Tom is like the professor in his deepest desires—for a vision that would comprehend the course of history, for an interior life independent of the pressures of polite society, for the freedom of intellectual play, and for a soul mate to share in his explorations. Tom is an explorer, an adventurer, a wanderer—in many respects another iteration of the type of the American hero: youthful, solitary, living outside the economy, not yet bound by feminine influence, not yet limited by the demands of practical life, able still to be indifferent to money and to pursue his ends with a purity of purpose that is necessarily sacrificed with the passing of adolescence into the compromises of adult life in modern culture.

The story Tom tells about himself is a southwestern romance full of marginal characters, adventure in open spaces, violence, discovery, and betrayal. It is also a spiritual bildungsroman—a tale of a young man's awakening and fall into experience through vital encounters with older men, with nature, and with the institutions of modern life. The tale is an odyssey through a series of dwellings, in each of which Tom's vision of the world becomes wider and his dreams larger. Tom's odyssey begins in Rodney Blake's one-room adobe, where the bed takes up most of the space and washing and shaving must be done on the patio. The tale then takes us to the open plains of New Mexico, where Tom and Blake ride the range with a herd of cattle for a season and live in a makeshift shack. They move at the end of the season to a cozy winter cabin, where they are joined by a "pitiful wreck of an old man," an English jack-of-all-trades who applies his skills as former orderly and valet to help them domesticate their rough environment and establish a semblance of family life. He earns his keep as their cook and begins with them to evolve a kind of family life in the cabin. Tom recalls, "Life was a holiday for Blake and me after we got old Henry. He was a wonderful cook and a good housekeeper. He kept that cabin shining like a playhouse; used to dress it all out with pinon boughs and trimmed the kitchen shelves with newspapers cut in fancy patterns. He had learned to make up cots when he was a hospital orderly, and he made our bunks feel like a Harvey House bed" (197).

Cather's description of the life of the three men in this "playhouse" gives a comic twist to the earlier depictions of domestic life, with its divisions of labor and underlying tensions. Tom recalls that "the three of us made a happy family" (197–198). The men at first have a fine time housekeeping together, content with a rusticity apparently impossible to women. Housekeeping becomes a form of recreation or elemental play. Ultimately, however, they run into the same deep conflicts of values that characterize the nether side of conventional family life. They live in a trifurcated economy: Henry is the functionary; Rodney, the heavy worker; and Tom, the dreamer and intellectual, encouraged to pursue his studies of Latin and his reading of the classics, excused from work for reasons of delicate health, and allowed in his quiet way to rebel against the foreman's prohibitions against solitary adventure in the canyons of the mesa. He is a youthful prototype of the professor, able by virtue of oddly similar protective structures, though free of the burdens of adult responsibility, to pursue his dreams. The trajectory of Tom's adventures reiterates in dramatic high relief that of the professor—first achieving his cherished goal, then experiencing diminishment, loss, and regret as his discovery is commercialized, vulgarized by contact with the world of men, and robbed of its virginity, like the land around it. The story not only reiterates the professor's in more epic dimensions but serves as yet another "allegory of the United States" in its broad outlines, telling once again the story of the Adamic hero whose innocence is lost and who is expelled from the garden by a sin not his own.

Tom's first view of the Blue Mesa is one of the most lyrical and telling moments in the book. Here the theme of the dwelling place becomes solemn, sacred, and epic:

> Far up above me, a thousand feet or so, set in a great cavern in the face of the cliff, I saw a little city of stone, asleep. It was as still as sculpture—and something like that. It all hung together, seemed to have a kind of composition: pale little houses of stone nestling close to one another, perched on top of each other, with flat roofs, narrow windows, straight walls, and in the middle of the group, a round tower.
>
> It was beautifully proportioned, that tower, swelling out to a larger girth a little above the base, then growing slender again. There was something symmetrical and powerful about the swell of the masonry. The tower was the fine thing that held all the jumble of houses together and made them mean something. It was red in colour, even on that grey day. . . . I felt that only a strong and aspiring people would have built it, and a people with a feeling for design. (203–204)

Cather's indictment of civilization lies in these last lines. What kind of people build the homes we create now? Tom has the professor's feel for composition—for life as art. And architecture combines the functional with the aesthetic in a way that is deeply humane. The loss of that proportion disturbs both the professor and Tom. Houses, buildings are there to be read, and they must speak a truth.

Tom returns from his first trip disinclined to tell anyone, even Rodney, about his sacred encounter with the cliff city. But later the two make the climb together. The account of this trip includes a long description from inside the city, deductions about the life of a peaceful, domestic people. "As Blake remarked, wind and sun are good housekeepers" (208). "Behind the cluster of houses was a kind of back court-yard, running from end to end of the cavern; a long low twilit space that got gradually lower toward the back until the rim rock met the floor of the cavern, exactly like the sloping roof of an attic. There was perpetual twilight back there, cool, shadowy, very grateful after the blazing sun in the front court-yard" (208–209). There are different spaces beautifully proportioned for different parts of life; light and shadow are part of the composition, which is once again reminiscent of a Dutch painting.

> One thing we knew about these people; they hadn't built their town in a hurry. Everything proved their patience and deliberation. The cedar joists had been felled with stone axes and rubbed smooth with sand, the little poles that lay across them and held up the clay floor of the chamber above, were smoothly polished. The door lintels were carefully fitted (the doors were stone slabs held in place by wooden bars fitted into hasps). The clay dressing that covered the stone walls was tinted, and some of the chambers were frescoed in geometrical patterns, one colour laid on another. In one room was a painted border, little tents, like Indian tepees, in brilliant red.
>
> But the really splendid thing about our city, the thing that made it delightful to work there, and must have made it delightful to live there, was the setting. The town hung like a bird's nest in the cliff, looking off into the box canyon below, and beyond into the wide valley we called Cow Canyon, facing an ocean of clear air. A people who had the hardihood to build there, and who lived day after day looking down upon such grandeur, who came and went by those hazardous trails, must have been, as we often told each other, a fine people. But what had become of them? (212–213)

These are the qualities Cather admires in both architecture and writing: the thing stands up to close scrutiny and is done with simplicity and precision. It is functional as well as aesthetic. It has a clear center, constellating its environment into a meaningful pattern. And it suggests more than is made explicit.

In time a mission priest, Father Duchene, comes and helps the two young men "read" the ruins. Henry dies and is buried there. Father Duchene's reading is a testimony to a lost civilization that seems to have taken with it the values and wisdom lost to the present generation:

> Their life, compared to that of our roving Navajos, must have been quite complex. There is unquestionably a distinct feeling for design in what you call the Cliff City. Buildings are not grouped like that by pure accident, though convenience probably had much to do with it. Convenience often dictates very sound design. . . . I see them here, isolated, cut off from other tribes, working out their destiny, making their mesa more and more worthy to be a home for man, purifying life by religious ceremonies and observances, caring respectfully for their dead, protecting the children, doubtless entertaining some feelings of affection and sentiment for this stronghold where they were at once so safe and so comfortable, where they had practically overcome the worst hardships that primitive man had to fear. They were, perhaps, too far advanced for their time and environment. . . .
>
> Like you I feel a reverence for this place. Wherever humanity has made that hardest of all starts and lifted itself out of mere brutality, is a sacred spot. Your people were cut off here without the influence of example or emulation, with no incentive but some natural yearning for order and security. They built themselves into this mesa and humanized it. (220–221)

The key words here are "care," "respect," "reverence," "careful," "humanizing," "natural." A good reader recognizes good construction. The priest's words make an appeal for this kind of reading.

On a mission of preservation, Tom travels to Washington, hoping to find federal money to protect the cliff city and its artifacts and perhaps an archaeologist at the Smithsonian who will "interpret all that is obscure to us" and "revive this civilization in a scholarly work" (202). But Tom experiences little success and much disillusionment with the way structures of government erode nonmercenary values. Tom fears for the survival of the mesa in its pristine beauty and historical integrity, afraid that he has somehow betrayed it by exposing it to human eyes. He returns to find that Rodney has sold the relics to a German speculator for four thousand dollars. Rodney offers Tom half the proceeds. Outraged at the betrayal, so reminiscent of that of Judas with his thirty pieces of silver, Tom compares Rodney to Dreyfus, asking, " 'You think I'd touch that money?' I looked squarely at him for the first time. 'No more than if you'd stolen it. You made the sale. Get what you can out of it. I want to ask you one question: did you ever think I was digging those things up for what I could sell them for?' " (244). The transformation of energy into artifact and then into money is deadening and degrading. This runs a close parallel to the professor's attitude about his own digging into the past via his histories.

Later, regretting what he sees as his own betrayal of the friendship, Tom returns to the mesa alone after looking for Rodney, who has disappeared. On that trip Tom finds that his experience of the mesa is profoundly different, informed as it is by the history of disillusionment and loss that now surround it:

> In a sense, that was the first night I was ever really on the mesa at all—the first night that all of me was there. This was the first time I ever saw it as a whole. It all came together in my understanding, as a series of experiments do when you begin to see where they are leading. Something had happened in me that made it possible for me to coordinate and simplify, and that process, going on in my mind, brought with it great happiness. It was possession."
> (250–251)

One of Cather's great themes comes to a head in these lines: we only fully possess the thing we have lost. Possession lies in comprehension, which depends on the backward glance of memory. The old Heraclitean paradoxes reassert themselves in Tom's "religious emotion" as he revisits the scene of his transformation: "And what you own is what you do not own"; and what you do not own is the only thing you own.[8] He experiences great intensities in this final sojourn close to the sun, re-reading the *Aeneid* with renewed understanding, overlaying it with the story of his own odyssey, finding in these ancient dwellings a spiritual home whose power resides partly in the fact that they cannot be possessed or dwelt in for long. The summer he spends there is, as he describes it later, "a life in itself" and gives new meaning to the idea of home. Home is the place to which the heart returns, the place where the epiphany has occurred, and the place we must leave in order, thereafter, to possess it in the heart, undiminished and glorified by memory, which returns to us the things we have lost in their first loveliness but at the cost of renunciation.

As in a fairy tale, Tom dies before his time and therefore remains fixed as an ideal image of the high-minded explorer whose innocence is still a virtue. His expeditions to the old cities of the cliff dwellers and his reverence for the simplicities and complexities of the old tribal cultures, living close to the earth, appropriating the goods of the earth proportionately and conservatively for the ends of survival, make him the kind of environmentalist hero who lends himself readily to the romantic imagination as a measure of what we have lost.

But the question Tom's story leaves us with is a vexing one and brings us directly up against the paradoxes and limitations of the romantic worldview: how long could he have maintained his delicate balance between inner and outer worlds, his freedom from sexual and institutional politics, the simplicity of his attitudes toward money and power? Already before his death, his discoveries had become objects of political contention. Tom's invention, an engine, both embodies and produces power of a kind Tom had not yet had to deal with. Power and money do not stay pure. After his death his money is used to build a home for the professor's daughter and her husband of a kind the professor is sure Tom would not have chosen.

Yet desire and creation and production belong to a cycle of transformations that is completed in socialization, politicization, and commodification of the objects rooted in ideas. And in the turning of that cycle, in the externalization of the interior world, lies the irony that Cather sees as the defining characteristic of modern life. The voice of the moralist sounds clearly in her work, and the message is a kind of jeremiad: we have lost the right relation between ideas and things, between desire and possession, between ambition and fulfillment, and so the world that is "so vast, so beautiful and so new" fails to satisfy our misplaced hungers. Our consumption is out of sync with our needs, and the uses to which we put the natural and material environment are exploitive and self-indulgent and therefore dangerous. In this conclusion she essentially reiterates the problem of American innocence identified by so many cultural historians as a central problem in our mythology, and the challenge she seems to pose her readers is to think how to regain a right relation with the material world after innocence is lost, after the garden has been violated, and after we are left in the thicket of our own entangled desires and misguided ends.

In the final book we return to the professor, alone in his house with his memories and Tom's. The moment of decision has come; the professor can no longer postpone the move. Returning from a vacation to find St. Peter still occupying the old house, Scott observes with uncomprehending amusement, "It never struck me, Doctor, that you were a man who would be keeping up two establishments. They'll be coming home pretty soon, and then you'll have to decide where you are going to live" (271). Scott has no idea what a monumental issue this is for his father-in-law.

As is his wont, St. Peter attempts one more escape into the past. He drifts into reveries and memories of the self that preceded family life. He feels near death or some transformation. Reflecting back up the first years of his friendship with Tom, the professor nostalgically concludes that they were "really the best of all," when he had come home to the "charming groups of three" composed of Tom and his two daughters, "in the hammock swung between the linden trees, in the window-seat, or before the dining-room fire" (125). The "charming groups of three" are, of course, the vision of an observer—something seen at close range but objectified and aesthetically distanced from the viewer. Once again the professor defines himself fundamentally as an outsider.

His melancholy deepens as he flashes through a mental album of sentimentalized family scenarios:

> Oh, there had been fine times in this old house then: family festivals and hospitalities, little girls dancing in and out, Augusta coming and going, gay dresses hanging in his study at night, Christmas

shopping and secrets and smothered laughter on the stairs. When a man had lovely children in his house, fragrant and happy, full of pretty fancies and generous impulses, why couldn't he keep them? Was there no way but Medea's, he wondered? (125–126)

This nostalgic glimpse of the past, casting Tom as the son St. Peter never had, once again reveals the professor's high romanticism. He is a man who seems fully to value things only in the loss of them, when, covered with the veil of memory, their outlines blurred, they can be beautified into cherished fictions against which to measure the harsh realities of actual life and time.

The professor thinks that if he is alive next summer, he will go to Outland's country "to look off at those long, rugged, untamed vistas dear to the American heart" (270). He wants to escape from houses. He wants to become Tom. He wants to escape into myth rather than confront life in its imperfection and muddiness. He wants both freedom and shelter from the risks freedom involves. Never more than at this stage of his story does the professor appear as a kind of Walter Mitty, consumed with dreams of glamour, unable to make of the very compromises of domestic life the material of his greatness, but stuck in a view of them as impediments to a hypothetical greatness forever prevented.

But he cannot stay ensconced in the past indefinitely. He is forced to make a decision about how to go on. He cannot live two lives. He may have "other lives to live" but cannot do so without cost. The choice he is facing presents itself as a life-or-death choice. The house that saw so much life is now fast becoming a tomb, as the next passage shows, and he must either consign himself to it or rise out of it to go on with his other life, a reluctant Lazarus facing a going-on that can be only a gradual descent and decrease.

The Professor went wearily upstairs and lay down on the couch, his refuge from this ever-increasing fatigue. He really didn't see what he was going to do about the matter of domicile. He couldn't make himself believe that he was ever going to live in the new house again. He didn't belong there. He remembered some lines of a translation from the Norse he used to read long ago . . . : For thee a house was built / Ere thou wast born; / For thee a mould was made / Ere thou of woman camest. Lying on his old couch he could almost believe himself in that house already. The sagging springs were like the sham upholstery that is put in coffins. Just the equivocal American way of dealing with serious facts, he reflected. Why pretend that it is possible to soften that last hard bed? (272)

He prefers the ease of death to the change that seems to cost so much more. As he lies there, the gas from the old stove overcomes him, and he falls into a stupor. Augusta appears fortuitously to save him. But in his brief brush with death some release has taken place that allows him to go on. He awakens with an unexpected feeling of resignation, able to accept the loss of his dreams and return to life with "the ground under his feet," having sacrificed ideals that he thought made life worth living but that ultimately were making it impossible to live. He awakens to accept life on diminished terms, aware that his loss and its attendant grief will never be understood by a family "happily preoccupied with their own affairs" and able to face the future with "fortitude" (283).

This final, rather melodramatic scene gives us Cather's tragic sense—or her pessimistic didacticism—at full strength. The professor will, we assume, move into the new house and resume his role as husband and father with docility, if not enthusiasm. It is a rather bleak resolution, one whose implications ripple out widely: the material world inevitably involves us in radical compromise of the very values that it is meant to enhance—high aspirations, wide perspective, a sense of grandeur, freedom, infinite possibility. The structures we need as sense-making and ordering devices signal the death of those energies that we might define as the impetus of life itself. And like the beds in old American homesteads that cradle both birth and death, the houses we live in are places where the possible life is lived out even as on the same spot of ground the impossible dreams of youth that motivate us to greatness are slowly entombed.

8

THE GREAT GATSBY
Awakening from the American Dream

Alfred Kazin once claimed of writers, "One writes to make a home for oneself, on paper."[1] That claim seems to capture with particular aptness the role of writing in Fitzgerald's life. His biographer, Arthur Mizener, says of him that "nothing was ever quite real to him until he had written about it."[2] Fitzgerald had a legendary ability to concoct fictions that for the time they lasted took on compelling reality not only for his audience but for himself. That capacity combined with the sense of himself as perennially on the margins of a magic circle defined by money and social position resulted in the now well-chronicled Fitzgerald legend—a glamorous decade of living in the public eye a life that was partly a fiction of which he was himself author, protagonist, and audience. Mizener records an incident in Fitzgerald's childhood that illustrates his capacity to make the figments of his imagination real both to others and himself and links his character in at least one respect closely with that of Jay Gatsby: "As a small boy Fitzgerald lived, as he said later, 'with a great dream' and his object was always to try to realize that dream. When he was four or five, for instance, he described his pony to his Grandmother McQuillan in minute detail; she was horrified that so small a child should have a pony, and it was not easy, after Scott's persuasive description, to convince her that the pony was quite imaginary."[3] The imagination and desire that drove fantasy to the very edge of reality seems epitomized in the man from the Midwest, son of an immigrant family that had a "history of dislocation and alienation,"[4] who built his dream into a house and won his woman until the dream burst like a bubble, taking his life and fortunes with it.

If there is something of Fitzgerald in Gatsby, there is certainly as much of him in Nick, the narrator who observes the legendary life literally from the margins, living in the shadow of

217

the mansion, watching it like a stage as the fabulous tale unfolds before him, a vicarious participant who in his detachment survives, like Ishmael, to tell the tale. Nick, also a boy from the Midwest, seems to have one foot in and one out of the world whose clamor and high drama both fascinate and exclude him. As the prototype of that midwestern boy, Fitzgerald lived in a home—or rather a series of homes, for his parents moved every year or two for much of his childhood—on "the periphery of St. Paul's finest residential street," a row of brownstones that Fitzgerald later called "a museum of American architectural failures." Mizener quotes from a letter Fitzgerald sent a friend from his home at 599 Summit Avenue where he locates himself "in a house below the average / Of a street above the average / In a room below the roof."[5] Always in the position of aspirant, given alternately to the snobbery of the climber and the reverse snobbery of the snubbed, he maintained a delicate balance for most of his career at that edge of the theater of action from which so many American narrators have told their ambivalent stories. Those narrations, which loom so large in our national canon, are forms of symbolic action that mirror the action of the protagonist in which the teller who tells the tale is, finally, the hero. This is the basic situation of *The Great Gatsby*, where, as David Minter puts it, Nick Carraway and Jay Gatsby are engaged in "parallel pursuits," the one building his dream into a house, the other building his observations and speculations into a story.[6]

Gatsby's house is probably the easiest among all the houses in our fiction to identify as the embodiment of the "American dream," a notion that incorporates a host of moral and social values and romantic ideals in complex relationship. Jay Gatsby, a self-made man from a poor and obscure background who has risen to wealth and power by sheer force of will and the inspiration of obsessive romantic love, incarnates a mélange of romantic prototypes that taken together fall just this side of caricature. The mansion he inhabits, which he did not build but bought, represents a naive effort to transplant European architectural and decorative tastes into an American setting, where they look hopelessly artificial and out of context. Gatsby is Captain Ahab in a domestic setting, whose passion is amorous rather than vengeful but whose obsession is just as blind. His house, devoted to an inappropriate purpose, is a mere shell around the vacancy of his life—a mockery of the idea of home, an empty facade constructed around an idea. Like Hawthorne, Fitzgerald recasts the most besetting questions of the American cultural conscience—questions of class conflict, expropriation and use of land, the morality of capitalism, and the coexistence of sexuality with innocence—in a contemporary setting. The houses that appear in the novel establish a spectrum along which we can locate and measure the relative values of the styles of American life they represent. Here again lines of class and gender become an important grid on which the architecture of the novel is designed.

When Nick Carraway leaves West Egg for the last time, sad and reflective after Gatsby's death, he walks across the yard to look once more at "that huge, incoherent failure of a house" (137). *The Great Gatsby* is, among other things, a sobering and even ominous commentary on the dark side of the American dream. Jay Gatsby's house is the visible result of determination, idealism, romantic love, and hard capitalism. But like so many American dreams, the idealism is not sufficiently grounded in wisdom, the romantic love is untempered by experience, and the capitalistic success the house represents is bought at a questionably high price.

In this novel we are visitors, like Nick, in a world of earnest materialism, where cars and garden parties and white suits and, most importantly, houses, serve, as in Wharton's fiction, as indices of success and taste but also of fantasy and desire and, beneath them, of lack and loss. We enter five dwellings in the course of the novel: Gatsby's grandiose "imitation of some Hotel de Ville in Normandy" (6), Tom and Daisy's Georgian colonial mansion, Nick's modest and nondescript rented cottage, Myrtle and George Wilson's ramshackle apartment over their gas station, and the vulgar, overfurnished Manhattan flat Tom keeps for his trysts with Myrtle. Each dwelling clearly mirrors the character of its inhabitants; Tom's and Gatsby's houses, and in a comically ironic fashion, Myrtle and Tom's apartment, are self-consciously designed and decorated to project a carefully designed public image. The poorer houses speak just as clearly of status, taste, and means, all, however, that are matters beyond the tenants' control.

Gatsby's house, like a formula romance, fulfills certain obvious, rather vulgar ideals. It is less an expression of a defined self than a declaration of achievement in received terms—the home of someone who can afford the very best and has taken care to find out what the "very best" is, though his fine possessions breathe no aura of refinement. Everything is "genuine"; the books in the library are real books, albeit uncut and unread; his shelves are full of shirts imported from England; his toiletries are burnished gold. The house, like Gatsby himself, is a decorative shell behind the glamour of which he seems to have disappeared into inexplicable and inappropriate seclusion.

Tom's house is likewise a self-conscious symbol of success, a fitting combination of traditional American design with French and Italian touches, an appropriate home for a Yale man. In it he houses Daisy, his most prized possession, with whom he lives in a state of suppressed tension, unreflectively conventional in his attitudes toward home and marriage. Inherited wealth has relieved him of the necessity of creating or imagining anything other than what money and prestige can buy. His ignorance and complacency throw Gatsby's awkward but self-reliant virtues into high relief. One of the great ironies of the novel is that Tom, the antithesis of the romantic hero, survives and wins, though not without heavy losses of his own, at Gatsby's expense.

Nick's "weatherbeaten cardboard bungalow," always seen in contrast to Gatsby's mansion, in whose shadow it inconspicuously stands, is a transition space for him. He does not own it, but he does inhabit it; he is an itinerant, rootless as yet, a kind of Ishmael in Eastern society, where he maintains the position of outsider and observer, forfeiting ownership and the intimacy of binding connections. He is free of his house, as he is free of most other identifying paraphernalia of adult life, and so is poised in a transitional, quasi-adolescent state, a state of relative innocence of the temptations of proprietorship as well as freedom from its responsibilities. He settles into West Egg feeling like "an original settler," filled with the optimistic sensation that "life was beginning over again with the summer" (5). This is the perspective of the *puer aeternus* (the eternal youth), the Huck

Finns and the Natty Bumppos who are nomads in a culture of settlers, planters, owners of houses and land.

Nick's general intention for himself during this golden summer is to become "that most limited of all specialists, the 'well-rounded man.'" He goes on to reflect on this objective, "This isn't just an epigram—life is much more successfully looked at from a single window after all" (5). The architectural metaphor here makes the common conflation of self and dwelling, both places from which one looks out on "life." It also underscores the practical value of limited perspective: the modern hero's predicament is to "see too much." Nick, like Quentin Compson, Stephen Dedalus, or even the Tiresias of *The Waste Land*, sees more than he can do anything about. He sees, in fact, through too many windows, cherishing a neutral and detached stance that makes him privy to multiple points of view but depriving him of the luxuries of conviction and passion.

Or perhaps it is just that the frame around Nick's window is extraordinarily large. His sees things on a broad canvas of history; his spatial sense grows quickly to cosmic dimensions; he looks at a house and sees the sky and stars behind it as part of the pattern. The perspectives Nick adopts about what he sees, which quickly move from the physical to the moral and metaphysical planes, derive from an old puritanical habit of mind: throughout the story he describes what he sees in terms of large, general dichotomies, polarities, oppositions. Everything is presented in terms of its opposite, beginning with the two points of land that form the poles of the story—East Egg and West Egg. Nick explains, "I lived at West Egg, the—well, the less fashionable of the two, though this is a most superficial tag to express the bizarre and not a little sinister contrast between them" (6).

Contrasts quickly assume symbolic value and are pushed in Nick's descriptions to extremities. The absence of a wide middle ground in his presentation of the geography of the social spectrum reiterates a commonplace in traditional American Protestant thought—that the middle is a radically uncomfortable place to be and in a sense an "unreal" place to remain; the individual tends toward one extreme or the other—heaven or hell. Middle means on the way up—or down. The points of stability on the spectrum of material life are likewise at the top or at the bottom.

Nick's hesitant description of the differences between the two similar strips of land works symbolically on a number of levels. They are equal and opposite entities: it seems that if one were fashionable, the other, to maintain some kind of necessary cosmic and social balance, would not be. Such contrasts appear to be the necessary order of things. Moreover, "fashionable" seems to be a term that masks the sharpness and depth of the differences it demarcates. Here, too, we find a vestige of an entrenched American habit of mind: surfaces are at odds with interiors; the body both mirrors and masks the soul. Appearances are both telling and deceptive. So "fashionable," a term that would seem definitively superficial, acquires a metaphysical resonance: Nick recognizes the contrast between fashionable and unfashionable areas as "bizarre" and "sinister." The words alert us to the fact that surface distinctions generally reflect in more palatable fashion profound and potentially unsettling differences. The Gothic note sounded here echoes frequently in descriptions of the material contrasts between Gatsby's house and Nick's, between New York and the Midwest, between Daisy and Myrtle.

Nick's house, significantly enough, is described as situated both at an extreme and "in between":

> My house was at the very tip of the egg, only fifty yards from the Sound, and squeezed between two huge places that rented for twelve or fifteen thousand a season. The one on my right was a colossal affair by any standard—it was a factual imitation of some Hotel de Ville in Normandy, with a tower on one side, spanking new under a thin beard of raw ivy, and a marble swimming pool, and more than forty acres of lawn and garden. It was Gatsby's mansion. Or, rather, as I didn't know Mr. Gatsby, it was a mansion, inhabited by a gentleman of that name. My own house was an eyesore, but it was a small eyesore, and it had been overlooked, so I had a view of the water, a partial view of my neighbor's lawn, and the consoling proximity of millionaires—all for eighty dollars a month. (6)

The essential feature of Nick's house, the aspect that provides its character, is its proximity to the neighboring mansions that almost obliterate it. It is interesting by association, not by any property of its own. This, of course, reflects Nick's own adopted persona: as a detached spectator whose involvement in the story he tells he belies by means of a bystander stance. He evaluates his own house as well as his neighbors' primarily in monetary terms; quantifying the difference of quality makes the contrast sharp and exact: the distance between twelve or fifteen thousand and eighty. This ludicrously extreme discrepancy serves to remind the reader of one more general truth: that in the United States such things can exist side by side. He describes his house as an "eyesore" but one that has made no eyes particularly sore because it has been "overlooked." The irony in the juxtaposition of these two designations is clear: it is Nick's own eyes that are "sore." His house is not a thing to be looked on but looked from. Its attractiveness lies in its views, as well as its "consoling proximity of millionaires."

Nick's house lies to the left of Gatsby's. In keeping with the symbolism assigned to spatial relations in this novel, the position of Nick's cottage may suggest the sinister or darker vantage point— the place in the shadow from which the more conspicuous world can be observed and evaluated. The house in this respect also reflects Nick's position in relation to the other characters.

The terms in which Nick describes Gatsby's house—a "colossal affair by any standard"—suggest a certain irony mixed with admiration; its grandioseness seems slightly vulgar; it is an imitation style borrowed from another culture in a kind of gratuitous and vulgar eclecticism, like so many things American, and set down in incongruous context. Gatsby's "forty acres" conform to the pattern of mythic elements that attach to Nick's presentation of Gatsby's house and person, forty being a biblical number of great symbolic significance frequently used to designate great stretches of time or space. The forty acres may by extension signify something as potentially limitless as the continent once seemed.[7]

In identifying Gatsby as the owner, Nick corrects himself: "Gatsby's mansion" suggests that the house is a function of the inhabitant. Correcting that phrase to "a mansion, inhabited by a gentleman of that name" not only reinforces the sense of mystery surrounding Gatsby's identity but alters the relation between the man and the house. The house is the essential; the man, the accidental.

After establishing these contrasts between Gatsby's house and his own as a matrix of the story, Nick adds a third term to the equation by taking us across the Sound to East Egg to receive our initial tour of Tom and Daisy's house:

> Their house was even more elaborate than I expected, a cheerful red-and-white Georgian Colonial mansion, overlooking the bay. The lawn started at the beach and ran toward the front door for a quarter of a mile, jumping over sun-dials and brick walks and burning gardens—finally when it reached the house drifting up the side in bright vines as though from the momentum of its run. The front was broken by a line of French windows, glowing now with reflected gold and wide open to the warm windy afternoon, and Tom Buchanan in riding clothes was standing with his legs apart on the front porch. (7)

Unlike Gatsby's fake French effect, Tom and Daisy's house is built in a style that dates back to the American Revolution and evokes a long history of American gentility. It is more organically unified with its surroundings, which indeed seem actively to have assimilated it—the grass and vines running, jumping, and drifting toward and over it, apparently eager to make it part of the natural landscape. The glowing French windows, a cosmopolitan touch, absorb the sun and open the interior to the warm afternoon wind. This is a place whose interior and exterior are in apparent harmony—a place apparently frank and hospitable and without mystery. Tom in his riding clothes on the front porch is the picture of a master on his own estate. He is an owner, a sportsman, an entitled member of the monied class, at home with luxury, situated between his house and his land, plainly in charge of both. His elevated position as well as his posture suggests symmetry, rootedness, stability, and command. He is a self-conscious representative of a class characterized by all these qualities, and his house and land are extensions of this persona.

Tom's comment on his own property is characteristically understated for effect:

> "I've got a nice place here," he said, his eyes flashing about restlessly. Turning me around by one arm, he moved a broad flat hand

along the front vista, including in its broad sweep a sunken Italian garden, a half acre of deep, pungent roses, and a snub-nosed motor-boat that bumped the tide offshore.

"It belonged to Demaine, the oil man." He turned me around again, politely and abruptly. "We'll go inside." (7–8)

Tom is both self-satisfied and dissatisfied with his property. Its details seem to escape him; he passes them by with a sweep of the hand while Nick takes them in one by one. Tom's sole comment on the rich and impressive property focuses not on its beauty or on his pleasure in it but on its pedigree. The name of the former owner gives the property much of its value for Tom, on whom forms of value other than those relating to money and status are largely lost.

Entering the house, Nick describes a scene that surely is one of the most memorable in the novel. In this dreamlike scene Nick's poetic fancy achieves a baroque eloquence that underscores both the dazzling inventiveness of his imagination and, correspondingly, his unreliability as a narrator, prone as he is to invest what he sees with his own imaginative whimsy. A little like Poe's distracted narrator in "The Fall of the House of Usher," Nick's visions are prophetic, if slightly unreal. Here in his vision of Tom and Daisy's living room the whole story of Tom and Daisy is prefigured in symbolic, surrealistic fashion, their incompatibilities of character made evident in the way they occupy space:

We walked through a high hallway into a bright rosy-colored space, fragilely bound into the house by French windows at either end. The windows were ajar and gleaming white against the fresh grass outside that seemed to grow a little way into the house. A breeze blew through the room, blew curtains in at one end and out the other like pale flags, twisting them up toward the frosted wedding-cake of the ceiling, and then rippled over the wine-colored rug, making a shadow on it as the wind does on the sea. The only completely stationary object in the room was an enormous couch on which two young women were buoyed up as though upon an anchored balloon. They were both in white, and their dresses were rippling and fluttering as if they had just been blown back in after a short flight around the house. I must have stood for a few moments listening to the whip and snap of the curtains and the groan of a picture on the wall. Then there was a boom as Tom Buchanan shut the rear windows and the caught wind died out about the room, and the curtains and the rugs and the two young women ballooned slowly to the floor. (8)

Tom and Daisy's house embodies the tensions between their characters. Before Tom enters the room it is "rosy-colored" and full of light and air. It lets in the outside; its walls, mostly window, are transparent and permeable. The whole room seems in motion, as the lawn did, and the two young women are borne on that motion, integrated into the environment by their billowing dresses, which replicate the breeze-blown curtains. To Nick the room seems all atmosphere, heady and dreamlike. Tom's first gesture on entering breaks the spell and brings everything "down to earth." This tension between the ethereal and the earthy recurs in numerous encounters between Tom and Daisy, whose respective masculinity and femininity, exaggerated to the point of cliché, constitute an antagonism that is also a profound bond of dependence; each is lopsided and incomplete without the influence of the other. And in this scene the house appears to be an epiphenomenon—a projection of the two selves that inhabit it, changing its aspect and atmosphere in response to the presence of each in turn. As Daisy's room it appears to Nick sensuous and sumptuous; the "wedding cake" ceiling and "wine-colored" rug suggest festivity and celebration. Daisy is a presiding spirit whose presence, here as elsewhere, seems literally to animate the room itself, whereas Tom's entry restores hard realism and reduces the objects in the room to their inanimate state.

Just as Nick gives us Tom and Daisy's relationship and character in terms of their house, so he reiterates this method of portrayal in bawdy comic form when we reach the New York West Side apartment where Tom and Myrtle carry on their affair.

The apartment was on the top floor—a small living-room, a small dining-room, a small bedroom, and a bath. The living-room was crowded to the doors with a set of tapestried furniture entirely too large for it, so that to move about was to stumble continually over scenes of ladies swinging in the gardens of Versailles. The only picture was an over-enlarged photograph, apparently a hen sitting on a blurred rock. Looked at from a distance, however, the hen resolved itself into a bonnet, and the countenance of a stout old lady beamed down into the room. Several old copies of *Town Tattle* lay on the table together with a copy of *Simon Called Peter*, and some of the small scandal magazines of Broadway. (23)

The tasteless incongruities of this anonymous little apartment again serve accurately to describe its oddly coupled inhabitants. The furniture suggests Myrtle's aspirations to taste and culture in the form of objects vaguely French and acquired with no attention to proper context—tawdry symbols of "culture" acquired ignorantly and housed inappropriately. Herein, as in many other particulars, Myrtle emerges as Gatsby's comic counterpart. The overenlarged photograph, too, suggests an entire lack of proportion. In the process of enlargement the picture has lost its clarity, sense, and significance, which can be recaptured only with effort by a discerning eye. Once Nick does distinguish the figure in the picture, it turns out to be a "stout old lady," and the reader cannot help noticing the similarities between the picture and Myrtle herself, large and loose and blurry, with her dull intellect and expanded form. The old lady of the picture and the ladies of the tapestries swinging in the gardens of Versailles dominate the room with exaggerated and overstylized forms of femininity, making the room coarsely seductive, as the femininity of the atmosphere Daisy evoked in her own living room awakens something subtler and more spiritualized. The reading material reiterates the impression of lowbrow vulgarity. Along with scandal sheets of the sort that pander to prurient and sensationalistic taste, the popular period piece, *Simon Called Peter*, suggests sentimental piety that makes cheap romance of religion.

In both serious and parodic fashion, Nick reverts repeatedly to the spiritual, religious, or cosmic dimensions of his subject. True to his puritanical habit of mind, everything is metaphor, and the social drama he witnesses enlarges by nuance to a cosmic scale. In the opening sentences of the third chapter Nick contemplates Gatsby's house from his obscure vantage point in a way that makes it a center point in a scene that takes on cosmic dimensions: "There was music from my neighbor's house through the summer nights. In his blue gardens men and girls came and went like moths among the whisperings and the champagne and the stars" (31). All the particulars are subsumed in an atmosphere of twilight and starlight, and all seem connected in a web of relations, at the center of which is the house. A similar effect is created in a subsequent scene where Nick is again watching the activity of Gatsby's guests, this time in daytime, on his private beach: "At high tide in the afternoon I watched his guests diving from the tower of his raft, or taking the sun on the hot sand of his beach while his two motor-boats slit the waters of the Sound, drawing aquaplanes over cataracts of foam" (31). Here again all the motion in the scene is somehow created or orchestrated by Gatsby, the invisible puppeteer enclosed in his mysterious house like the Wizard of Oz behind his screen.

Nick continues to observe, from various vantage points at various times of day, the life of the house next door, thereby accumulating a string of impressions that he fuses like a time-lapse photographer, noticing the cars that come and go for weekend parties, the servants and gardeners who emerge from their invisibility to prepare and dismantle the elaborate sets, as if the house and garden were a theater or circus. When we return to "real time," Nick describes a party on a particular summer night in elaborate, jeweled detail, down to the old-fashioned cordials and the instruments in the hired orchestra. The mind's eye of the reader is made to flit with dizzying rapidity about the fantastic scene, taking in its colorful details in distinct but shifting kaleidoscopic patterns. Again the dimensions shift radically and rapidly from the cars parked five deep in the drive to the vast nighttime cosmos: "The lights grow brighter as the earth lurches away from the sun" (31). Gatsby's house is once again made to seem the center of the universe, as it seems the center of the social world in such succinct visions as, "On Sunday morning while church bells rang in the villages alongshore, the world and its mistress returned to Gatsby's house and twinkled hilariously on his lawn" (47).

Nick eventually appears at one of these parties and the camera moves closer, first among the colorful, anonymous guests and then to the interior of the house, which until now has remained a wide, blank facade situated as an appropriate backdrop to the spectacle. Meeting Jordan Baker at the party, Nick attaches himself to her conveniently, as he knows no one else. Finding that he has never met his host, Jordan embarks on a search for the missing Gatsby. Nick recalls the odd quest, during which Gatsby's absence becomes more conspicuous and almost palpable: "The bar, where we glanced first, was crowded, but Gatsby was not there. She couldn't find him from the top of the steps, and he wasn't on the verandah" (35). The search for Gatsby in his own house once again provides a Gothic touch to the tale: the director and host, the governing presence and first cause, is absent. Everything within the wide scope of his powerful reach is apparently under his control, but he is elusive, subject of much rumor and local legend and rapidly evaporating into a fiction. As Nick and Jordan hunt for him, it becomes apparent, as it does each time we enter the mansion, that its most conspicuous and peculiar quality is its emptiness. Evidences of life within it, like the man doing his exercises in an upstairs bedroom, the occasional servant, and the guest loitering in the library, seem purely incidental. There is no evidence of "life" of a deeper and more proper kind.

The peek into the library provides a moment of comic relief. It is "a high Gothic library, panelled with carved English oak, and probably transported complete from some ruin overseas" (35)—like the Normandy facade, an imported design that bespeaks borrowed elegance. Nick and Jordan surprise a curious visitor who is unabashedly marveling at the "realism" of the room as an achievement in effect. He is handling one of the expensive volumes pulled off a shelf:

> "Absolutely real—have pages and everything. I thought they'd be a nice durable cardboard. Matter of fact, they're absolutely real. Pages and—Here! Lemme show you. . . . See!" he cried triumphantly. "It's a bona-fide piece of printed matter. It fooled me. This fella's a regular Belasco. It's a triumph. What thoroughness! What realism! Knew when to stop, too—didn't cut the pages. But what do you want? What do you expect?"
>
> He snatched the book from me and replaced it hastily on its shelf, muttering that if one brick was removed the whole library was liable to collapse. (36)

Particularly in this scene we encounter the irony of separation of form and function. The very "authenticity" of Gatsby's library, the perfection of its completeness, combined with the obvious fact that the books are unread and the room is unemployed for its ostensible purpose, once again reinforces the sense that this is a movie set fashioned by an expert master-designer who went to such lengths to create appearances that the surfaces even have interiors. But these interiors, like his house, are, for all their authenticity, false; they are surfaces in their turn. Failing the ends for which they are created, they lack "soul." Then, too, the suspicion that the library was "probably transported complete from some ruin overseas" suggests an incongruity more skillfully and elaborately brought off but not unlike the imported tapestried furniture in Myrtle's and Tom's Manhattan apartment, slightly ludicrous when out of proper context.

The theme of incongruity is continued in Nick's speculations about Gatsby himself. Like Faulkner's Thomas Sutpen, Gatsby is a mythic character of unknown origins, whose reclusiveness adds to his mystery. The known and observable facts about him do not add up to a story. Nick reflects, "I would have accepted without question the information that Gatsby sprang from the swamps of Louisiana or from the lower East Side of New York. That was comprehensible. But young men didn't—at least in my provincial inexperience I believed they didn't—drift coolly out of nowhere and buy a palace on Long Island Sound"(38). Just as the house does not "add up," so the man himself seems a series of incongruous surfaces. There is no sufficient explanation for either. The lack of history and aesthetic integrity is itself an old theme in American cultural mythology. In this respect Gatsby is a parody of what James might have called the "American type," an intruder on foreign shores, lacking cultural, architectural, and often familial context, piecing together a persona and a past out of available materials and a patchwork of notions derived from some piecemeal form of autodidacticism—a self-made man in the worst sense, both powerful and pathetic, clever and abysmally ignorant, lacking the cultural formation that can be provided only in a setting of consensual values and shared tastes.

The biblical overtones that recur in Nick's rhetoric add another dimension to the depiction of Gatsby as ur-American—another of the "American Adams" described by R. W. B. Lewis as our native hero.[8] The roll call of people "who came to Gatsby's house" that summer, for instance, reads a little like the first chapter of Matthew—a long list, ending with the formulaic phrase, "All these people came to Gatsby's house in the summer" (49). This ceremonial rendering casts Gatsby's house as a pilgrimage spot where the faithful come to worship an elusive god of wealth.

Over time as Nick becomes acquainted with his neighbor, the magnified image disintegrates and is replaced by a rather disappointingly amiable but ordinary man, who, Nick finds, has little to say. "So my first impression, that he was a person of some undefined consequence, had gradually faded and he had become simply the proprietor of an elaborate road-house next door" (49). Like his house, Gatsby seems to be vacant, somehow. He, too, is mostly facade, impressively designed and properly functioning but oddly inhuman, impenetrable, and incapable of intimacy. He seems at times a property of the house rather than vice versa.

Eventually Nick learns the history of the building of Gatsby's mansion, partly from Jordan, a thirdhand source who is as willing to be a truth-teller as a liar, both of which she seems to do with perfect aplomb, thereby making it difficult to determine what status to assign her claims. Realizing that Gatsby built the house expressly so that he would be just across the bay from Daisy humanizes him for Nick. "He came alive to me," he recalls, "delivered suddenly from the womb of his purposeless splendor" (60). The love motive gives Gatsby a soul, and the mystery becomes a romance. The house is not an inexplicable anomaly but a means to an end—a performance for Daisy's benefit, a gift, a self-exhibition for her viewing. Interestingly enough, the absurd disproportion of Gatsby's magnificent gesture does not disturb Nick; this extravagant romanticism is another deeply rooted American attitude. Gatsby assumes a place among a long line of passionate, fanatical heroes, his purposes a little lower than Captain Ahab's but understandable in terms just as cosmic. And Nick, like Ishmael with Ahab, participates vicariously in Gatsby's wild quest, watching from an inconspicuous vantage point, storing up the tale to tell.

When Nick returns home one night, after Gatsby's decision to arrange a tryst with Daisy, he turns the corner and is "afraid for a moment that my house was on fire." It seems to him that the whole peninsula is ablaze, until he sees that the eerie luminosity is merely Gatsby's house with lights on in every room. Nick wonders if it is another wild party, but no sound comes from the house. Running into Gatsby on the lawn, Nick comments, "Your place looks like the World's Fair." Gatsby's answer is revealing: " 'Does it?' He turned his eyes toward it absently. 'I have been glancing into some of the rooms' " (62). The disproportion between Nick's perception from the outside of the blazing light of the house and Gatsby's own obliviousness to its effect creates another incongruity. Gatsby apparently notices very little, except what relates directly to the object of his obsession. The light, like other forms of energy that seem to radiate from the house, does so without his apparent knowledge or understanding. Gatsby's effects far exceed his designs, which are unifocal and exclusive. This fact gives his intricate calculations an odd quality of innocence; he is a man not fully conscious, childlike in his desires and means. But a man who is a child is a frightening thing, unnatural, having more power than he can judiciously wield, and once again a certain ominous strain is played on the familiar American theme of dangerous innocence.

When Daisy comes for the appointed meeting with Gatsby, she greets Nick with characteristic superlatives that seem, like Gatsby's grand gestures, much form without substance: "Is this absolutely where you live, my dearest one?" (65). Like Gatsby, Daisy is a dangerous innocent. Her innocence is a habitual posture of such long standing that it almost completely conceals a shrewd, suppressed, and somewhat bitter adult. Leaving the two of them in his living room, Nick retreats discreetly to his backyard and contemplates Gatsby's house as he waits for a decent interval to give them the privacy they have wanted:

> There was nothing to look at from under the tree except Gatsby's enormous house, so I stared at it, like Kant at his church steeple, for half an hour. A brewer had built it early in the "period" craze a decade before, and there was a story that he'd agreed to pay five years' taxes on all the neighboring cottages if the owners would have their roofs thatched with straw. Perhaps their refusal took the heart out of his plan to Found a Family—he went into an immedi-

ate decline. His children sold his house with the black wreath still on the door. Americans, while occasionally willing to be serfs, have always been obstinate about being peasantry. (67)

This capsule history of the house heightens the ludicrousness of the incongruities already observed. The house has its own peculiar history, quite apart from Gatsby's peculiarities. It has always been someone's attempt to create or recreate an artificial setting for a private fiction. Nick's comparison of the mansion to Kant's church suggests that the house will, through him, acquire yet another layer of significance as catalyst and symbol, a focal point of the story he has to tell that will become legend and outlive the house itself. Like Miss Rosa, who tells the story of Faulkner's Thomas Sutpen, Nick has appropriated Gatsby's house and made it into a story, in that way symbolically claiming it as an inheritance.

When Nick returns to Gatsby and Daisy in the living room, they insist on taking him with them to tour Gatsby's house. Gatsby looks over his house as if he had never quite seen it: " 'My house looks well, doesn't it?' " he asks. " 'See how the whole front of it catches the light.' " As he scrutinizes it, he observes, " 'It took me just three years to earn the money that bought it.' " Nick, puzzled, asks, " 'I thought you inherited your money' " (68). Gatsby doesn't miss a beat. He claims he did but lost most of it during the "big panic." The mystery of Gatsby's house now shifts ground; the question in Nick's mind is no longer one of ends but of means.

Like Tom's, Gatsby's interest in his own house, apart from its effect on Daisy, is in its public appearance and economic value rather than its livability. The house is a dream translated into effort, translated into money, translated into stone. Gatsby's roving eyes see the effect of that chain of causes, where others see through lenses of envy or desire an image of home life they want to believe is possible, thrilled with the "colossal vitality" of Gatsby's illusion. It is significant, too, that he takes such credit for and pride in a house he neither designed nor built but chose. It seems in every particular to express his own idiosyncratic exhibitionism, but it also clearly represents a kind of ambition not peculiar to Gatsby, revealing him as a type rather than the anomaly he at first seems. The approach the three take to the house is carefully staged for visual effect:

> Instead of taking the short cut along the Sound we went down the road and entered by the big postern. With enchanting murmurs Daisy admired this aspect or that of the feudal silhouette against the sky, admired the gardens, the sparkling odor of jonquils and the frothy odor of hawthorn and plum blossoms and the pale gold odor of kiss-me-at-the-gate. It was strange to reach the marble steps and find no stir of bright dresses in and out of the door, and hear no sound but bird voices in the trees. (69)

The theatrical effects are not lost on Daisy; they are, in fact, a perfect vehicle for her equally theatrical responses. The silence and the natural fragrances give the place a new aura of mystery, a different, and perhaps more believable, dimension. The distinctive odors of flowers in the gardens are suddenly perceptible, and what was simply a stage setting acquires at this viewing depth and subtlety. Nick is awed at this change in the house's aspect; the palpable emptiness of the house and garden strikes him as slightly ominous: "As we wandered through Marie Antoinette music-rooms and Restoration salons, I felt that there were guests concealed behind every couch and table, under orders to be breathlessly silent until we had passed through. As Gatsby closed the door of 'the Merton College Library' I could have sworn I heard the owl-eyed man break into ghostly laughter" (69).

Here, as elsewhere, the house appears as a haunted mansion and Gatsby's own life insufficiently real to offset the ghostliness. The house is a museum piece, a remnant of past styles of decoration and past styles of social intercourse; the term *feudal* suits the house's inappropriate and awkward splendor, which is lost on the American landscape without its retinue of peasantry to provide a setting for the jewel. But only Nick perceives the house this way. It is his consciousness of history and his sensitivity to implication that endow the house with resonance. Like the narrator who guides us through the House of the Seven Gables, he projects on the house his own consciousness, infusing it with sinister meaning that proceeds from his own inhibitions and apprehensions. He is a prophet of sorts, reading signs and portents where his companions see only plaster and stone.

After a tour of "period bedrooms swathed in rose and lavender silk and vivid with new flowers," luxurious dressing rooms and pool rooms and elaborate bathrooms, passing by a nameless tenant doing his exercises, the three come to Gatsby's own apartment: "a bedroom and a bath, and an Adam study." Nick observes that Gatsby's bedroom was "the simplest room of all—except where the dresser was garnished with a toilet set of pure dull gold" (69–70). The simplicity of Gatsby's own living quarters in the midst of the magnificent house is both ironic and poignant. In his "Adam study," aptly named, he suddenly appears almost Thoreauvian in his isolation, solitude, and unpretension. At the heart of all this magnificent falsehood lies something very simple and true: Gatsby leads an unpretentious, almost austere private life, driven by one single-minded desire, unworldly in his apparent indifference to all his material wealth.

Gatsby's only concern is Daisy. Both he and the house are transformed by the alchemy of her presence, animated and given value entirely by her appreciation. Nick observes, "He hadn't once ceased looking at Daisy, and I think he revalued everything in his house according to the measure of response it drew from her well-loved eyes. Sometimes, too, he stared around at his possessions in a dazed way, as though in her actual and astounding presence none of it was any longer real. Once he nearly toppled down a flight of stairs" (69).

The eyes that see the house provide its character. Later, when Tom appears at one of Gatsby's parties, Nick remarks that the house seems "peculiarly oppressive" under Tom's gaze. The whole matter of assigning value is of course complicated by the fact that Nick's values, despite disclaimers meant to suggest that he is a merely neutral and transparent recorder of events, heavily overlay his own observations of the house; the further we proceed in the story, the more the house is described in terms of Nick's own morally weighted speculations.

The conclusion of the house tour brings us to a moment of quiet climax. Gatsby shows Daisy how if he stands on the dock, he can see her house across the bay. Artlessly, he confides, "You always have a green light that burns all night at the end of your dock" (70). Suddenly he is uncharacteristically oblivious to Daisy's reaction to this bit of sentiment, and we see him for just a moment absorbed in some interior reflection, on which Nick speculates: "Possibly it had occurred to him that the colossal significance of that light had now vanished forever. Compared to the great distance that had separated him from Daisy it had seemed very near to her, almost touching her. It had seemed as close as a star to the moon. Now it was again a green light on a dock. His count of enchanted objects had diminished by one" (71).

At this point the diminution of Gatsby's great dream begins. Romance dissipates like a bubble on contact. Like the blurred picture in Myrtle's apartment, the descent into reality here is a comic diminishment: the beacon of romance and promise is a mere green dock light. At this moment we begin to contemplate the dark side of American romanticism: that the ideal will not withstand the pressure of experience. And for Gatsby, oriented entirely toward creating the fantasy, the touch of reality leaves him not only disappointed but baffled because he cannot adjust his behavior to its mundane irregularities; he does not know quite what to do next. Gatsby's mansion, like Gatsby's self, is the realization of a patently adolescent dream, and having the means to embody that dream and insulate himself in it, he has remained perennially adolescent, created for himself a private world in which he can do that. But it is a posture that cannot be maintained indefinitely.

Nick's reflections in chapter 6 about Gatsby's creation of his own fictitious identity parallel the history of the house provided in the previous chapter:

> I suppose he'd had the name ready for a long time. . . . His parents were shiftless and unsuccessful farm people—his imagination had never really accepted them as parents at all. The truth was that Jay Gatsby of West Egg, Long Island, sprang from his Platonic conception of himself. He was a son of God—a phrase which, if it means anything, means just that—and he must be about his Father's business, the service of a vast, vulgar, and meretricious beauty. So he invented just the sort of Jay Gatsby that a seventeen-year-old boy would be likely to invent, and to this conception he was faithful to the end. (75)

This passage exposes and critiques several aspects of what can readily be identified as a composite of those characteristics commonly called the "American character"—an idea of self drawn from a religious model and based on the belief in an Emersonian and Platonic idealism and the autonomy of the self, the complex assimilation of religious doctrine to pragmatic capitalism that makes acquisition a virtue paid for by a certain suppression of awareness that can be accomplished only by fostering perpetual innocence, a posture increasingly difficult to maintain as the demands of adult life make it increasingly inappropriate and ineffectual. The necessary fate of the American romantic is to die young or end in abject failure because he has hitched his wagon to an impossible dream. We do not, as a people, admire compromise, though it may be the only virtue that ensures survival. Indeed, survival itself on such terms seems a dubious and guilty business; the hero had better die before he has to grow up. Otherwise he will have to choose whether to be alive or to be heroic because, in these terms, the two are incompatible. Nick's account here of Gatsby's construction of his own image betrays Nick's romantic bent as well. Rather than exposing Gatsby as a sham, the account conveys a certain admiration of Gatsby's successful fictionalization of his own life—a writerly admiration for imaginative shaping of the material—and indeed elevates that fiction to the status of a great myth.

In a subsequent encounter, Nick attempts, however, to temper Gatsby's inevitable disillusionment by injecting a small note of realism:

> "I wouldn't ask too much of her," I ventured. "You can't repeat the past."
> "Can't repeat the past?" he cried incredulously. "Why of course you can!"
> He looked around him wildly, as if the past were lurking here in the shadow of his house, just out of reach of his hand. (84)

Like Ahab's, Gatsby's monomania grows into megalomania. An assumption of omnipotence is necessary to sustain his illusions. Admission of limitation would be admission of defeat. He must, in fact, defy time—the absolute conundrum that condemns the ideal of eternal youth and innocence. As at so many other points, we have here another episode in the allegory of American experience and the American experiment, whose nobility is proportionate to its pathetic impracticality and visionary myopia.

Gatsby's attainment of his goal brings his fantastic effort to a speedy end. The anticlimax moves rapidly. Suddenly "the lights in his house failed to go on one Saturday night—and, as obscurely as it had begun, his career as Trimalchio was over" (86). The house has served its purpose and is no longer useful because it has never been turned to any purpose other than to impress Daisy. As she begins actually to visit Gatsby in the afternoons he fires his servants; he is reduced to intrigue and caution to avoid gossip. His insularity, once a kind of purity of devotion, is now a strategy of self-protection. He dismantles the whole show, just as he erected it, for her. As Nick puts it, "So the whole caravansary had fallen in like a card house at the disapproval in her eyes" (86). The card house is a perfect image: a fragile structure that delights precisely by its delicate balance and utter pointlessness except to prove that it can stand for a moment in unlikely poise before falling.

Naturally, Daisy cannot measure up to Gatsby's dream. She never aspired to the power with which he has invested her. The excess of his adoration dooms Gatsby's love affair to failure. Daisy in person is a reality, not a fiction he can control by the power of his imperial imagination. His treatment of her as the princess of his private fairy tale incapacitates him for an authentic adult relationship. Like his house, Daisy is real to him only as a figment conjured in the universe of his own mind.

The inevitable showdown between Gatsby and Tom is more than a necessary element in a melodramatic formula plot. The two men are equal and opposite quantities in this allegory of American life and character. In comparison to Gatsby's magnificence, glamour, and extravagance of imagination, Tom appears to be stunted, dense, and pedestrian. Yet it is Tom who is capable not only of survival but of making the compromises necessary to make and keep a home and family—admittedly on questionable terms, but keep them, all the same. The incompatibilities and conflicts that strain his relationship with Daisy are of human dimensions and effect perhaps a necessary tension that at least holds out the possibility of tempering both people in their masculine and feminine excesses to some kind of livable balance.

The confrontation takes place on "neutral turf" because Gatsby, lunching uncomfortably at Tom and Daisy's, confides to Nick, "I can't say anything in this house, old sport" (91). Each of the men is overwhelmed by the power signified in the other's property. Tom artlessly reveals his bitter sense of inferiority by attacking what he finds most impossible to compete with in Gatsby's conspicuous worldly success: "I know I'm not very popular. I don't give big parties. I suppose you've got to make your house into a pigsty in order to have any friends—in the modern world" (99).

Tom, like Gatsby, sees a house as a medium of exchange. Gatsby represents, moreover, something about the "modern world" that Tom finds enormously threatening because it unsettles his notion of himself as a member of an empowered and privileged class whose entitlement is a heritage. When we first meet Tom he is attempting in rather simplistic fashion to explain the theories of a book he has been reading, *The Rise of the Colored Empires*, deriving from it a position that "Nordic" races need to defend themselves against displacement by inferior peoples. Gatsby, as an upstart, an intruder from outside the ranks of northeastern aristocracy, represents just the kind of intrusion and illegitimate empowerment that Tom finds repugnant and fearful. He is an old colonial in the modern world and as ludicrous in his unexamined traditionalism as Gatsby is in his high romanticism. What they share is a myth of the power of property and masculine privilege. Daisy, the object of the contest, serves mainly as pretext to the ideological battle being played out in the context of romantic farce.

Daisy returns in Gatsby's car while Tom follows with Nick and Jordan. Symbolically, she chooses Gatsby as a companion in adventure, but their destination is the home she shares with Tom and a return for her to the secure, if difficult, realities of domestic life. Gatsby's last act of devotion is to protect her chivalrously from the consequences of her own recklessness by assuming blame for the accident, though she was driving. Back at the Buchanans' house, late at night, both Gatsby and Nick linger in the dark yard, watching the theater of domestic life before them in the lighted windows of the Buchanan house. Nick tiptoes up the verandah steps and watches through an aperture in the curtains Tom and Daisy at the kitchen table earnestly engaged in discussion. What is actually going on between them is left to speculation, but a wife and husband face to face across their own kitchen table is a scene that suggests engagement, stability, relationship. There is no fantasy here. Tom deals in concretes—problems and solutions. He and Daisy need each other, flawed as they are in their respective excesses.

Gatsby, however, is sufficient unto himself, despite his grand passion. He is powerful and actual only in the private world of his own imagination. He needs Daisy as an icon, not as a woman. Nick finds him in the yard: "He put his hands in his coat pockets and turned back eagerly to his scrutiny of the house, as though my presence marred the sacredness of the vigil. So I walked away and left him standing there in the moonlight—watching over nothing" (111). This is as cynical as Nick has allowed himself to be about Gatsby's obsession. Its hollowness has been fully revealed, and for Gatsby not to acknowledge defeat makes him a fool. Gatsby's situation here, out in the dark, gazing on Tom and Daisy's house as so often before, but this time at close range, is an ironic recapitulation of the opening scene where he stands, arms outstretched toward the green light on their dock, in an act of worship. But the power of his imagination to body forth his dreams fails in battle with the hard, unromantic realities of Tom and Daisy's necessary, if disillusioned, partnership. Their house is a barrier Gatsby cannot penetrate, but, indeed, he diverts defeat by making it a shrine and attempting to restore her to the status of sacred object. Only the devotion is bought now at the price of profound denial, and what was romantic fiction becomes sordid falsehood.

Home once again in West Egg, Nick visits Gatsby in his house, to find it, like its master, reduced, diminished, and squalid with defeat:

> His house had never seemed so enormous to me as it did that night when we hunted through the great rooms for cigarettes. We pushed aside curtains that were like pavilions, and felt over innumerable feet of dark wall for electric light switches—once I tumbled with a sort of splash upon the keys of a ghostly piano. There was an inexplicable amount of dust everywhere, and the rooms

were musty, as though they hadn't been aired for many days. I found the humidor on an unfamiliar table, with two stale, dry ciga-rettes inside. Throwing open the French windows of the drawing-room, we sat smoking out into the darkness. (112)

Gatsby's house is a ruin, a hollow shell with apparently random objects floating around in it like debris after a flood. Bereft of its purpose, the house is an enormous, awkward, embarrassing incongruity. Sitting on the porch, Gatsby fills in for Nick the long story of Daisy and his house, now something like a per-sonal creation myth. He had visited her as an officer in a house more beautiful than any he had ever seen that "was as casual a thing to her as his tent out at camp was to him."

> There was a ripe mystery about it, a hint of bedrooms upstairs more beautiful and cool than other bedrooms, of gay and radiant activities taking place through its corridors, and of romances that were not musty and laid away already in lavender, but fresh and breathing and redolent of this year's shining motor-cars and of dances whose flowers were scarcely withered. . . . But he knew that he was in Daisy's house by a colossal accident. However glorious might be his future as Jay Gatsby, he was at present a penniless young man without a past, and at any moment the invisible cloak of his uniform might slip from his shoulders. (113)

He felt, thereafter, "married to her." And his long period of constructing his image and his house in pious imitation of that house he mostly imagined, for a woman he mostly imagined, was based on a bond forged in a moment of magical vision into which he had never since bothered to inquire. From this pas-sage it becomes clear why it seemed to Gatsby that the only way to win Daisy was to build a house. He had always understood her as the animating spirit of a house that was itself in some sense the object of his passion. He wanted to build a grander house than the one she had inhabited and to attract her there like a fly into a more luminous web.

After Gatsby's death, Nick meets Gatsby's father, an insouciant old midwestern farmer whose admiration for his son betrays a profound ignorance of him. The elder Gatsby pulls a picture from his wallet in the midst of their conversation: "It was a photo-graph of the house, cracked in the corners and dirty with many hands. He pointed out every detail to me eagerly. 'Look there!' and then sought admiration from my eyes. He had shown it so often that I think it was more real to him now than the house itself" (131). Like his son, the old man has sustained himself on an illusion for which reality offers no substitute—an image of an image of an image. He adds that Gatsby had, two years previously, bought him the house he lives in now. Gatsby's father was the one person besides Daisy to whom Gatsby needed to prove his worth. Typically, he chose to do so by means of a house, another Pyrrhic victory that won him gratitude and admiration but no real familial love or intimacy.

At the end of his tale, Nick grows expansive when reflecting on his own role in a drama he begins to recognize as cultural allegory. He reminisces about returning home to the Midwest from his Eastern prep school:

> I am part of that, a little solemn with the feel of those long winters, a little complacent from growing up in the Carraway house in a city where dwellings are still called through decades by a family's name. I see now that this has been a story of the West, after all—Tom and Gatsby, Daisy and Jordan and I, were all Westerners, and perhaps we possessed some deficiency in common which made us subtly unadaptable to Eastern life. (134)

Westerners here are defined as people who know themselves and are known by their families and the houses they live in—rooted and grounded by brick and wood and stone in the land they have claimed and farmed and populated with rectilinear streets and wide-verandahed homes. The assumptions that define a life like that are not transferable to this place on the edge of the urban wasteland—the stabilities do not hold; the virtues give no assurance of reward.

Nick takes one last look at Gatsby's house before leaving for good and sees that the grass on that lawn has grown as long as his own. It is already a scene of decay and desolation—fodder for legend-makers, gossipmongers, and storytellers. He sees a taxi drive past and point, and he muses, "Perhaps it was he who drove Daisy and Gatsby over to East Egg the night of the accident, and perhaps he made a story about it all his own" (136). The house has become the material of legend—not the legends of Gatsby's own fashioning but those of any curious passerby. And the grass, the line of demarcation that separated Gatsby's manicured property from Nick's, has lapsed into similar unkemptness. The house has begun its descent into the landscape.

Nick takes a moment to wander into Gatsby's yard and contemplate once more "that huge incoherent failure of a house." Then he wanders down to the shore and lies on the sand, where his perspective broadens to the cosmic:

> As the moon rose higher the inessential houses began to melt away until gradually I became aware of the old island here that flowered once for Dutch sailors' eyes—a fresh green breast of the new world. Its vanished trees, the trees that had made way for Gatsby's house, had once pandered in whispers to the last and greatest of all human dreams; for a transitory enchanted moment man must have held his breath in the presence of this continent, compelled into an aesthetic contemplation he neither understood nor desired, face to face for the last time in history with something commensurate to his capacity for wonder. (137)

That "great failure of a house" comes finally to symbolize a whole way of life, a misguided cultural quest, imitative and invasive and irreverent, imposed without discretion or discernment on a land indiscriminately appropriated and exploited. The house once again provides a point of reference from which to contemplate the cosmos and the long stretch of history whose culmination seems to have been an abandoned, pretentious, and useless building on the site of a ruined wilderness.

The narrative has come full circle. Nick is alone, as he was at the beginning, on the edge of things, in transition, uprooted, belonging nowhere in particular, and therefore in a position to assume the privileged stance of prophet. He is as prototypical a figure as Gatsby himself, like Ishmael and Huck Finn a wanderer who survives to tell the tale and who can tell it only because it is about a life he has consented not to live, choosing rather to be the only kind of prophet we credit, a "son of man" who, though the foxes have their holes and the birds their nests, has "nowhere to lay his head"—a man who will consort with "publicans and sinners" but remains pure in his detachment, mobile, unworldly, unhoused, and therefore free.

9

ABSALOM, ABSALOM!
A House Divided

In 1955 Faulkner published an article in *Harper's Magazine* entitled "On Privacy. The American Dream: What Happened to It." The article was part of an intended series of essays on American mores he planned in retaliation for repeated attempts by the press to publicize his personal life. The piece is a paean to the American dream as "a sanctuary on the earth for individual man: a condition in which he could be free not only of the old established closed-corporation hierarchies of arbitrary power which had oppressed him as a mass, but free of that mass into which the hierarchies of church and state had compressed and held him individually thralled and individually impotent."[1]

The first few pages review with similar rhetorical flamboyance the noble history of American individualism as epitomized in the hope of freedom to carve out a place in the world, make a home, and live in it in individual privacy, not as a part of the mass. He follows this sweeping manifesto with a story of several successful attempts to violate his privacy that were protected under the claim of freedom of the press, which "can postulate to itself complete immunity to violate the individualness—the individual privacy lacking which [one] cannot be an individual and lacking which individuality he is not anything at all worth the having or keeping" (68). His subsequent reflections on the misconstructions and misuses of American freedoms that threaten to turn the principles of freedom into instruments of oppression drive deep and close to the heart of the motivating vision that informs his fiction. Taste and responsibility as those humane qualities that temper the law are, he declares, all that distinguish liberty from license. He diagnoses the atrophy of these qualities as a sickness that "goes back to that moment when in place of freedom we substituted immunity for any action to any recourse, provided merely that the act be performed beneath the aegis of the empty mouthsound of freedom" (69).

These distinctions—between freedom and license and between those with taste and responsibility and those without—are constants among the many dividing lines by which we can classify the characters who populate Faulkner's Yoknapatawpha—as diverse and tragic in their blind struggles over fate and freedom as the American types from which they are drawn. The figure of Thomas Sutpen looms as large as Captain Ahab's among literary portraits of American individualism turned to misguided ends, whose exercise of freedom becomes a form of violation and ends in the destruction of a grand design.

Sutpen's story, told and retold in *Absalom, Absalom!* starts and ends in urgent tête-à-têtes between storytellers who are makers and bearers of a legend bound to trace the path of the "magnificent defeat" of a grand design, its foundations weakened by pride:[2]

> From a little after two o'clock until almost sundown of the long still hot weary dead September afternoon they sat in what Miss Coldfield still called the office because her father had called it that—a dim hot airless room with the blinds all closed and fastened for forty-three summers because when she was a girl someone had believed that light and moving air carried heat and that dark was always cooler, and which (as the sun shone fuller and fuller on that side of the house) became latticed with yellow slashes full of dust motes which Quentin thought of as being flecks of the dead old dried paint itself blown inward from the scaling blinds as wind might have blown them. (7)

On this first page of *Absalom, Absalom!* at what is for us the beginning of the story, though we are later to find that it is far from a beginning, young Quentin Compson sits captive, listening to the tale of the rise and fall of the house of Thomas Sutpen. Entrapped in the room, entrapped by the code of courtesy that keeps him there, entrapped by the tale itself, Quentin, like Miss Rosa, becomes a bearer of a legend that grows to occupy him to the point of obsession, as it has occupied her for forty-three years of her long, static, memory-ridden life.

The two characters seem at this moment suspended in time. As in a dream, the passage of actual time seems distorted. Pages, apparently hours, later Quentin observes, "It should have been later than it was; it should have been late, yet the yellow slashes of mote-palpitant sunlight were latticed no higher up the impalpable wall of gloom which separated them; the sun seemed hardly to have moved" (22). The story goes on and on, turning in on itself, as time stands still, caught with the light and the dust and the hot air in the small space of a dim hot airless room. Miss Rosa keeps the blinds closed despite the heat because of a notion someone once had and passed on to her that it is cooler that way. It is not. And herein we have our first clue to the character of Miss Rosa and to her relation to the immediate world. Quentin watches flecks of paint dancing in the light beams borne on an imaginary wind. But they are not flecks of paint, and there is no wind. And herein we have our first clue to how Quentin sees.

Miss Rosa has summoned Quentin to tell him the story of Thomas Sutpen, to pour it into him as into a receptacle, to transmit responsibility for it to him and there by rid herself of the obsession that has consumed her for four bitter decades. She has cast herself as chronicler and guardian of local legend, a sibyl waiting out her time, condemned to endless remembering and rehearsing of events that, having witnessed, she is compelled to prophesy. Sutpen's story has become her fate as, in a larger sense, it has become a local creation myth, a prototypical and paradigmatic story of the South. Entrusting this story with its mysteries and undisclosed secrets to Quentin imposes on him a burden of manifold obligations that he only begins to divine as he sits spellbound, a half-willing listener. She begins at the beginning, with the mysterious and portentous arrival of Thomas Sutpen and his entourage in Jefferson in 1833:

> A man who rode into town out of nowhere with a horse and two pistols and a herd of wild beasts that he had hunted down single-handed because he was stronger in fear than even they were in whatever heathen place he had fled from, and that French architect who looked like he had been hunted down and caught in turn by the negroes—a man who fled here and hid, concealed himself behind respectability, behind that hundred miles of land which he

took from a tribe of ignorant Indians, nobody knows how, and a house the size of a courthouse where he lived for three years without a window or door or bedstead in it and still called it Sutpen's Hundred as if it had been a king's grant in unbroken perpetuity from his great grandfather—a home, position: a wife and family which, being necessary to concealment, he accepted along with the rest of respectability as he would have accepted the necessary discomfort and even pain of the briers and thorns in a thicket if the thicket could have given him the protection he sought. (16)

In one sentence, Miss Rosa provides the "fable" that unfolds in all its convoluted complexities in the following three hundred pages: the story of the rise and fall of the house of Sutpen—a recasting of the tale of creation, the fall, and its consequences or, as many readers have recognized, a recasting of American history with its grand, theocratic designs; its tragic divisions; and its degeneration by greed, miscegenation, and violence. Indictment and judgment as well as the insight of one who knows intimately of whom she speaks are implied in her words: "strong in fear," "concealed himself behind respectability," "the protection he sought." This is a story of a usurper who has seized illicitly the inheritance of the sons and built an empire on a wrongful claim. Miss Rosa's telling begins a long project of reconstruction; she rebuilds the house of Sutpen in words of her own, taking possession of his house and land by the power of the spoken word. Like a haunted prophet crying, "Set down this, set down this," she enjoins Quentin to inscribe the story in writing and take it abroad and sell it. The long trajectory of building and destruction will then be complete: an idea bodied forth in house and formal gardens and sprawling plantation, passed from hand to hand, sold piecemeal, diminished, and finally burned, becomes a story to be written and sold for money, she suggests, that might serve to furnish Quentin's own house someday.

In the little dark room where we first see them, the old woman and the young man sitting opposite each other resemble a medium with her half-willing client, summoning a ghost from the dead. The spirit of Thomas Sutpen inhabits the story, the room, the woman. As she unravels the long tale, her little dried legs swinging beneath her chair, Quentin, listening, discerns an alien presence evoked by her monotonous recitation: "The ghost mused with shadowy docility as if it were the voice which he haunted where a more fortunate one would have had a house" (8).

Thomas Sutpen did have a house, one "torn violently" out of the wilderness, built on stolen land, by a man who "came from nowhere" and was of unknown origin and pedigree. At its most literal *Absalom, Absalom!* is the story of that house—a story of expropriation, settlement, empire-building, destruction, and dubious hope of reconstruction on questionable terms. Like Poe's house of Usher, the house, the structure at the center of this novel, is symbolically reiterated in every element of the story, indeed in the circuitous, symmetrical, and secretive design of the story itself, and reveals itself as the shape of a universe, its design a caricature of southern life, its fate the fate of a people.[3]

Each of the four narrators, Miss Rosa, Quentin, Quentin's father, and Shreve, attempts to reconstruct from fragmentary and elusive data some lost and irrecoverable vision incarnated in the house of Sutpen. Miss Rosa is driven by revenge; Quentin, by a sense of inherited obligation; Mr. Compson, by a historical and legal interest in facts; Shreve, by the fascination of the Other. Like Sutpen with his grand design, each is pursuing a vision of something that, when attained, will have the completeness and inevitability of revelation. The ultimate "narrator" is the reader, who, like them, is involved in piecing together conflicting and fragmentary stories to achieve a moment of whole sight. Like the image in a kaleidoscope, the story keeps shifting, tantalizingly redistributing its discrete elements in new and intriguing but unstable patterns of meaning. Characters, narrators, and the narrative itself are comprehensible only as functions of labyrinthine cultural, legal, familial, psychic, and linguistic structures as deceptive and illusory as Sutpen's great "shell" of a mansion, whose purpose was defeated in the very act of building. If it were a simple moral tale, the moral of Sutpen's story might be that all efforts to impose structure on chaos and conquer the wilderness ultimately fail, that the enterprise of civilization is doomed because all our endeavors to raise up our houses and lives out of the primordial mud are built on falsehood and crumble to dust in our wake. Yet even as a story of defeat, the magnificence of the design and the courage, audacity, and even presumption of the builder are portrayed in heroic terms, and the story of the house of Sutpen is a tragedy of classic dimensions.

Quentin measures Miss Rosa's bitter story of how Sutpen seized his land and built his house against the more dispassionate, or at least more sympathetic, account he has received from his father, who received it from his father, who described to him how the suspicious and apprehensive citizens of Jefferson watched the invasion and transformation of their countryside:

> As General Compson told his son, Quentin's father, while the negroes were working Sutpen never raised his voice at them, that instead he led them, caught them at the psychological instant by example, by some ascendancy of forbearance rather than by brute fear. Without dismounting (usually Sutpen did not even greet them with as much as a nod, apparently as unaware of their presence as if they had been idle shades) they would sit in a curious quiet clump as though for mutual protection and watch his mansion rise, carried plank by plank and brick by brick out of the swamp where the clay and timber waited—the bearded white man and the twenty black ones and all stark naked beneath the croaching and pervading mud. (37)

The respect in this portrayal contrasts sharply with the tone of Miss Rosa's description of the same events:

> So he and the twenty negroes worked together, plastered over with mud against the mosquitoes and . . . distinguishable from one another by his beard and eyes alone and only the architect resembling a human creature . . . working in the sun and heat of summer and the mud and ice of winter, with quiet and unflagging fury. (38)

The problem here and throughout for Quentin, and for us, is how to interpret the paradoxical unorthodoxies by which Sutpen disturbs the universe of Yoknapatawpha county and threatens the locals' sense of fundamental proprieties.

The ambiguity of Sutpen's character and the nature of his errand in the wilderness are complicated for the reader by the dissonance among the various narrators' accounts. As Quentin

conceives it, the building of Sutpen's house is at its very incep-
tion an act of violence and presumption, not unlike the satanic
will to "be as God" implied in the story of the original sin. Sutpen appears as a creature not fully human, emerging out of "no
discernible past," of dubious origins and with dubious and alien
servants to expropriate land that was neither granted nor sold
him, wreaking his will on it, building a house "apparently out of
nothing"—a repeated phrase that suggests a preternatural dimension in these events.

> Out of quiet thunderclap he would abrupt (man-horse-demon)
> upon a scene peaceful and decorous as a schoolprize water color,
> faint sulphur-reek still in hair clothes and beard, with grouped be-
> hind him his band of wild niggers like beasts half tamed to walk up-
> right like men, in attitudes wild and reposed, and manacled among
> them the French architect with his air grim, haggard, and tatter-
> ran. Immobile, bearded and hand palm-lifted the horseman sat;
> behind him the wild blacks and the captive architect huddled qui-
> etly, carrying in bloodless paradox the shovels and picks and axes of
> peaceful conquest. Then in the long unmaze Quentin seemed to
> watch them overrun suddenly the hundred square miles of tranquil
> and astonished earth and drag house and formal gardens violently
> out of the soundless Nothing and clap them down like cards upon
> a table beneath the up-palm immobile and pontific, creating the
> Sutpen's Hundred, the *Be Sutpen's Hundred* like the oldentime *Be
> Light.* (8–9)

This remarkable passage gives us Sutpen as a demon-god and
the house as a monument to the magnitude of a usurper's presumption. The "man-horse-demon" hybrid conjures a pagan
image of a centaur or other weird half-breed that straddles a
boundary between two discrete orders of being. The sulphur-
reek suggests hell; the slaves with him are alien and hybrid creatures, paradoxical, too, in their "wild repose."

Thomas, the twin, the dubious disciple, author of an apocry-
phal and rejected gospel: much can be read into the name
chosen for this elusive figure who can be reached only by speculation. And the name of Sutpen hovers close to the name of
Satan, who in his defiance disrupted the divine order to establish "death's other kingdom." Miss Rosa observes, "He wasn't
even a gentleman. He came here with a horse and two pistols

and a name which nobody ever heard before, knew for certain was his own anymore than the horse was his own or even the pistols, seeking some place to hide himself, and Yoknapatawpha County supplied him with it" (3). The fugitive who claims the land he is banished to and makes it his kingdom threatens not only the inhabitants of the land but the whole existing order. The dispossessed who takes possession is the archetypal American, guilty and triumphant in his self-proclaimed entitlement.

The figure of Sutpen, "immobile, bearded and hand palm-lifted" on his horse bears, however, a shocking similarity to the figure of God the Father in medieval paintings, static, flat, hand lifted eternally in blessing over the riotous earth. The only verb in this passage that describes Sutpen's movement is "abrupt"—an adjective pressed into service to connote action, not movement so much as the sudden apparition of a ghost moving neither from nor toward but breaking through some invisible barrier that separates orders of existence. In every respect this passage gives us Sutpen as a preternatural figure.

In a shift we come to recognize as a characteristic modulation from one plane of story to another, the narrator moves beyond Miss Rosa's actual description into Quentin's private elaboration of it: "Then in the long unamaze Quentin seemed to watch them." The figures and action become more and more archetypal and stylized as they pass from her memory to his imagination. In Quentin's version the scene broadens from portraiture to landscape, and a sudden moment in time becomes an epoch as the invaders "overrun" the "hundred square miles of tranquil and astonished earth." The scene becomes mythic and epic as Quentin "watches" Sutpen's hordes "drag house and formal gardens violently out of the soundless Nothing and clap them down like cards on a table beneath the up-palm immobile and pontific" and concludes with a final vision of Sutpen as God, creating his own order out of Nothingness by simple command. The house and formal gardens signify establishment of order in the wilderness.

The image of cards on a table, however, strikes an insidious note in this creation myth; the gesture is a gamble, the gambler a careless and violent man, the house a gesture of, what? defiance? presumption? challenge? in any case the signature of one whose claim and character are open to dispute, though his power is not. Quentin, rehearsing the story to himself, embroidering on it as he listens, reflects, "Who came out of nowhere and without warning on the land with a band of strange niggers and built a plantation—(Tore violently a plantation, Miss Rosa Coldfield says)—tore violently" (9). Pausing over the verb in this way underscores the paradox of building that is also destroying, amounting to a rape of nature, surprised and violated like a woman forced to suffer the attacks and bear the child of a stranger. The house, in this light, becomes something monstrous and unnatural, not an extension of the natural setting but a scar on it.

As the final sentence implies, the erection of this house represents an order wrenched out of proper context. The men who build it are dark, captive men, portrayed as beings of a lower order, except for the curious French architect whose ambivalent presence and eventual escape suggest Sutpen's limitations. Sutpen needs the aid of this foreign and civilized intelligence to carry out his plan. He cannot himself civilize this wilderness because he is himself of the wilderness, so he attempts to turn the forces of civilization to his own primitive purposes.

The figure of the French architect adds a comic element to what might otherwise be a solemn reiteration of the Edenic myth. The incidental characterization of Sutpen's mansion in *Requiem for a Nun* as "something like a wing of Versailles glimpsed in a Lilliput's Gothic nightmare" suggests, William Ruzicka points out, "the presence of French Baroque details in the stylistic vocabulary of the house, provides a reference for conjecturing overall dimensions, and recommends certain images of grandeur and scale."[4] The allusion furthermore calls up images of baroque garden-palaces in which a "world" is divided in half and the sovereign is situated at the center; this allusion therefore highlights the magnitude of Sutpen's pretensions and caricatures them in the pathetic figure of the architect.

The ambiguous nature of Sutpen's achievement is represented most vividly in the comic contrast between him and his captive French architect, a poignant Chaplinesque figure in whose person the remnants of civilized gentility are diminished and pathetic, dwarfed in the shadow of Sutpen's primal, mud-covered body, yet whose education and expertise are necessary to the completion of his scheme. Quentin's father describes the architect as

> a small, alertly resigned man with a grim, harried Latin face, in a
> frock coat and a flowered waistcoat and a hat which would have created no furore on a Paris boulevard, all of which he was to wear
> constantly for the next two years—the somberly theatric clothing
> and the expression of fatalistic and amazed determination—while
> his white client and the negro crew which he was to advise though
> not direct went stark naked save for a coating of dried mud. This
> was the French architect. Years later the town learned that he had
> come all the way from Martinique on Sutpen's bare promise and
> lived for two years on venison cooked over a campfire, in an unfloored tent made of the wagon hood, before he so much as saw any
> color or shape of pay. (35)

A later addendum to this portrait details the architect's confused role in Sutpen's project:

> They worked from sunup to sundown while . . . the architect in his
> formal coat and his Paris hat and his expression of grim and embittered amazement lurked about the environs of the scene with his
> air something between a casual and bitterly disinterested spectator
> and a condemned and conscientious ghost—amazement, General
> Compson said, not at the others and what they were doing so much
> as at himself, at the inexplicable and incredible fact of his own
> presence. (39)

But Quentin measures this parodic characterization against the evidence of something more substantial, a contribution more essential and significant than these comic vignettes seem to imply:

> He was a good architect; Quentin knew the house, twelve miles
> from Jefferson, in its grove of cedar and oak, seventy-five years after it was finished. And not only an architect, as General Compson
> said, but an artist since only an artist could have borne those two
> years in order to build a house which he doubtless not only expected but firmly intended never to see again. . . . That only an
> artist could have borne Sutpen's ruthlessness and hurry and still
> manage to curb the dream of grim and castlelike magnificence at

which Sutpen obviously aimed, since the place as Sutpen planned it would have been almost as large as Jefferson itself at the time; that the little grim harried foreigner had singlehanded given battle to and vanquished Sutpen's fierce and overweening vanity or desire for magnificence or for vindication or whatever it was . . . and so created of Sutpen's very defeat the victory which, in conquering, Sutpen himself would have failed to gain. (39)

In his tattered finery, huddled on a wagon among a throng of "half-naked savages," the architect embodies a number of paradoxes: he represents the cumulative knowledge and culture of European civilization that the settlers of this American wilderness both scorn and depend on. Though he provides the requisite expertise for Sutpen to carry out his plan, the architect's authority and status remain unacknowledged, and in fact he becomes an object of contempt to the very man who depends on him to establish a kingdom in the wilderness. It is the architect who exercises the curbing force by which Sutpen would destroy himself, who tempers and refines and controls. He is the force of civilization: seasoned and tolerant and steeped in compromise. He is the hidden intelligence behind the mythic silhouette of Thomas Sutpen, the conquering hero and claimant to this fated land. As such the architect's presence belies the mythic notion of Sutpen as a demigod who emerged out of nothing and nowhere. The Frenchman brings Sutpen down to size, gives him human dimensions, and, as Sutpen's complement and counterpart, throws into relief Sutpen's limitations and excesses.

At one point Miss Rosa describes the architect as a man "who looked like he had been hunted down and caught in turn by the negroes" (16). Like Europeans terrified of "going native" among primitive peoples, the high culture the architect represents cannot survive the conditions of the American wilderness. His final escape, abandoning the savage master and his wild band to their own devices, signals the end of the period of design and construction and the beginning of the long saga of degeneration and destruction. Quentin describes that escape in provocative terms when he recreates the scene for Shreve:

and [Sutpen] got his dogs and his wild niggers out and hunted the architect down and made him take earth in a cave under the river bank two days later. That was in the second summer, when they had finished all the brick and had the foundations laid and most of the big timbers cut and trimmed, and one day the architect couldn't stand it anymore or he was afraid he would starve or that the wild niggers (and maybe Colonel Sutpen too) would run out of grub and eat him or maybe he got homesick or maybe he just had to go. . . . So I reckon the niggers never did know what the architect was there for, supposed to do or had done or could do or was, so maybe they thought Sutpen had sent him, told him to go away and drown himself, go away and die, or maybe just go away. (219)

The speculations progressively trivialize the architect's purpose and fate, reducing him to pathetic insignificance. When the architect leaves, Sutpen in fact celebrates by declaring a holiday from work on the house: "And Grandfather . . . brought some champagne and some of the others brought whiskey and they began to gather out there a little after sundown, at Sutpen's house that didn't even have walls yet, that wasn't anything yet but some lines of bricks into the ground but that was all right because they didn't go to bed anyhow" (219). The bacchanalian scene not only signals a temporary cessation of labor, however; the departure of the architect, leaving Sutpen to his own inscrutable and idiosyncratic devices, represents the end of the period of controlled and methodical building. In a kind of inverted banishment from Eden, this departure is the beginning of a new and ominous chapter in the Sutpen saga. The nearly finished house remains in a curiously unfinished state, as if the subtleties of civilizing detail are beyond Sutpen's ken, and the master lives in the house in inappropriate primitive simplicity:

So it was finished then, down to the last plank and brick and wooden pin which they could make themselves. Unpainted and unfurnished, without a pane of glass or a doorknob or hinge in it, twelve miles from town and almost that far from any neighbor, it stood for three years more surrounded by its formal gardens and promenades, its slave quarters and stables and smokehouses; wild turkey ranged within a mile of the house and deer came light and colored like smoke and left delicate prints in the formal beds where there would be no flowers for four years yet. (39)

Miss Rosa's judgment is that Sutpen had "builded even better in evil than he could have hoped" (30). His master plan, his grand design, his scheme to claim and populate his square of earth, was indisputably magnificent but for a fatal hubris running through every aspect of it like a disease in the blood. She remembers the period of desperate completion when the seeds of Sutpen's own destruction began to flower almost before his house was a habitation: "Because the town now believed that it knew him. For two years it had watched him as with that grim and unflagging fury he had erected that shell of a house and laid out his fields, then for three years he had remained completely static, as if he were run by electricity and someone had come along and removed, dismantled the wiring or the dynamo" (42).

At the end of those three years of primitive solitude, Sutpen went after a wife, as part of his plan, in a similarly calculated and inhuman way: "He had apparently marked down Miss Coldfield's father with the same cold and ruthless deliberation with which he had probably marked down the French architect" (42). But at this stage no one could name the evil he was wreaking. On the face of things, for a man to build a house and court a wife might seem eminently natural and right. Yet for Sutpen to engage in these rituals invested them with a sinister significance no one at the time was able to explain because they proceeded out of a state of "ontological poverty"—an incapacity to sense or assign meaning or to care for and enjoy the things he possessed. Building and creating served essentially egotistical, imperialistic ends.[5]

No one could specify what crime he had committed, perhaps because the scope of the crime was beyond the law itself. As Quentin's father reflects, "Heretofore, until that Sunday when he came to church, if he had misused or injured anybody, it was only old Ikkemotubbe, from whom he got his land—a matter between his conscience and Uncle Sam and God" (44), a matter of justice beyond the jurisdiction of existing laws and perhaps even outside the scope of contemporary conscience. But that Sunday, when he came to church to court his bride, the town began to watch his deceptively conventional enactment of the rituals of domestication with a deepening sense of foreboding: "They just waited while reports and rumors came back to town of how he and his now somewhat tamed negroes had installed the windows and doors and the spits and pots in the kitchen and the crystal chandeliers in the parlors and the furniture and the curtains and the rugs" (44). To Quentin, Miss Rosa recounts this scene of preparation as the laying of a trap for Ellen, her sister, the innocent bride Sutpen was to drive to distraction and death by his monomaniacal plans, in which she figured only as a functionary, a necessary piece of the furniture of his house, and a means to the end of establishing a legitimate lineage.

Miss Rosa returns to the theme of building in evil as she reflects on Sutpen's considerable but dubious achievement: "But then, so had vanity conceived that house and, built it in a strange place and with little else but his bare hands and further handicapped by the chance and probability of meddling interference arising out of the disapprobation of all communities of men toward any situation which they do not understand" (51). Sutpen's tragic flaw, by her account, is his incomprehensibility, his mystery, his keeping of some secret that, unacknowledged, festers into contagion. The house and the family are doomed insofar as they are perceived as extensions of his awful and sinister presence, and so, indeed, they become for the people of Jefferson appendages proliferating on the body of a monster.

In every respect Sutpen's house is a "house divided against itself," conceived and wrought in ambivalence and laid on a foundation of violence proportioned by guilt. The land was stolen from the Indians through brute power. The house was built on an economy of slave labor; the balance of power between master and slaves was a delicate one, the line between them thin. The legitimate heirs were shadowed by mulatto siblings of uncertain status with complex claims on the place and its proprietors.[6] It was a place where whites came in the front door and blacks in the back, yet where whites and blacks led an oddly parallel existence, the lines of demarcation between them increasing in import in inverse relation to the gradual obliteration of conventional barriers: they conducted "the same parties; the identical music from identical instruments, crude fiddles and guitars, now in the big house with candles and silk dresses and champagne now in dirt-floored cabins with smoking pine knots and calico and water sweetened with molasses" (98). The women Sutpen allowed into his house threatened him like Delilahs, emasculating presences that he tolerated only by various strategies of resistance and defiance, allowing them no exercise of power that might threaten his own. Race, class, and gender were all lines of division that defined the conflicting forces operative in this house from the beginning. Sutpen's miscegenation blurred and weakened the lines of family structure and claims of inheritance.

Lines of color in this story are contiguous with lines of legitimacy; miscegenation therefore appears to undermine legitimate lines of inheritance. What is white diminishes and dies or becomes detached, removed from the land and the inheritance. What is black survives: primitive, without social or political status, but triumphant in survival and repossession. The house of Sutpen, bigamist, miscegenist, intruder, imperialist, whose energies are divided between his public and his hidden life, ends like the house of Usher, which finally opens along the crack that extends to its foundation, crumbles, and sinks to oblivion, returned to the earth as if in final punishment for satanic pride.

The multiple rifts within the house of Sutpen come to a head in the story of the two sons, Henry Sutpen and Charles Bon, who in their fashion reiterate the Old Testament stories of two sons divided by laws of inheritance or legitimacy: Cain and Abel, Isaac and Ishmael, Jacob and Esau. Here, most importantly, the house of Sutpen breeds within itself the seeds of its own destruction. Henry is described as a "grim humorless yokel out of a granite heritage where even the houses, let alone clothing and conduct, are built in the image of a jealous and sadistic Jehovah" (109)—a product of a harsh southern Puritanism whose inherent contradictions create a moral universe that is a field of intolerable tension, driving those who live by its dictates to a state of radical uncertainty coupled with fanatical compliance. Charles, Henry's urbane, worldly counterpart, is free of the puritanical obsession and guilt that weaken the legitimate line of Sutpen.[7]

The bond of intimacy that grows between Henry and Charles is proportionate to their fated opposition. They build a "rapport not like the conventional delusion of that between twins but rather such as might exist between two people who, regardless of sex or age or heritage of race or tongue, had been marooned at birth on a desert island: the island here Sutpen's Hundred; the solitude, the shadow of that father with whom not only the town but their mother's family as well had merely assumed armistice rather than accepting and assimilating" (99). Henry finally rides away with his half brother and "abjure[s] his home and birthright" (106) to go to New Orleans, Bon's world, where, Quentin's father reflects, "I can see him corrupting Henry gradually into the purlieus of elegance, with no foreword, no warning, the postulation of come after the fact, exposing Henry slowly to the surface aspect—the architecture a little curious, a little femininely flamboyant, and therefore to Henry opulent, sensuous, sinful" (110). And after that initiation and after Bon's revelation of his identity and his incestuous intentions toward Judith (his half-sister), one brother is compelled to destroy the other, as Miss Rosa dramatically recalls the denouement of the tragedy: "I saw Henry repudiate his home and birthright and then return and practically fling the bloody corpse of his sister's sweetheart at the hem of her wedding gown" (18). It is finally the "illegitimate" line that accedes to the inheritance, just as did the Gentiles, who, according to Christian theology, acceded to the inheritance promised to the chosen people, who had lost the vitality of faith and passion required to sustain it.

Both sons leave home and repudiate their father. Both return to meet their fate: Charles, to be killed; Henry, to wither into living death and eventually to perish at the hands of Clytemnestra, his mulatto half-sister. Reentering the house, each is doomed and ensnared in its secrets. When Bon returns home, Sutpen realizes that the moment of his return portends the destruction of the household. The potential of an incestuous alliance with Judith, the necessity as it seems to him of keeping the secret of Bon's identity that would prevent that alliance, the high stakes of either keeping or revealing the secret, all come to him as he invites Bon into his house for the first time as an adult. Sutpen is aware of the fatal import of his act even as he opens the door:

> He stood there at his own door just as he had imagined, planned, designed, and sure enough and after fifty years the forlorn nameless and homeless lost child came to knock at it and no monkeydressed nigger anywhere under the sun to come to the door and order the child away; and Father said that even then, even though he knew that Bon and Judith had never laid eyes on one another, he must have felt and heard the design—house position, posterity and all—come down like it had been built out of smoke, making no sound, creating no rush of displaced air and not even leaving any debris. And he not calling it retribution, no sins of the father come home to roost; not even calling it bad luck, but just a mistake. . . . So he invited Bon into the house. (267–268)

The fatal moment that begins the long decline and fragmentation of his household comes by Sutpen's own invitation when he allows Charles, knowing the consequences, to return to the house a fully empowered and conscious man, a son become a rival and a threat, an alien whom Sutpen can neither deny nor acknowledge, the bastard offspring who has become the father's sign of contradiction. The history of the house of Sutpen, like any genealogical history, can be told only as a series of divisions. In a house built as a personal empire, such divisions can mean only vitiation of power. In the house's original integrity it was, Miss Rosa supposes, a double of its maker, whose ethos has survived the house's many changes of hands and character. It was, she recalls,

> as though his presence alone compelled that house to accept and retain human life; as though houses actually possess a sentience, a personality and character acquired, not so much from the people who breathe or have breathed in them inherent in the wood and brick or begotten upon the wood and brick by the man or men who conceived and built them—in this house an incontrovertible

affirmation for emptiness, desertion; an insurmountable resistance to occupancy save when sanctioned and protected by the ruthless and the strong. (85)

Sutpen lived there at first in inviolate solitude—a kind of fierce virginity and original innocence from which every change represented descent. In that state, his house had a kind of integrity that was a direct and symbolic manifestation of the man himself, roughly magnificent, cold, unfeminized, monolithic. Therein the house was "true," if truth can be attributed to the incarnations of self that are bodied forth in man's creations. Indeed, Mr. Compson describes the Thoreauvian simplicity of Sutpen's first years in the great house as something oddly akin to virtue:

> For the next three years he led what must have been to them [husbands and bachelors in town] a perfect existence. He lived out there, eight miles from any neighbor, in masculine solitude in what might be called the half-acre gunroom of a baronial splendor. He lived in the Spartan shell of the largest edifice in the county, not excepting the courthouse itself, whose threshold no woman had so much as seen, without any feminized softness of window-pane or door or mattress; where there was not only no woman to object if he should elect to have his dogs in to sleep on the pallet bed with him. (39–40)

> And he lived out there for almost five years before he had speaking acquaintance with any white woman in the county, just as he had no furniture in his house and for the same reason: he had at the time nothing to exchange for them. (62)

Sutpen's marriage to Ellen Coldfield represents the first "violation" of this virginal integrity. The marriage is a concession to worldly norms, a compromise with the dictates of civilized life that here, as in so many American novels, is represented as an ambiguous attainment. Miss Rosa recalls the figure of Sutpen years after his marriage as having become portly:

> The flesh came upon him suddenly, as though what the negroes ... called the fine figure of a man had reached and held its peak after the foundations had given away and something between the shape of him that people knew and the uncompromising skeleton

of what he actually was had gone fluid and, earthbound, had been snubbed up and restrained, balloonlike, unstable and lifeless, by the envelope which it had betrayed. (80–81)

With marriage come the world and the flesh. The "uncompromising skeleton," like the blueprint of the grand design, is condemned to be fleshed out in imperfect and degenerating form—incorruptible idea made flesh and, like the house he built, subject to moth, dust, and corruption. The process of corruption begins in giving away something of his power to a wife, who, however unassuming, serves as a necessary evil who will provide him heirs and continuity even as she undermines the purity of his solitude. Ellen represents the beginning of loss— an old and common misogynistic notion deeply embedded in the fiercely patriarchal ethic Sutpen represents. Marriage already creates a house divided against itself, making of home a locus of the ancient sexual battles that, once entered into, leave no one unscarred.

When by this uneasy alliance Sutpen's house becomes Ellen's as well, his control over his domestic domain is compromised. This submissive woman breaks his hegemony and subverts his fanatical purposes. Yet for Ellen the house is a prison. Her predicament is classic: his dream, his house, the walls he erected around nothing, constitute the boundaries of her own existence. The house becomes the stage on which she must act out the drama of her own usurped destiny. His house is her fate, and she is in a real sense more wedded to the house than to the man. Miss Rosa, recalling bitterly Ellen's fatal consent to this captivity, is not completely baffled by this complicity. It has about it the ironic inevitability of the typical: "It may have been," Miss Rosa reflects, "for the sake of that big house and the position and state which the women realized long before the men did that he not only aimed at but was going to attain" (52).

Miss Rosa knows what it cost her sister to enter that house as Sutpen's bride. She calls it "that house for which she had exchanged pride and peace both" (15). Despite children and prosperity, Miss Rosa describes the house and Ellen's life in it as barren. "I saw her almost a recluse, watching those two doomed children growing up whom she was helpless to save. I saw the price she had paid for that house and that pride" (18). Miss Rosa views her sister as having vanished into "an edifice like Bluebeard's" and there become "a mask looking back with passive and hopeless grief on the irrevocable world, held there not in durance but in a kind of jeering suspension by a man who had entered hers and her family's life before she was born with the abruptness of a tornado, done irrevocable and incalculable damage, and gone on" (60). The images of natural disaster Miss Rosa appropriates to describe Sutpen's actions and effects suggest again her ironic sense of the inevitability of the tragedy she retails. Bitter as she is, her business is not to blame Sutpen but simply to reveal him as a source of impersonal and tragic evil in whose given nature it is to destroy.

Ellen's children, and later her sickness and death, score the house with further lines of division. The fatal relation of her two children to Sutpen's illegitimate half-breed son and daughter place them, too, on the stage of an antique tragedy, doomed to be the innocent agents of division and destruction. Judith and Henry are passive where Clytie and Charles are active, their whole fate a function of circumstance rather than choice. Already in their generation the vitality of Negro blood gains a kind of moral ascendancy. In geometric progression the house of Sutpen is divided into two and then four conflicting interests and claims.

For awhile, as her mother lies sick and dying, the house is Judith's. She runs it with Clytie's, and eventually with Miss Rosa's, help, gradually transforming it into a nunnery of sorts.

> And Judith. She lived alone now. Perhaps she had lived alone ever since that Christmas day last year and then year before last. . . . She lived in anything but solitude what with Ellen in bed in the shuttered room, requiring the unremitting attention of a child while she waited with that amazed and passive uncomprehension to die; and she (Judith) and Clytie making and keeping a kitchen garden of sorts to keep them alive; and Wash Jones, living in the abandoned and rotting fishing camp in the river bottom which Sutpen had built after the first woman—Ellen—entered his house and the last deer and bear hunter went out of it where he now permitted Wash and his daughter and infant granddaughter to live. (125)

Miss Rosa joins the household for a time on Ellen's death, entering into its barren life but not its secrets. She recalls being kept from a particular room in the house by Judith, then mistress in her mother's stead.

> "Don't you go up there, Rosa." That was how she [Judith] said it: that quiet, that still, and again it was as though it had not been she who spoke but the house itself that said the words—the house which he had built, which some suppuration of himself had created about him as the sweat of his body might have produced some (even if invisible) cocoon-like and complementary shell in which Ellen had had to live and die a stranger, in which Henry and Judith would have to be victims and prisoners, or die. (138–139)

Miss Rosa goes on to give an account of her time in Sutpen's house:

> I stayed there and waited for Thomas Sutpen to come home. . . . I waited for him exactly as Judith and Clytie waited for him: because now he was all we had, all that gave us any reason for continuing to exist, to eat food and sleep and wake and rise again: knowing that he would need us, knowing as we did (who knew him) that he would begin at once to salvage what was left of Sutpen's Hundred and restore it. . . . I who had kept my father's house and he alive for almost four years, Judith who had done the same out here, and Clytie who could cut a cord of wood or run a furrow better . . . than Jones himself. (154)

The women live in inviolate celibacy as Sutpen did in his first days as proprietor of the house. In his absence it has become a peculiar nunnery, inhabited by three women each of whom has her own claim on his house and on him. Miss Rosa identifies Sutpen's house with Sutpen's person. They seem dependent but are actually utterly independent of the man whose spirit so holds them spellbound. "So we waited for him," she goes on.

> "We led the busy eventless lives of three nuns in a barren and poverty-stricken convent: the walls we had were safe, impervious enough, even if it did not matter to the walls whether we ate or not. . . . We kept the house, what part of it we lived in, used; we kept the room which Thomas Sutpen would return to—not that one which he left, a husband, but the one to which he should return a sonless widower, barren of that posterity which he doubtless must have wanted who had gone to the trouble and expense of getting children and housing them among imported furniture beneath crystal chandeliers—just as we kept Henry's room, as Judith and Clytie kept it that is. (155)

Finally, she recalls the years of Sutpen's absence and his return:

> Not absent from the place, the arbitrary square of earth which he had named Sutpen's hundred: not that at all. He was absent only from the room, and that because he had to be elsewhere, a part of him encompassing each ruined field and fallen fence and crumbling wall of cabin or cotton house or crib; himself diffused and in solution held by that electric furious immobile urgency and awareness of short time. . . . We were right about what he would intend to do: that he would not even pause for breath before undertaking to restore his house and plantation as near as possible to what it had been. (160)

The plantation has diminished to a tiny fragment of its original dimensions. On the day he proposed, he knew "definitely and at last exactly how much of his hundred square miles he would be able to save and keep and call his own on the day when he would have to die, that no matter what happened to him now, he would at least retain the shell of Sutpen's Hundred even though a better name for it would now be Sutpen's One" (168).

Eventually the house becomes Clytie's house, the illegitimate mulatto daughter, on all counts a dubious claimant to her father's inheritance. By legitimate laws of inheritance the house should have gone to Sutpen's son, but legitimate and illegitimate sons cancel one another out, and the house falls to the half-breed, illegitimate daughter—a situation that in every respect, by the laws of Sutpen's world, is a regrettable devolution. Like so many domestic slaves, Clytie is an intimate of the house from the time she is born, and she survives to destroy it. It is, in fact, more her house than Ellen's. The gradual passing of the house into feminine control parallels the gradual fading of the "white" power in the household into "black." The house is finally burned down by Sutpen's illegitimate half-black daughter in a suicidal act of insubordination, subversion, and triumph. It is the inevitable fate of such a house, the only resolution possible, fatalistically proving the proverb that a house divided against itself cannot stand.

Now, at the time of this telling, Judith, Clytie, Henry, Charles, Ellen, and Thomas Sutpen are dead. What remains of the house of Sutpen resides in the memory of Miss Rosa Coldfield. Miss Rosa, as Faulkner might put it, "negatives" each of the other main characters. She is the sister who never became the wife, the maiden aunt who raised children she never bore, the perpetual guest in a house that is never her home. She is at various points a counterpart to Ellen, believing she will be Sutpen's wife but never becoming one in fact; a counterpart to Judith in filial duty, teaching and supporting her in the business of taking over the household on her mother's death, a contemporary, though belonging to Ellen's generation; a counterpart to Clytie in her similarly ambiguous position as intimate in a household to which she can exercise no legal or moral claim; and, most importantly, a counterpart to Sutpen himself. Miss Rosa is the only character in the story who is Sutpen's equal. Her lust for revenge is equal in its fanaticism to his lust for possession.

Characteristically, Faulkner doubles Sutpen's saga of displacement and degeneration in the story of Miss Rosa Coldfield's house. Miss Rosa's house, once her father's, and the house in which her father took his own life, is a counterpart to the house of Thomas Sutpen in a number of ways—a place as small and penurious as his is grand and flagrant in its magnificence, characterized by a Puritanism as small-minded and squalid as Sutpen's fanatical heterodoxy is unabashedly voracious. "So for the first sixteen years of her life she lived in that grim tight little house with the father whom she hated without knowing it—that queer silent man whose only companion and friend seems to have been his conscience and the only thing he cared about his reputation for probity among his fellow men" (60).

Like Sutpen's house, Coldfield's is a place of secrets to which Miss Rosa becomes privy by subversion and indirection:

Miss Rosa's childhood was passed, that aged and ancient and timeless absence of youth which consisted of a Cassandra-like listening beyond closed doors, of lurking in dim halls filled with that presbyterian effluvium of lugubriuous and vindictive anticipation, while she waited for the infancy and childhood with which nature had confounded and betrayed her to overtake the disapprobation regarding any and every thing which could penetrate the walls of that house through the agency of any man, particularly her father, which the aunt seems to have invested her with at birth along with the swaddling clothes. (60–61)

Like Ellen, Miss Rosa "kept her father's house . . . until the night the aunt climbed out the window and vanished" (64), quietly waiting for the inarticulate battle between her and her father to terminate in the death of one or the other. Coldfield's house becomes a place, like Sutpen's house, of sickness and suicide in which survival is a matter of endurance of a kind that hardens the soul in bitterness. She inhabits it not as a home but as a tomb, sustained by memory and desire for revenge like the shades in hell, keeping watch over her father's last days as Clytie later does Henry's, harboring his secrets and her own and waiting for them to apotheosize in the moment of death.

> [Coldfield] had closed his store permanently and was at home all day now. He and Miss Rosa lived in the back of the house, with the front door locked and the front shutters closed and fastened. He spent the day, the neighbors said, behind one of the slightly opened blinds with the big family Bible in which his and his sister's birth and his marriage and Ellen's birth and marriage and the birth of his two grandchildren and of Miss Rosa, and his wife's death . . . had been duly entered in his neat clerk's hand. . . . That night he mounted to the attic with his hammer and his handful of nails and nailed the door behind him and threw the hammer out the window. (82)

When Quentin finds Miss Rosa, the "little grim house" has regressed to a state of "impregnable solitude" (88). Miss Rosa's final revenge on the man whose rise and fall determined the trajectory of her own tragic existence is to have the last word. She comes into her inheritance after the death of Sutpen and the destruction of his house by assuming his story as her property. By right of inheritance, by right, we might say, of simple endurance, it has become hers. She, who views herself as the "rightful" wife of Thomas Sutpen, the barren woman whose line is stopped, takes her inheritance by subversion: she is in possession of Sutpen's story, and as storyteller, the whole "house of Sutpen" belongs to her. There is no one now with any vested interest to prevent the story from being told as she wishes to tell it.

She has nothing left to her but this story, and her right to it is something she establishes insistently. She is an eyewitness to the events she wants Quentin to set down; like the women of the Gospels passing an oral tradition to the four writers, she presses Quentin into service as witness to her testimony. "I lived for two years under the same roof with him" (19), she reminds Quentin. And yet she has been excluded from the deepest secrets of the Sutpen household, the secrets borne by blood, and so her claim to privilege is ambiguous. This is her bitterness—to have been condemned to the role of excluded intimate. As a child, she recalls, "though Ellen was my own sister and Henry and Judith my own nephew and niece, I was not even to go out there save when papa or my aunt was with me and. . . . I was not to play with Henry and Judith at all except in the house" (21).

Rosa believes, however, that precisely as a function of her marginal position in relation to this family, she has a privileged perspective on the events she relates. She claims for herself an oracular status, recalling how aware she was of things the members of Sutpen's own household seemed oblivious to:

> "Even when I saw it for the first time that I could remember I seemed already to know how it was going to look just as I seemed to know how Ellen and Judith and Henry would look before I saw them for the time which I always remember as being the first. . . . I only knew, as soon as papa and I crossed the threshold, that he was not there: as though with some almost omniscient conviction, knowing that he did not need to stay and observe his triumph." (26)

In another memory she is a child, "standing motionless beside that door as though trying to make myself blend with the dark wood and become invisible, like a chameleon, listening to the living spirit, presence of that house, since some of Ellen's life and breath had now gone into it as well as his, breathing away in a long neutral sound of victory and despair, of triumph and terror, too" (27).

For Miss Rosa reality has diminished as memory has enlarged. Everything about Miss Rosa represents diminishment. When Quentin answers Miss Rosa's summons, he observes that her house seems "smaller than its actual size . . . with an air, a quality of grim endurance as though like her it had been created to fit into and complement a world in all ways a little smaller than the one in which it found itself" (10). Miss Rosa's person answers the same description as he finds her sitting in the dark, suffocating, tomblike hallway, full of "slow heat-laden time," very still—a "small figure in black which did not even rustle, the wan triangle of lace at wrists and throat" (10–11).

In this house of the dead, as if in concession to its pull toward death, Miss Rosa gives away her inheritance to Quentin, like Esau's "mess of pottage," as a commodity to be sold, to be converted by the alchemy of the marketplace into furniture for his wife's house, should he have one: "So maybe you will enter the literary profession as so many Southern gentlemen and gentlewomen too are doing now and maybe some day you will remember this and write about it. You will be married then I expect and perhaps your wife will want a new gown or a new chair for the house and you can write this and submit it to the magazines" (9–10).

This is her final revenge: to give away Sutpen's story, in so many ways representing the "secrets of the South" and its shame, to be put before an anonymous public in a degraded form, a commodity to sell in the marketplace. She shows Quentin a way to build his house on the ruins of Sutpen's. But with the story she gives him a charge: to find out the mystery of the house. "There's something in that house," she tells him. "Something living in it. Hidden in it. It has been out there for four years, living hidden in that house" (172). To take possession of his inheritance, Quentin must find out what that something is.

Quentin himself is neither detached nor objective about the story he hears. It comes to him, as it has to Miss Rosa, as a destiny. It was Quentin's great-grandfather, General Compson, who had been Thomas Sutpen's friend and foil, his confidant and supporter in the early days when he came like a wild man out of the wilderness bewildering the town and leaving behind him a trail of suspicion and apprehension. The general was the Starbuck to Sutpen's Ahab, friend and mate to a man of whose purposes he remained somehow innocent. "It was General Compson," Quentin learns, "who offered to lend Sutpen the money to finish and furnish his house, and was refused" (41).

Quentin, more than any other candidate for this epic task of reconstruction, is in a position to revise and qualify Miss Rosa's weighted tale. Seeming more definitive in its rational account of the man and his endeavor, the sympathetic portrait of Sutpen transmitted through Quentin's judicious father, a lawyer, whose father knew Sutpen, and who has seen the documents and read the accounts written in local record, throws Miss Rosa's intensely dramatic, highly charged version of the story into the realm of fiction and myth-making. It is left to Quentin to measure the epistemological validity and the worth of the variant versions of the story. As Quentin absorbs Sutpen's story, filtering it through his own prismatic consciousness, it takes on new mythic significance; what has been for Miss Rosa defining family lore becomes on the larger canvas of Quentin's cosmic imagination a southern epic with cultural implications that extend far beyond his own fatalistic sense of predestined inculpation. What she describes he understands prescriptively; he recognizes the pattern of Sutpen's rise and fall, his building and destroying, as a prophetic formula.

Quentin is called, like one of the reluctant prophets, to receive and bear a message to and about his people that his own people will not heed and that outsiders will not comprehend. Sutpen's story is given to him for several reasons: because as a descendant of Sutpen's friend and confidant, General Compson, Quentin has a right to the story; because Quentin is a literary man, someone who can tell the story and shape it and who knows enough to tell it faithfully but also enough to recognize the consequences of truth-telling; because he will translate the story into new terms for a new generation; because he is mobile. He will take the story and escape with it. Borne into the North, published in magazines, as Miss Rosa hopes, the story of Sutpen will grow to the dimensions of myth, and Sutpen will be flung on the world like the image of Jesus, to be distorted and battered and betrayed in a thousand ways by just such readers as the good-hearted Shreve, who are fascinated but do not understand.

Quentin is neither builder nor destroyer but is a demoralized "savior" whose psyche and body provide a vacant space in which all of history and myth are reiterated, shrunken to the confines of a single tortured mind condemned to "forge," like Stephen Dedalus, "the conscience of his race." Quentin is a "second Adam," whose inheritance is legend, story, myth. His childhood was full of names and stories, which were his inheritance: "His very body was an empty hall echoing with sonorous defeated names; he was not a being, an entity, he was a commonwealth. He was a barracks filled with stubborn back-looking ghosts still recovering, even forty-three years afterward, from the fever which had cured the disease" (12).

Quentin's historical position as inheritor prevents him from becoming a builder. Rather than a plantation in the wilderness, he constructs a house of fiction made of the remnants gathered from his father and grandfather and Miss Rosa. His is the burden of reconstruction, the desolate task of rebuilding out of the heap of broken images that lay scattered abroad in the South after the Civil War. Like a reluctant prophet, he does not want the task, and yet it seems there is no one else. So he takes the burden of the story and begins the patchwork process of fitting pieces together, listening, gathering material, shaping it, honing it, giving it new words, substituting his words for Miss Rosa's or hers for his, matching her words to his father's and grandfather's, comparing accounts, claiming none of them, his only authority consisting of the profound and oppressive sense of his destiny lying in the task. The first step in assuming this burden is to witness the final destruction of Sutpen's house. With Miss Rosa Quentin makes his fatal pilgrimage for this purpose:

> The drive seemed interminable. He knew the place. He had walked from the gate to the house as a child, a boy, when distances seem really long (so that to the man grown the long crowded mile of his boyhood becomes less than the throw of a stone) yet now it seemed to him that the house would never come in sight: so that presently he found himself repeating her words: "If we can just get to the house, get inside the house," telling himself, recovering himself in that same breath: "I am not afraid. I just don't want to be here. I just don't want to know about whatever it is she keeps hidden in it." But they reached it at last. It loomed, bulked, square and enormous, with jagged half-toppled chimneys, its roofline sagging a little; for an instant as they moved, hurried toward it Quentin saw completely through it a ragged segment of sky with three hot stars

in it as if the house were of one dimension, painted on a canvas curtain in which there was a tear; now, almost beneath it, the dead furnace-breath of air in which they moved seemed to reek in slow and protracted violence with a smell of desolation and decay as if the wood of which it was built were flesh. (366)

Quentin enters the house, finds it dark, slips along a dark passage to open the door for Miss Rosa. Clytie, who is already there, strikes a match. She has "a bunch of enormous old-fashioned iron keys, as if she had known all the time that this hour must come and that it could not be resisted" (368–369). When the fire starts he watches with ironic detachment: "It would be a good three minutes before it could reach the house, the monstrous tinder-dry rotten shell seeping smoke through the warped cracks in the weather-boarding as if it were made of gauze wire and filled with roaring and beyond which somewhere something lurked which bellowed, something human since the bellowing was in human speech, even though the reason for it would not have seemed to be" (375). Even as the house is utterly demolished, its mystery speaks from the ruins and remains to haunt the witnesses.

In a dorm room at Harvard, far from home and South, and because there is no one else to tell, Quentin transmits this legend, betraying the secrets of the tribe, to a "Gentile"—a stranger, a northerner, a Canadian, his roommate, Shreve. The extent of Quentin's personal investment in the story becomes, to his horror, more and more evident as he attempts to reconstruct it for Shreve. In the face of a truly disinterested, albeit fascinated, audience, Quentin's own psychic investment in Sutpen's story as personal and cultural myth and his inability to explain the way it has shaped his consciousness or to rid himself of his compulsive sense of involvement in it drive him finally to desperate silence, defeat before the inexplicable, which closes over him and his tribal secrets like water, drowning the words with which he flails to keep afloat.

Shreve cannot possibly grasp the story's meaning and in receiving and retelling it distorts and falsifies it. As Quentin lapses into silence, Shreve takes over the task of narration, pursuing with the excitement of an archaeologist the fragments that will provide clues to the mysteries of this history. His reconstructions are bound to be false. In the hands of this stranger the house of Sutpen will be entirely remodeled. Shreve invests the story with his own uninvested enthusiasm and with an ironic note of comedy. He characterizes Aunt Rosa as "this old dame that grew up in a household like an overpopulated mausoleum" (176) and Sutpen as "this Faustus who appeared suddenly one Sunday with two pistols and twenty subsidiary demons and skuldugged a hundred miles of land out of a poor ignorant Indian and built the biggest house on it you ever saw and went away with six wagons and came back with the crystal tapestries and the Wedgwood chairs to furnish it and nobody knew if he had robbed another steamboat or had just dug up a little more of the old loot" (178).

In telling the story to Shreve, Quentin completes the turn of a large tragic cycle; just as Sutpen brought foreign influence onto American soil, brought his West Indian natives and his French architect, and forged a life and a home out of borrowed and stolen elements, so Quentin is paying the penance for that heritage of invasion, miscegenation, and betrayal by betraying in his turn. He is giving away the story of the South to an outsider, a northerner, who will neither appreciate nor comprehend it with anything but a detached, or even prurient, fascination with what seem to him peculiarities, aberrations, inexplicable allegiances, and passionate enmities clung to from a past that keeps invading and taking over the present. Once again Quentin reviews for Shreve the story whose telling has assumed such shifting shapes, built and rebuilt and condemned to be rebuilt again. Like Thoreau, Quentin has appropriated the ramshackle remains of another man's building to shave and fit and fashion into something habitable for himself. But his experiment does not work. Shreve takes over the story as Quentin lapses into inarticulate silence. He cannot tell the story here, in this place, to this uncomprehending listener. And so he is left with silence, his house of fiction collapsed about his ears, and we, like Shreve, are left to overtake the reconstruction.

Like Quentin, the author has, as it were, given away his inheritance to an anonymous audience. The secrets of the South are written and sold, plowed back into the economy, sold in the marketplace, perhaps to buy a chair for the house. The word become flesh becomes words again in an old tragic cycle of building and destruction. To tell is to create and simultaneously to destroy. We assume our place after Shreve in the lineage of illegitimate inheritors. Throughout the novel we are being invited to participate in the business of reconstruction. We are given the materials of a story, as Quentin is, filtered through multiple minds, shaped by the pressures of several distinct relationships in which some events are suppressed and others exaggerated. And out of these "broken images" we seek to fashion a whole that will incorporate all the pieces left as detritus from the past.

For us, as for these explorers of the past, two accounts surface that, juxtaposed, reveal the magnitude of what has been achieved and destroyed. One is a written recollection by General Compson: "You have seen the rotting shell of the house with its sagging portico and scaling walls, its sagging blinds and plank-shuttered windows, set in the middle of the domain which had reverted to the state and had been bought and sold and bought and sold again and again and again" (213). The other record is Sutpen's own account of his magnificent defeat—as explained to General Compson—which is full of a poignancy and an immediacy that serve as a ground and measure for the tales Sutpen's story has spawned: "You see, I had a design in my mind. Whether it was a good or a bad design is beside the point; the question is, where did I make the mistake in it, what did I do or misdo in it, whom or what injure by it to the extent which this would indicate. I had a design. To accomplish it I should require money, a house, a plantation, slaves, a family—incidentally of course, a wife. I set out to acquire these, asking no favor of any man" (263).

The story, like the house, is a structure erected around a vacancy—a betrayal of history, a confession, and a defense. It is a place to enter into with curiosity and distrust because ghosts lurk there. It is a structure of deferred meaning, virtual meaning, almostness. The structure is never closed; the house is never quite finished. In it there are chambers within chambers—stories within stories. Faulkner's narrative is a place we enter; like Miss Rosa's "office," it is an enclosed place, dim, hot, airless, where things circulate but do not escape. Like Quentin's mind, it is a repository for layers on layers of history, and history has become story, has become legend, has become myth, has become destiny, has become mirror for the individual psyche that seeks to comprehend the whole and so encompass it or inhabit it. We are involved in spite of ourselves in the business of building and habitation.

How do we become comfortable in such an imaginative space—with many mansions superimposed on one another? We start by learning to live in suspension, to wait and listen as Miss Rosa does at many half-closed doors, to gather the mysteries that remain unexplained. The inscape of the sentence teaches us how to do this waiting and listening. Faulkner's sentences are edifices that, like the whole narrative, have many chambers and doors that open into unexpected places. In a single sentence we can shift planes or frames of reference several times. A sentence is a structure within which we must maneuver through passageways to find the exit. We infer at the beginning what the end will be but must keep correcting our assumptions as we move through it, hitting walls as in a maze, and having to retreat and seek another passageway. If in the end the resolution is not found, we are propelled on to the next sentence to begin the puzzle again. The following sentence, for instance, about the French architect, leads us through a maze, slowing us at every turn, teaching us to be alert to the relations expressed, ambiguous, complex, and multiplying in their complexity as the wave crests:

> Not, General Compson said, the hardship to sense and the outrage to sensibility of the two years' sojourn, but Sutpen: that only an artist could have borne Sutpen's ruthlessness and hurry and still manage to curb the dream of grim and castlelike magnificence at which Sutpen obviously aimed, since the place as Sutpen planned it would have been almost as large as Jefferson itself at the time; that the little grim harried foreigner had singlehanded given battle to and vanquished Sutpen's fierce and overweening vanity or desire for magnificence or for vindication or whatever it was (even General

Compson did not know yet) and so created of Sutpen's very defeat
the victory which, in conquering, Sutpen himself would have failed
to gain. (38–39)

This passage pulls several grammatical tricks: it confuses
antecedents, thereby forcing the reader to review earlier information to see how things are joined; it uses parallel constructions that seem to promise closure but fail to close and veer instead into a new clause by means of a colon or semicolon; it
deconstructs its main claim—that the architect has achieved
some kind of victory—by refusing to name what has been vanquished, substituting instead several possibilities, leaving it at
"whatever it was," emphasizing the dissolution of the object
with the parenthetical "(even General Compson did not know
yet)," reminding us that our main source of information is unreliable; and, finally, it ends by leading us into a syntactical maze
that demands a doubling back and reassessment of the possibilities of logical meaning. Each element opens a door on an array
of possibilities; going through one door, we find ourselves led
back to the place we thought we had left. We are kept in a realm
of uncertainty, as in a hall of mirrors with the repeated "or,"
leaving possibilities open, the whole thing setting history in the
conditional tense. What is called for is insight, vision, even inspiration. We cannot be passive listeners—in listening we, too,
become interpreters and authors, assuming responsibility for
what we hear. We are therefore challenged to be those who
"have ears to hear," to see past the dazzling surface to the grand
design, to be, ourselves, readers of blueprints and architects
willing to restore, reconstruct, and renovate the crumbling
structures of the past.

If *Absalom, Absalom!* is a moral tale, it is of the kind told in the
parable of the man who built his house on sand. In that spirit its
epigraph might be drawn, appropriately enough, from the Old
Testament, itself so full of stories of building and destruction:
"Except the Lord build the house, they labour in vain that build
it" (Psalm 127:1).

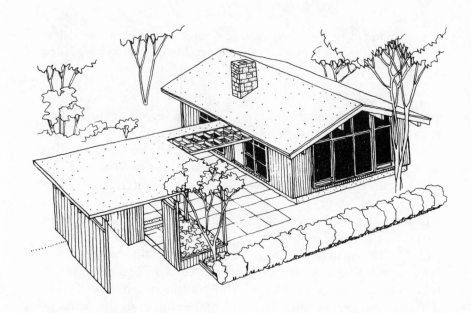

10

POSTWAR SUBURBAN FICTION
American Dream as Nightmare

The exodus from cities to suburbs after World War II began one of the most significant demographic shifts in American history and was a reaffirmation of the American dream in concrete, commercial terms. The ideal of the freestanding single-family dwelling with lawn, carport, and a bedroom for everyone came, by virtue of ingenious community planning, energetic marketing, and the GI bill, within range for a larger number of families than ever before. Experimental communities such as Kaiserville in the West and Levittown in the East carried in their blueprints not only a new set of practical possibilities but a set of values keyed to a new kind of consumerism. Homes were affordable and available. Things to fill those homes were multiplying at a staggering rate. Sears catalogs, Tupperware parties, and Chevrolets became visible indices of comfort, stability, and success.

American writers recognized and responded to these changes in a burgeoning body of writing that could be defined as a subgenre—a "literature of the suburbs." A whole generation of writers who witnessed the dramatic transition from Depression to war to domestic complacency began almost as soon as the wave of consumer prosperity crested to document with deepening irony the insidious effects of suburban life. Updike, Irving, French, and many others have contributed during the past three decades to raising Americans' collective consciousness about the issues of class, gender, and moral perspective generated by suburbanization. The short stories discussed in the following pages have been selected as representative of the progressive appropriation of "suburbia" as a literary trope among American writers. In these stories, as in many others, suburbs appear as places where living space has become confining, isolating, and fragmenting and where apparent order and even gentility effectively conceal a darker side of life and reduce romantic ambitions to confused and surreptitious longings.

Georgia McKinley's "The Crime" is a story about the dislocation, disruption, and fear caused by the encroachment of a suburban development on a small rural village in the deep South.[1] The main characters, two white redneck hunters and their black servant, watch from their hunting lodge in the local hills as a new shopping center and rows of stucco houses invade the landscape like floodwater spreading. Not only their sport is threatened; so are their sense of dominion and the exploitive separate peace they have been able to strike with the blacks in their town by virtue of a laissez-faire local government. Suburbia, these three men realize, means theaters where both blacks and whites are admitted together. It means neighborhoods where they live next door to one another. It means the encroachment of "civilization" on a primitive order that has become institutionalized not only for these whites, who have retained power, but for this black man, whose subjugation is the only way of life he knows. This story makes the equal and opposite dangers of blind conservatism and thoughtless progressivism disturbingly apparent.

Some Saturdays, we are told as the story opens, the two white men do not go hunting but sit on the front porch of their little lodge, drinking bourbon and staring out at "the rows of houses which had crept out from the city to menace their land" (137). On this particular Saturday the hunters have picked up their servant, Leroy, from his daughter's "flimsy little house" at the edge of town to avail themselves of his services for the day. As the white men drive along the highway toward their lodge, they comment on the changed countryside: "Look at that, look at that. . . . They're putting up another damned motel here. . . . We used to shoot quail there, you remember that?" They gaze in growing distress out the car window at "a whole city of bright little houses, row upon row, acre upon acre, off to the edge of sight" where "flat land had lain so long in black plowed fields or empty prairie grasslands," and one of them mutters bitterly, "Now isn't that a *damnable* shame." Leroy, too, is looking out the window, and his puzzled unconcern contrasts sharply with the white men's outrage. For seven years he has witnessed their ritual anger on rides to and from the hunting lodge as they have passed the ubiquitous land development sites, with their alien workers "coming in with bulldozers and piles of bright new wood, and leaving behind them unfinished boxes" (142). Having little to lose, Leroy does not share their fear and suspicion over the changing landscape, though he does come to realize that the good hunting in the hills will not last for long.

McKinley portrays the suburbs as a large organism in movement and the human characters sitting immobile, watching it move. Time is compressed; a seven-year process is observed as though through time-lapse photography. The landscape changes but the characters do not, and the landscape seems to be a kind of monster that is moving in to devour them. These suburbs are recognizable as the kind immortalized by Malvina Reynolds's song, of the same era, about "little boxes." McKinley's rhetorical repetitions reiterate the repetitive, predictable design of the rectilinear tracts. Moreover, the "rows and rows" of houses evoke comparison with the furrows of a planted field. The houses appear to be some alien crop, like inorganic weeds, that has invaded the "black plowed fields."

The dimensions of the housing development are left deliberately, threateningly vague. It stretches "off to the edge of sight," a phrase that hints at uncontrolled spreading with nothing to stop its imperialistic progress. That spread is described in terms that suggest violence and wounding. "The little box houses had almost reached them now," she writes, "and already the County had cut a highway straight across their land, slicing open the red clay earth with machines and leaving it healed with a wide grey macadam scar" (143). The anonymous, alien force behind the machines is never named; as vague as the boundaries of the development is the plan or intelligence behind it, which seems arbitrary and hostile and inevitable. Nowhere is there any indication that any of the characters, black or white, contemplates any kind of response to the expansion of the suburbs other than passive hostility or, in Leroy's case, mildly distressed curiosity.

Mr. Underwood, one of the two white men, while gazing out toward the new shopping center ironically reminds Leroy that there are "lots of colored moving into that area" and then reflects bitterly, "They'll meet. Have to come a street with new white houses on one side and new colored houses on the other." And, he continues, "the first thing you know it'll be possible, it'll be *legal* for some black son of a bitch to move in next door to any of us." At this point Leroy deliberately begins not to hear the conversation. Instead, he drifts off into comforting fantasies and leaves the white men "jabbering." He finds a place to sit in the yard away from the other two and withdraws into himself:

> Slowly, helplessly he dropped his eyes from the hills, down down, until they rested upon a small circle of ground at his feet and found there many comfortable and familiar things: scalloped brown leaves and tiny acorns from the scrub oak trees, shining stalks of dry grass, some wing feathers of a mallard. . . . He knew that if you sat still in the direct sun, even in winter, you could pull its heat straight through your skin until you had a pool of warmth inside you. (146)

This steady diminishment of perspective to the immediate circle around and then within Leroy's body becomes a lyrical moment that encapsulates the action of the entire story: the shrinking of the boundaries of an old way of life, the necessity of withdrawal into oneself in the face of social forces beyond one's power to combat or even to contemplate. Leroy, who has learned survival through passivity over many years of practice, poses a complex foil to the two men who now find themselves in an analogous position of helplessness and are outraged. All three sense the change.

The many analogies between Leroy's position as indulged victim and that of the two white men can hardly be missed: they, too, belong to a class of people whose wants are presumably being provided for by impersonal, nameless powers beyond their control—housing, convenient shopping, cleanliness, order, predictability. The needs that are not being met are harder to name and are therefore suppressed or ignored. And the two men's adaptations to change will inevitably be as ineffectual as Leroy's: they can engage in impotent gestures of defiance or comfort themselves with nostalgic memories and fictions that will provide them that small place in the sun into which they can withdraw and be warmed as the land around them disappears.

W. D. Weatherill's "The Man Who Loved Levittown" traces the obliteration of rural landscape from a different perspective— that of the enthusiastic buyer of one of the new tract homes that supplanted acres of potato farms on Long Island after the war.[2] Out of the army and eager to begin a new life with his wife away from his parental home, Tommy DiMaria ventures out across the Brooklyn Bridge to hunt for a job as an airplane mechanic and, stopping in a local cafe, finds himself in the midst of a microeconomic crisis: "Farmers inside look me over like I'm the tax man come to collect. Bitter. Talking about how they were being run off their places by these new housing developments you saw advertised in the paper, which made me mad because here I am a young guy just trying to get started, what were we supposed to do . . . live on East Thirteenth Street the rest of our lives?" (1).

Curious, he drives farther out of town to investigate. "Sure enough, here's this farmhouse all boarded up. Out in front is an ancient Chevy piled to the gunwales with old spring beds, pots and pans. Dust Bowl, Okies, *Grapes of Wrath* . . . just like that" (1). A bit further on, he sees the skeletons that have driven the farmers off their land: half-built houses with "baby grass" and posts waiting for street signs standing expectantly on each corner. As he watches, a truck of workers stops in front of one of the structures, and a crew leaps out, installs bathroom plumbing in it, and moves on in fifteen minutes to the next. He comes on "a guy in overalls planting sticks in little brown patches stamped out of the grass" (3), asks what he would have to pay for "one of these babies," and finds that he is talking with Bill Levitt himself, who magnanimously takes the eighty-three dollars Tommy has with him as a down payment on a seven-thousand-dollar home. Thus begins the story of the house of DiMaria in Levittown.

There follows a brief chronicle of twenty years of occupation, settlement, renovation, and organization of this model American suburb. Carrying three jobs between them to pay the mortgage, spending weekends enhancing their small estate with new porch, shrubbery, and a neighborhood swimming pool, the DiMarias find themselves happily surrounded with similar and like-minded families. Tommy shares tools and Saturdays with his fellow veterans, now fathers, who start the local Little League and attend the local PTA. From a much later vantage point he looks back on those years of building with unabashed nostalgia and pride: "I'll never forget those years. The fifties. The early sixties. We were all going the same direction. . . . Thanks to Big Bill Levitt we all had a chance. You talk about dreams. Hell, we had ours. We had ours like nobody before or since ever had theirs. SEVEN THOUSAND BUCKS! ONE HUNDRED DOLLARS DOWN! We were cowboys out there. We were the pioneers" (4).

This heroic reconstruction of the early years of Levittown as an American utopia precedes a long descent into a tale of American tragedy. The dream has lasted twenty years—long enough to raise one generation of children and trees, long enough to remodel bedrooms and install covered patios, knock out a few walls, and build a homogeneous, congenial, and fairly complacent little community that shares yards and expertise and a small conspiracy to filch free electricity from the power company by rigging the meters.

Now, as Tommy puts it, the end begins to come. With a few stock characters from the 1960s the writer sketches the outlines of a demographic shift that brings into the town not just a new generation but a new ethos. Into the house next door, which the first "defector" from Tommy's generation of neighbors has vacated to move to Florida, move a couple of young aliens: a sandaled, beaded, braless, and brash woman with a husband comic in his worldly ignorance (who thinks Levittown is an Indian name). Into the next house, sold by a neighbor for six times what he paid, moves a preoccupied, aggressive "sheepherder," as Tommy christens him, who threatens to shoot Tommy's dog if he wanders onto the lawn. Tommy's efforts to create community meet with repeated rebuffs. He shares almost nothing with these people. At first he is philosophical about the situation and regards them only with regretful condescension:

> You have to wonder about them to begin with. Here they are starting off where we finished, everything took us so long to get they have right away. They're sad more than anything . . . sadder than the old-timers moving south. Shopping centers, that's it. If it's not in a mall they don't know nothing. And talk about dreams, they don't have any. A new stereo? A new Datsun? Call those dreams? Those aren't dreams, those are pacifiers. Popsicles. . . .What will the

sheepherders be able to say they did when they get to be our age? . . . Evaded the draft. Bought a Cougar. Jogged. (7)

But Tommy is fighting the tide. One by one his old neighbors join the exodus to Florida, and he finds himself outnumbered not only by unfamiliar faces that range from cool to hostile but also by invading forces of real estate brokers pressuring him to sell out to househunters willing to pay inflated prices and tax assessors whose reevaluation of his property consumes much of what he has saved. His children move out, his wife dies, his dog is killed in what appears to be an intentional "accident," and, as a final blow, the power company catches up with his longstanding gimmick and charges him years of back payment for stolen electricity. Tommy's final act of defiance is to prevent the house he has held onto with such fierce pride of ownership from falling into the hands of profiteering philistines: he drags a can of gasoline in from the garage and wanders from room to room, soaking the accumulated possessions of half a lifetime, planning one last event for the neighbors, who can "see what fifty-five thousand dollars, thirty-two years, looks like going up in smoke." Then, he thinks, he will head out, first to his sisters, and then maybe south, though not, he declares emphatically, to Florida.

Tommy's anguish and resentment at the passing of a way of life are presented in this story with a delicately balanced mixture of irony and pity. It is left to the reader to decide which side to take in a struggle to maintain a dream whose failure is inevitable. And the unanswered question lingers with the image of the little rows of "boxes"—is it in the nature of the planned and packaged community to produce the kind of consumerism that leads to the community's diminishment into an atomized, anomalous collection of self-preoccupied people who buy homes for their resale value, fence off their lawns, and carry shields of protectiveness and suspicion? The dream, it seems, was also an illusion—of stability, insular contentment, and a growing collection of material comforts that were supposed to add up to a kind of earned peace for the returned warrior and innocence regained in the mutual protections of the nuclear family. A reader of the generation after almost has to regard the dream itself with a certain dubiousness, if not irony, and perhaps to wonder if its disintegration may not leave room for a vision more variegated and more malleable, shaped to the complex contours of a culture in which "home" can and does and perhaps should have a thousand faces.

The theme of diminishment and nostalgia for a nobler, freer past is replayed in a different key in John Cheever's "The Country Husband," a story about the burial of primitive vitality under the genteel rituals of suburban life in the Northeast.[3] Here the protagonist, Francis Weed, finds himself struggling to maintain vital contact with the part of himself that feels and acts authentically, even primitively. In a state of alienation brought on by a brush with death, he begins to penetrate the polished surfaces of suburban life and to intuit what powerful mythic forces are contained explosively not only within himself but behind all the placid housefronts along his quiet street. Suddenly suburbia is a dangerous place waiting to explode from the pressure of its own repressions.

Francis, who has just been evacuated from a plane that came near crash landing, returns home from his brush with death to find dinner nearly ready, his wife preoccupied, his children quarreling, and no one capable of hearing or understanding the enormity of what he has just been through. His wife, Julia, is an immaculate housekeeper, which we gather from an extended description of a living area in which "nothing had not been burnished." "It was not the kind of household where, after prying open a stuck cigarette box, you would find an old shirt button and a tarnished nickel. The hearth was swept, the roses on the piano were reflected in the polish of the broad top, and there was an album of Schubert waltzes on the rack" (247–248). All this order contrasts markedly with the absence of tranquillity among the family members. To escape the dinner table bickering, Francis retreats to the back garden for "a cigarette and some air." There he hears the familiar sounds of neighbors' voices; sees the neighborhood menace, a dog named Jupiter who steals meat from people's barbecues, leaping a hedge; and listens to doors slamming and the hum of lawn mowers. Jupiter is one of the free-roaming creatures in this neighborhood of carefully separated yards and little squares of privacy.

In the course of the story the smooth surfaces of Francis's life of routine and fixed customs begin to crack. He starts to experience an upsurging of the unconscious, to endow ordinary events with mythic significance, and to resist the civilizing restraints that filter out the greater portion of what takes place in his mind and heart. He suddenly looks at the baby-sitter and is touched to his core by her beauty, which evokes a passion in him he would not have believed himself capable of. He recognizes a new French maid at a neighbor's party as a woman he had seen publicly stripped and shaved in a small town in France during the war as punishment for living with a German soldier, but even as her identity dawns on him he realizes there is no one to whom he can confide it without violating all the proprieties by which his neighbors regulate their carefully controlled existence, where the shocking, the grotesque, the obscene, bear no mention. He finds himself suddenly so irritated by one of the loquacious "leading women" of the community that he insults her to her face and then confronts his wife's wrath when his inexplicable rudeness finds its way back to her through the quick and efficient local grapevine.

As the story progresses, what seems to impel Francis to his uncharacteristic improprieties is a realization he is hard put to articulate: that the forms of life in Shady Hill are insufficient to the magnitude and variegation of the inner life, that most of what is worth feeling and saying cannot be acknowledged there, that life is a series of artificially perpetuated rituals that have long since lost their meaning.

Francis eventually consults a psychiatrist when he himself begins to be alarmed by his own behavior. The prescribed therapy is woodwork, and when we last see Francis he is hard at work in his cellar building a coffee table. As evening wears on, he hears all the familiar neighborhood sounds. Then night falls, and in a final line we are given a glimpse of Francis's dreamlike state: "Then it is dark; it is a night where kings in golden suits ride elephants over the mountains" (274). Like the protagonists in the other stories, Francis ends in acquiescence to the demands and constrictions of the way of life imposed on him by an ethic that seems to have evolved with the Dutch colonial houses and department store furniture. The notion of the "suburban way of life" is clearly under attack in this story, though Cheever seems to concede that these are "good people" who are legitimately engaged in the pursuit of happiness as they understand it; they are in their blindness and shallowness perhaps no more blind and shallow than the fickle human race is wont to be. The question of to what extent the random communities formed as suburbs contribute to those things that destroy the soul is definitely raised but left to the reader to judge.

The themes of loss, disruption, and institutionalized hypocrisies are offset in each of these stories by recognition of the complexities of the changes described. None of these stories is sentimental—indeed, the sentimentalities of the protagonists in each are exposed as just as much a sham as the false values motivating those who threaten their pieties. All the stories are both ironic and ambivalent in presenting the spread of suburbs, rectilinear streets, shopping malls, and chrome and glass kitchens as an outgrowth of a complex of needs and values that are not all bad. In the tradition of the jeremiads that characterize our literary tradition, these stories are warnings but not condemnations. As a culture still firmly grounded in our Puritan foundations, we are uncomfortable with our own hard-won comforts. Moreover, our romantic legacy makes us wary of possessions and practices that separate us from nature; we tend in many ways to harbor the same distrust of "civilization" that drove Thoreau out to Walden Pond and caused Huck Finn to "light out for the territory." What each of these writers does, like many others of their generation, is to reassert the continuity of the pervasive social and metaphysical concerns that have most distinctively characterized our native tradition, bound as it has been to a history of settlement and conquest whose morally ambiguous victories have left each generation uneasily contemplating the cost of its own achievements.

11

HOUSEKEEPING AND BELOVED
When Women Come Home

Marilynne Robinson's *Housekeeping* and Toni Morrison's *Beloved* may seem at first glance to have little in common other than the slightly deteriorated houses in which they are both set.[1] The first is the story of a young woman from an isolated, white, middle-class Idaho mountain community of the 1950s who is summoned back to her family home to care for it and her two orphaned nieces. She finds a home too much to care for. One of a number of recent "bag lady" heroines in American fiction and drama, Sylvie prefers riding the rails and living under the sky to the domestic duties that bind her to a material world fast filling with used newspapers and empty tin cans. The "stuff" of daily existence assumes a ludicrous absurdity as she tries to cope with what seem to her pointless rituals of housekeeping, failing to understand what they have to do with real life. The second is the story of three black women—a freed slave, Baby Suggs, her daughter-in-law, Sethe, and her granddaughter, Denver—who live in a clapboard house in Ohio near the river they crossed to freedom. The house is haunted by the spirit of another granddaughter, Beloved, killed by her mother to keep her out of the hands of white men who might do her harm. Each of the women has her own peace to make with the past, with the free black community among whom they are constructing a new life in the ambiguous time of "reconstruction," and with the ghost who haunts them.

Though each novel can and should be read in relation to a distinct tradition whose recurrent themes have much to do with race, class, and region and with the shifting terms of feminist vision in the 1980s, I propose here to consider them under the rubric of house and home as ideas in relation to which women in every generation and in every situation have had to "work out their salvation" and define their identities. One important difference between the issue of domestic life in these stories and in those of Chopin, Gilman, and Wharton is the absence of men as rule-givers and overseers of hearth and home. The actuality of women living without men is acknowledged here and addressed as a situation well within the range of the normal, though a long suppressed fact of American life unaccounted for in our mythology, which so liberally depicts the romantic adventures of men without women.

The houses in both novels are female places, housing three generations of women. The women in the middle generation—Sylvie in *Housekeeping* and Sethe in *Beloved*—are struggling to find a balance between continuity and change, between healing the wounds of their own past and finding a way with few resources and little guidance to raise the daughters in their care. Both Sylvie and Sethe remember pasts full of death—killing, suicide, accident—and both work through the particular kinds of craziness these memories have visited on them toward some version of life that will allow them freedom from the burden of a grisly past that is now part of a family mythology in which they are implicated as heirs. Their "craziness" sets them apart from other women: both their houses are conspicuously isolated, not only by fences but by an atmosphere of difference and an attitude of indifference, from the communities that surround them and are stigmatized, taboo, objects of curiosity and apprehension to the neighbors. To both, visiting ladies from the community, representing the forces of propriety and solidarity, come to bear gifts, spy, and gossip.

In both novels home is a place where women come to terms with themselves and their own choices and the choices of their female elders, which have come down to them as a destiny that they will not claim unchallenged because they cannot. The issues of each new generation are not those of their mothers; the women who had to spend their lives working for the freedom to own and keep a house or pioneering in hostile territory to establish a home have left those homes as a legacy to their daughters and granddaughters, who, inheriting them, experience a different set of challenges as a result of ambiguous privilege.

The granddaughters, growing up in these "haunted" houses, have their own separate peace to make with a past from which

they are even further removed and whose tragedies they understand only in the fragmentary way a person comes to understand family lore and history. In the paradoxical way in which
growing up so often involves a reversal of generational roles,
the young women in each novel come into their inheritance
in the moment they assume responsibility for their own lives
and in doing so either outgrow or become caretakers of their
guardians/mothers. In *Housekeeping* the two possible responses
to Sylvie's final rejection of domestic life as female destiny are
played out in the choices her two nieces make. Ruth, the older,
ultimately joins Sylvie in burning the house and running away,
and they become a pair of female refugees, like Huck and Jim,
from a civilization whose proprieties and prejudices make no
sense to them. Lucille, the younger, like Sethe's Denver, leaves
Sylvie and Ruth in their disheveled and disintegrating household to make a place for herself in the community and find a
home among people she comes to recognize as her people.
Denver's role is more redemptive than Lucille's; in a time when
Sethe has succumbed to the mental distress her haunted house
of memories has heaped on her, Denver forges a connection between home and community, finds employment among white
people and a strong network of mutual support among the
blacks from which her mother had cut off contact, and becomes
a force of renewal and normality in her household.

Both novels have important wilderness scenes—moments of
revelation take place in clearings out beyond the edges of town
that become sacred spaces where an escape from domestic life
into magical or spiritual time is possible. Like the forest scenes
in *The Scarlet Letter*, where Hester's erotic and visionary potential momentarily comes alive and transforms her, these flights
into the wilderness are portrayed in both stories as moments of
grounding, renewals of contact with primary sources of spirituality and vitality—moments when contact with things invisible
and too subtle to penetrate the walls of houses restores the energy, vision, and sense of purpose that give the women the
strength they need. Sylvie habitually retreats from the house
when domestic life overwhelms her, sometimes simply to the
backyard, sometimes to a secret place to which she finally takes
Ruth to experience with her the magic of the lake, the woods,

and a ramshackle, deserted hovel buried in those woods, which serves as a vehicle for Sylvie's fantasies of escape and transcendence. The trip is an initiation ceremony at which a tacit pact is sealed between the two—an implicit conspiracy of renegades who from then on begin their gradual retreat from the civilities of home and town life. For Baby Suggs, the clearing is the site of prophetic visions and visitations of power and holiness. People follow her there and are healed. She preaches to them and becomes an instrument of grace, binding them to one another in an effusion of love and ecstasy. Months after Baby Suggs' death, Sethe goes to the clearing to remember and pray and seek the grace that seems to have departed from her house and her heart; the spirit of Baby Suggs visits her there, and the light touch of her ghostly fingers are enough to "lift her [Sethe's] spirits to the place where she could take the next step" (95). The renewing power of the wilderness, nature as the temple of God and habitation of spirits, an old American theme, is replayed here with peculiar significance in relation to the lives of women to whom the land has never belonged except as a vehicle of secret fantasies of freedom and a place of periodic escape from the duties of domestic life.

In light of these striking similarities, the differences between the two novels may become more significant as the meanings of house and home for black and white women in their respective historical situations unfold. For Sylvie, as for her two elderly aunts, the house is an inherited burden; the privilege of ownership, an unwelcome obligation; and the American dream, an unsettling pastiche of childhood memories, disillusionments, and possessions that weigh like ball and chain on feet that long for the freedom to wander. For Baby Suggs and Sethe, the house is a refuge, an achievement, and a gift entrusted to their stewardship, something they own, who have never known the privilege of ownership, and to which they bring a special expertise in "housekeeping," having long kept others' houses, and in hospitality, having developed a talent for the kind of sharing that wrings power and celebration out of repression and deprivation. In *Housekeeping* the inheritor longs to shed the burden of her heritage and wander like Ishmael, unconstrained by the burdens of legitimacy. The house is her antagonist. In *Beloved* a slave woman become heir and home owner emerges for the first time into a position of legitimate entitlement and social empowerment, assuming a place in the local economy, keeping a house, making it a home, welcoming into it a man, starting a life in freedom and responsibility. It is revealing to compare how these two domestic dramas unfold on their different stages and how they respectively recast some very old questions about female destiny.

In Sylvie, Robinson has put a new twist on the well-established American tradition of the nomadic hero, the lone wanderer, the refugee from a degenerate civilization, the image of innocence regained. Sylvie is happiest riding the rails and sleeping on park benches. Long out of contact with her family, she defected not out of ill-will but out of the need of the chosen to follow a road less traveled, an innocent response to an ironically monastic vocation in a setting of Protestant capitalism turned ritualized consumerism wholly out of sympathy with the ideal of the solitary ascetic. She marches to Thoreau's "different drumbeat," but the consequences of her difference are complicated manyfold because she is a woman; eccentricities that make a man the object of curiosity and even ridicule make a woman the object of suspicion and scandal.

Sylvie's childhood home is in the tiny mountain town of Fingerbone, of which Ruth, her niece and the narrator of the story, observes, "Fingerbone was never an impressive town. It was chastened by an outsized landscape and extravagant weather, and chastened again by an awareness that the whole of human history had occurred elsewhere" (62). The town was "shallow-rooted"; it was plagued with yearly floods and had succumbed once to fire. Sylvie's father had come to this scene of dogged defiance of nature's discouragements, drawn to its harsh magnificence after a childhood in a Midwest sod house, a "mere mound, no more a human stronghold than a grave" (3), and had built a home for his family. Like many pioneer dwellings, its construction is crude, the work of a determined man who knew "nothing whatever of carpentry," but it serves its proud purpose and stands as a monument to self-sufficiency. Ruth remembers that "its fenestration was random" and that "its corners were out of square" but that its builder "had had the good judgment to set it on a hill," from which perch of safety its inhabitants could, like Noah and his family, watch their neighbors struggle with the yearly floods (74). There is something essentially comic in these struggles; the myths of American know-how and the self-reliance of hardy pioneers are gently mocked in Ruth's depiction of the consequences of the ineptitude and maladaptive habits that subjected the settlers of this mountain town to repeated misunderstandings of nature in unfamiliar guises. The settlers built their houses

> of planks nailed to a frame vertically, and strips of wood perhaps two inches wide nailed on at each seam to close the chinks. If the house began to lean, the chinking sprang loose and the pine knots popped out and as often as not the windowpanes fell and the door could only be opened with increasing effort, until finally it could not be closed. I imagine that this kind of building was a habit acquired in a milder climate. I do not know why it was persisted in, for it turned people out of house with a frequency to startle even Fingerbone. (156)

Homesteading in this place was a tenuous accomplishment. Not only did nature threaten continually to overwhelm efforts at domestication; it was a place that seemed to spawn transients in its frontier tolerance for a shifting population, whose "shanties and lean-tos under the bridge and along the shore" defined the margins between town and wilderness. Recalling her childhood fascination with these hoboes fashioning their makeshift shelters, Ruth reflects, "The sorrow is that every soul is put out of house. Fingerbone lived always among the dispossessed" (179). To be a possessor in their midst was a constant reminder of the achievements of survival and settlement—achievements that belonged to the grandparents' generation. With his death in a bizarre railroad accident that becomes a mainstay of local legend, and later his wife's, the house so proudly erected on its unyielding mountainside begins slowly to fall into disrepair. The floods occasionally fill the basement or lick at the porch and floorboards, though being on a hill, the house is not as ravaged by the rising lake as are those houses nearer the shore.

The grandmother's role in settlement was one of pushing the roots down further into the hard soil, consolidating the gains, and ensuring the future of the house to which she had come as a pioneer bride. She lived the life of a good wife in Fingerbone, her religion a version of some commonsense notion of hard work and domestic tranquillity, and cherished a vision of life as "a road down which one traveled, an easy enough road through a broad country, and that one's destination was there from the very beginning, a measured distance away, standing in the ordinary light like some plain house where one went in and was greeted by respectable people and was shown to a room where everything one had ever lost or put aside was gathered together, waiting" (10).

The values that inform this vision are those of settlers clinging to the simple civilities that connect the patterns of a new life emerging from the disruptions of migration with an old order where continuities were assured and categories were intact. Among the settlers' ambitions was the hope of reestablishing the institutions of that order in their new environment as part of the business of domesticating the wilderness and passing them on as an inheritance. Ruth recalls that because her grandmother owned both her house and a little money,

> she always took some satisfaction in thinking ahead to the time when her simple private destiny would intersect with the great public processes of law and finance—that is, to the time of her death. All the habits and patterns and properties that had settled around her, the monthly checks from the bank, the house she had lived in since she came to it as a bride, the weedy orchard that surrounded the yard on three sides where smaller and wormier apples and apricots and plums had fallen every year of her widowhood, all these things would suddenly become liquid, capable of assuming new forms. And all of it would be Lucille's and mine. "Sell the orchards," she would say, looking grave and wise, "but keep the house. So long as you look after your health and own the roof above your head, you're as safe as anyone can be," she would say, "God willing." (27)

But her certainties do not transfer along with her assets. Keeping the house is not the same sacred task to Sylvie and her sister as it was to their mother. In the transition from one generation to the next, values have been displaced, and the relationship among work, acquisition, accumulation, and satisfaction has been disrupted. The older daughter, Helen, marries a man who takes her away to Seattle, where she finds herself living

> in two rooms at the top of a tall gray building, so that all the windows—there were five altogether, and a door with five rows of small panes—overlooked a narrow white porch, the highest flight of a great scaffolding of white steps and porches. . . . Since all the windows were in a line, our rooms were as light as the day was, near the door, and became darker as one went farther in. In the back wall of the main room was a door which opened into a carpeted hallway, and which was never opened. It was blocked, in fact, by a big green couch so weighty and shapeless that it looked as if it had been hoisted out of forty feet of water. Two putty-colored armchairs were drawn up in a conversational circle. Halves of two ceramic mallards were in full flight up the wall. As for the rest of the room, it contained a round card table covered with a plaid oilcloth, a refrigerator, a pale-blue china cupboard, a small table with a hotplate on it, and a sink with an oilcloth skirt. (20–21)

The apartment is a badly designed box, a place in which to survive, but incapable of properly housing the rituals of social life. The reduced family lives in reduced circumstances with space reduced to the essentials so that the distinctions between one living function and another are not borne out in the plan of the house but are mingled in an all-purpose room.

This is a house halfway between the house of Helen's birth and the complete disintegration represented by Sylvie's nomadic life, a halfway mark in the progressive diminishment of the grandfather's realized dream. Helen makes her final escape from it in a borrowed car with which she sails off a cliff to a dramatic suicide after having deposited her young daughters with her mother at the family homestead. On the grandmother's death her two maiden sisters come to look after the children. Ruth recalls, "They were almost destitute, and the savings in rent, not to mention the advantages of exchanging a little hotel room below ground for a rambling house surrounded by peonies and rose bushes, would be inducement enough to keep them with us until we came of age" (28). But the burdens of householding outweigh the advantages, and the aunts find themselves daunted not only by the realities of home maintenance but by the idiosyncrasies of the old house and their own nightmarish visions of what might happen to it, the children, and themselves in the event of natural disaster. When they cannot take it anymore, they set about locating Sylvie and send her a message to come home. "I have often wondered," Ruth muses, "what it seemed like to Sylvie to come back to that house, which would have changed since she left it, shifted and settled" (48).

The reader can soon surmise what it felt like to Sylvie. She makes a valiant attempt to domesticate herself, to tone down her peculiarities and play mother to her abandoned nieces, but she literally and figuratively keeps bumping into the walls and furniture, unaccustomed to the constraints and niceties of indoor life. Her odd habits involve the girls in teaching her what they need in the way of care and housekeeping. But she is not a quick learner, and the house seems to be in league against her efforts at compromise. The spring after her arrival, for the first time in memory, the annual floods reach the house. Ruth recalls, "Water poured over the thresholds and covered the floor to the depth of four inches, obliging us to wear boots while we did the cooking and washing up. We lived on the second floor for a number of days. . . . If we opened or closed a door, a wave swept through the house, and chairs tottered, and bottles and pots clinked and clunked in the bottoms of the kitchen cabinets" (61–62).

Unlike the aunts, however, Sylvie meets this invasion of natural forces with serene and even amused detachment. In the midst of the flood she seizes Ruth in a fit of gnomic amusement and sloshes about the kitchen with her in an impromptu dance. The floodwater not only displaces the furniture within the house but seems to have reconfigured the landscape. Lucille looks out the front door in the midst of it and observes, "I don't think the Simmons' house is where it used to be." Sylvie replies, "It's so hard to tell." The landscape becomes, by a combination of flood, mist, and Sylvie's fluid perceptions, a running watercolor in which boundaries of time and space fluctuate disturbingly.

Recalling this time of cold exile to the upper rooms of the house, and looking out on a landscape both familiar and strange, Ruth lapses into musing on the resonances of the small material world around her:

> Every spirit passing through the world fingers the tangible and mars the mutable, and finally has come to look and not to buy. So shoes are worn and hassocks are sat upon and finally everything is left where it was and the spirit passes on, just as the wind in the orchard picks up the leaves from the ground as if there were no other pleasure in the world but brown leaves, as if it would deck, clothe, flesh itself in flourishes of dusty brown apple leaves, and then drops them all in a heap at the side of the house and goes on. (73)

Here at its most appealing is the transcendent point of view that governs this footloose heroine and the niece who tells her story. Sylvie identifies in her deepest being with the rhythms of nature and the large cycles of seasonal change and geological movement. It is hard for her to take seriously the minutiae of daily existence in this house, which loses its significance against the vast backdrop of her imagination. She is a woman who has made the world her home, for whom, as for Thoreau and Ishmael, the sky is her roof and the wide earth itself a home she knows to be safe and habitable.

Life with Sylvie seems continually to threaten boundaries. She is a nocturnal animal, her circadian rhythms attuned to something other than human activity. The girls discover her several times awake and sitting in a dark house in a state of inexplicable and weird contentment, unwilling to turn on the lights that would restore their sense of normality. "She seemed" Ruth muses, "to dislike the disequilibrium of counterpoising a roomful of light against a worldful of darkness. Sylvie in a house was more or less like a mermaid in a ship's cabin. She preferred it sunk in the very element it was meant to exclude" (99).

Her unpredictable behavior creates an atmosphere that seems to invest the house itself with an aura of Gothic animation that bewilders the girls and keeps them in a sleepless state of vigilance over the habits of this aunt who in her way seems never to have been housebroken: "We thought we sometimes heard her leave the house [at night], and once when we got out of bed, we found her playing solitaire in the kitchen, and once we found her sitting on the back porch steps, and once we found her standing in the orchard" (83). She seems to have brought with her some wild natural influence that begins with small intrusions of the outside world into the house—leaves unswept on the floors that make a sound of "lifting and alighting" when the door is opened.

Over time Ruth begins to sense something preternatural in the random motion of these bits of outdoors: "I noticed that the leaves would be lifted up by something that came before the wind, they would tack against some impalpable movement of air several seconds before the wind was heard in the trees. Thus finely did our house become attuned to the orchard and to the particularities of weather, even in the first days of Sylvie's housekeeping. Thus did she begin by littles and perhaps unawares to ready it for wasps and bats and barn swallows" (85). Sylvie, true to her name, seems an agent of natural forces who has come to seduce the house and its young inhabitants back to a state of nature.

While she is there the house begins to degenerate more rapidly and visibly by virtue of her active disregard for conventional standards of housekeeping. Things fall apart, and whatever center was once there, perhaps in the person of a woman trained to the tending of hearth and home, does not hold under Sylvie's haphazard regime. Once when Lucille's birthday candles set the curtains on fire, Sylvie "[beat] out the flames with a back issue of *Good Housekeeping*, but she . . . never replaced the curtain" (101). The niceties of order and cleanliness are lost on Sylvie, whose mind is on loftier, or at least airier, matters. She abandons her duties sometimes for whole days to make unannounced excursions to a hidden spot across the lake—"a little valley between two hills where someone built a house and planted an orchard and even started to dig a well. A long time ago" (137). The ghostly remnant of someone's abandoned settlement charms her with the mystery of its past and its seclusion, which make it a perfect setting for a visitation of spirit or at least for moods of fantastic speculation. When Ruth sees the place, on the occasion of her first illicit foray into the woods with Sylvie on a school day, she sees it at first with ordinary eyes and has to learn to see the magic Sylvie sees. Remembering that first trip to the little house slowly returning to nature, Ruth reflects:

> Abandoned homesteads like this one were rare . . . so perhaps all the tales of perished settlers were at root one tale, carried off in every direction the way one cry of alarm is carried among birds through the whole of the woods and even the sky. It might have been this house that peopled all these mountains. When it broke it might have cast them invisibly into the wind, like spores, thousands from one drab husk, or millions, for there was no reason to believe that anyone ever had heard all the tales of unsheltered fold that were in these mountains, or that anyone ever would. (157)

Never quite able to enter fully into Sylvie's fantastic vision, Ruth is nevertheless initiated on this shared pilgrimage, and as her desire for such moments of vision and for wild, natural things begins to deepen, the thin lines that bind her to civilization, such as it has survived in the little outpost town, begin to fray. She knows, despite the stories she and Sylvie invent, that the little ruin does not secretly shelter elfin children long since abandoned there, not because the story is unlikely but because its logic is faulty: if there were children there in that magic place, they would have to be "light and spare and thoroughly used to the cold," and it would be "almost a joke to them to be cast out into the woods, even if their eyes were gone and their feet were broken" (159). Ruth begins to become, like Sylvie, a creature of the outdoors, learning to live there the way a child learns to take possession of the house she lives in, as gradually its dark corners become less mysterious and her sense of authority to inhabit it grows into a proprietary claim. She learns to love and inhabit the darkness, to become a creature of the night: sleeping one night in the woods, she remembers, "I simply let the darkness in the sky become coextensive with the darkness in my skull and bowels and bones. Everything that falls upon the eye is apparition, a sheet dropped over the world's true workings. . . . Darkness is the only solvent" (116). Like Sylvie, Ruth begins to shed her attachments to the material culture of home and hearth like a skin grown too tight. "It is better to have nothing, for at last even our bones will fall. It is better to have nothing" (159).

These nature women are innocent, but not sentimental, grateful but not evangelical about their private mysticism. Ruth recalls that "the deep woods are as dark and stiff and as full of their own odors as the parlor of an old house. We would walk among those great legs, hearing the enthralled and incessant murmurings far above our heads, like children at a funeral" (98).

But as Ruth's intimacy with Sylvie and her habits of mind deepens, Lucille begins to find herself alienated from them both, distressed and disoriented by what she sees not as friendly interminglings of nature into the life of the household but as threatening intrusions of chaos and distressing manifestations of pointless neglect. Sylvie collects things. Newspapers and cans seem to have a vague intrinsic value; she is not sure what to do with them or even, in a sense, what to make of them. So they pile up in corners, awaiting some revelation of their place in the order of things, and the house gradually takes on the aspect of a junk heap while Lucille, like the sorcerer's apprentice, tries desperately to devise strategies to maintain some semblance of order. The issue of housekeeping becomes a point of contention, driving her to take decisive measures in the interests of her own proper upbringing. "There were other things about Sylvie's housekeeping that bothered Lucille," Ruth recalls.

> For example, Sylvie's room was just as my grandmother had left it, but the closet and the drawers were mostly empty, since Sylvie kept her clothes and even her hairbrush and toothpowder in a cardboard box under the bed. She slept on top of the covers, with a quilt over her, which during the daytime she pushed under the bed also. Such habits (she always slept clothed, at first with her shoes on, and then, after a month or two, with her shoes under her pillow) were clearly the habits of a transient. They offended Lucille's sense of propriety. (102–103)

Lucille's distress puts the reader in a curious position of recognizing, in the midst of sympathizing with the endearing oddities of Sylvie and Ruth, that it is Lucille who represents the will to order, socialization, and "normality." She is the one trying to preserve what in ordinary life most of us regard as sane forms of accommodation and maintenance of civilized standards. Yet in the context of the novel, her efforts seem pathetic, slightly small-minded, common. Ruth, for a time, finds her loyalties divided between her aunt, whose fanciful freedom compels her heart, and Lucille, whom she senses is being lost to her. She tries to emulate Lucille's adaptations to the norms of social life, accompanying her to town one day to meet with friends, but her efforts fail miserably, and she begins to hear in herself the fateful sound of whatever voice called Sylvie to her unorthodox destiny. Returning from her unsuccessful foray into local society, she looks up at the house and experiences a strange shock of recognition, as if "something I had lost might be found in Sylvie's house" (124). At the same time, she sees it with Lucille's eyes: "As I approached the house I was newly aware of the changes that had overtaken it. The lawn was knee high, an oily, dank green, and the wind sent ripples across it. It had swamped the smaller bushes and the walk and the first step of the front porch and had risen to the height of the foundation. And it seemed that if the house were not to founder, it must soon begin to float" (124–125). Images of water, floating, dissolution, and random movement are associated throughout the book with Sylvie.

Ruth is learning gradually to adapt herself to this medium; she is acquiring a deep quality of fluidity, what in its best manifestation the ancients called "the way of water," which is the way of the wise man. She is not simply succumbing but is actively seeking some quality of knowing she recognizes in her mercurial aunt, whose wisdom looks so distressingly like ineptitude and foolishness. While Ruth spends a night in a stolen boat on the lake with Sylvie, her apprehensions dissolve into rumination and then into a dream in which first the boat and then her body fill with water to bursting. "Then, presumably, would come parturition in some form." The image fades into self-reflection: "What is thought, after all, what is dreaming, but swim and flow, and the images they seem to animate?" Our thoughts "mock us with their seeming slightness. If they were more substantial—if they had weight and took up space—they would sink or be carried away in the general flux. But they persist, outside the brisk and ruinous energies of the world" (162–163). She realizes that perhaps it was some vain seeking to unite with the flow under the surface of things that prompted her mother's suicide. And with these thoughts she drifts into sleep "between Sylvie's feet, and under the reach of her arms" (163), curled in the hull of the boat.

Despite the germination and fruition of this magical relation with Sylvie, the loss of Lucille is a costly one for Ruth. Having a sister around, she recalls, is like having a light on in a house at night. Lucille is associated with images of light, as Sylvie is with images of darkness. Lucille represents to Ruth the safety of the known, the conventional, the comforts of ordinary life. She is tempted at moments to retreat to those comforts but finds herself increasingly unable to. After Lucille leaves, the authorities threaten to take Ruth away, too, and this threat propels Sylvie into a tragicomic frenzy of domestic activity, a last-ditch attempt to restore her credibility and learn the ways of her kind. She stages a great bonfire of old newspapers and phone books as Ruth watches, transfixed, "I saw the fiery transfiguration of a dog, and the bowl he ate from, and a baseball team, and a Chevrolet, and many hundreds of words. It had never occurred to me that words, too, must be salvaged, though when I thought about it, it seemed obvious. It was absurd to think that things were held in place, are held in place, by a web of words" (200). Sylvie sends for seeds to frame the house with flower beds in the spring and hangs a new yellow curtain in the kitchen. She is suddenly "full of purpose, which sometimes seemed like hope" (201).

But they are not her purposes, and they fail in translation. Ruth hides in the orchard the evening the sheriff comes to negotiate her removal and is overcome once again by an alien vision of things: the house with its lighted windows "stood out beyond the orchard with every one of its windows lighted. It looked large, and foreign, and contained, like a moored ship—a fantastic thing to find in a garden" (203). Ruth resurrects in her visionary moments Thoreau's old question, "What is a house?" in strange, fantastic terms that detach it from all the notions that make a house seem so elemental a grounding force. She imagines a house as something that might be transformed to fit needs not dreamed of by generations not yet mired in the wreckage of their own progress and wonders what that house would have to be like: "Imagine that Noah knocked his house apart and used the planks to build an ark, while his neighbors looked on, full of doubt. A house, he must have told them, should be daubed with pitch and built to float cloud high, if need be. . . . A house should have a compass and a keel" (184). This house has neither but weighs them down, tying them to the mores of the little community and the duties it has defined for them, preventing these two visionaries from tasting life in the way that all adventurers have longed to taste it, and so they decide to set themselves free.

The only recourse is to burn the house and leave on the next train. What might turn into a scene of high melodrama or sentimental tragedy is redeemed and deepened by the comic difficulties of the arsonists: "The house was as dank as the orchard, and would not burn. Oh, the doilies on the couch blazed a while, and they left smoldering rings on the arms, but Sylvie slapped those out with her hand, saying they were worse than nothing" (208). Sylvie's strange unfamiliarity with domestic objects extends even to an inability to destroy them effectively. Like the newspapers and tin cans, the house itself baffles her in its resistances. Finally, however, Sylvie and Ruth manage a conflagration and escape before the townspeople have a chance to stop them. As the fugitives make their way across the bridge in the dark, the house burning behind them, they feel what Kundera would call a "lightness of being"—an exhilaration of freedom from possession. In her flight Ruth imagines the burning house "all turned to fire, and the fire leaping and whirling in its own fierce winds" and "the spirit of the house breaking out the windows and knocking down the doors, and all the neighbors astonished at the sovereign ease with which it burst its tomb, broke up its grave" (211). It seems not a destruction but a transformation, an apotheosis, a releasing of the elements of the house to some other, freer form.

This novel challenges us to reimagine the American dream of home ownership. Sylvie has it and does not value it. The home does not have any of the symbolic, and little of the practical, importance for her that it did for her mother. Her mother collected family photos; Sylvie burns them—not out of hatred or rebellion but because such gathering and preserving seem irrelevant. She has, like Thoreau, "other lives to live." Sylvie is among a number of bag lady types featured in recent American writing. Certainly the plight of the homeless is anything but romantic; yet there is a romance of homelessness that has nearly as long a history in our culture as the dream of home and property ownership. The values reflected in that romance are counterweights to the domestic virtues that stabilize home and family. Sylvie and her predecessors are reminders of the dangers of the insularity, complacency, and too-comfortable materialism that accompany the very successes we are admonished to pursue. And they are symbols of a kind of radical freedom that needs to be exercised by the occasional eccentric or rebel to help the rest remember what freedom looks like and to drive us back to the fundamental paradoxes that keep desire and fulfillment from becoming greed and complacency: that voluntary renunciation can bring unsuspected richness and involuntary possession, unbearable impoverishment.

Possession, to the dispossessed, however, brings its own awakenings, especially to those who understand the material world as part of a subtle and complex spiritual economy that transcends the logic of the marketplace. Understood in their true significance, things become animated by the energies of the people who use them. *Beloved*, one of the most haunting "ghost stories" in American fiction, opens with a bald affirmation of that mysterious dimension of the material world: "124 was spiteful." One twenty-four is the address of a gray and white house on Bluestone Road in Cincinnati, once a way station for escaped slaves, a gathering place for the shifting population of black men and women on their way to somewhere better. It is a place full of spirit and history. As one character puts it, "Compared to 124, the rest of the world was bald" (41). At the story's beginning it is home to three women who have been abandoned by their men through death or desertion: Baby Suggs, an escaped slave, a holy woman, preacher, and minister to the local community; Sethe, escaped from the same plantation and now living with Baby as her daughter; and Denver, Sethe's half-grown daughter. No one comes to 124 anymore; evil things have happened there, and a restless spirit troubles the house and makes it "spiteful." The house contains not just a ghost but a secret.

In a moment of desperation, threatened with death or worse by white slave-catchers standing on the threshold of this house, Sethe killed her own baby. Now the baby's spirit inhabits the place. The house is "palsied by the baby's fury at having its throat cut" (5). The sideboard moves when Sethe calls out the ghost. The house pitches when a man appears from Sethe's past to make love to her. Denver comes home one day to see in the living room a "pool of red and undulating light" (8). Strange phenomena like these are not, however, occasion for terror so much as for a kind of vexed tolerance. The erratic appeals of the invisible fourth inhabitant must be reckoned with as surely as must the demands of the dying Baby Suggs. Indeed, the ghost seems not so much an inhabitant as the soul of the house itself; Denver has come to regard the house as a person rather than a structure, so accustomed is she to its preternatural rumblings.

The house has some peculiar features. Like Pilate's house in Morrison's *Song of Solomon*, it has only one door. Baby Suggs boarded up the back door because she did not want to make the journey to the outside kitchen anymore (207). Like the houses of Hawthorne and Poe, this is a house haunted by a guilty and ambiguous past, weakened by the battles of sexes and generations, and located in a town but not of it—a house isolated in its own metaphysical space by virtue of the unexpiated evil that sets it apart. It is a place possessed by a power that inhabits it and entraps all its inhabitants in a common and isolating fate. In the course of the story, boundaries between present and past, living and dead, animate and inanimate, fade and dissolve, and the reader is left uneasily pondering the fragility of rational categories of experience.

But *Beloved* fits only marginally into the American Gothic tradition as it is generally defined. The questions it raises are different from those posed by traditional "ghost stories." It is not, for one thing, a tale of terror. Within the context of black Christianized folklore, intrusions of the supernatural into ordinary life are taken more or less for granted, regarded with respect but not surprise. Moreover, the radical individuality that has so defined white American culture is far less a part of black consciousness; bonds of common suffering, ambiguous genealogical lines, and a religious tradition that evokes experiences of transcendent unity make the issue of establishing individual identity much less pressing than that of establishing communal identity. The presence of a restless spirit in a household is a demand to be reckoned with but not a threat to sanity or a challenge to some model of reality from which such occurrences are categorically excluded.

The main characters in this novel are the three women, a man, and a ghost whose presence is manifest first in the hauntings and then in the form of a young girl who inexplicably appears, stays, and gradually comes to dominate the will and intentions of the others, thereby turning household life to her hungry purposes. The three generations of women represent successive stages in emergence from enslavement and endangerment. Baby Suggs, who spent most of her life at the plantation of "Sweet Home" as personal slave to the plantation's mistress, having been freed, continues her life of service by ministering to the physical and spiritual needs of the fleeing and displaced. Like Faulkner's Dilsey, Baby Suggs has "seed de first and de last" and finds nothing human to be alien or anomalous. She acquires the status of local saint by the immense capacious tolerance and absorbency that make her an agent of healing and her home a general place of refuge.

Sethe, married to one of Baby Suggs' sons, arrives at 124 in need of that healing after she gave birth on her escape route, sent her child on ahead, and nearly died in crossing the river. She remains to care for Baby and the house and her own children, but her staying is sealed as an irrevocable fate the day she kills her baby daughter to save her from white men who have come into the yard threatening and tormenting the black fugitives. After that event Sethe's orientation turns away from community and toward what family remains to her. Her sons eventually leave her. Isolated and ostracized, she turns inward, enclosing herself, her daughter, and her memories behind the door that once stood open to so many travelers. Her story is a simple tale of survival and sorrow complicated by the one desperate act that has defined her and become her fate.

Denver, Sethe's surviving daughter, suffers that fate unhappily; it is an inherited burden, something that does not for her, as it does for Sethe, betoken the exaction of a just payment for sin committed but rather a dismal foreclosure of possibilities in the actual world. She grows up largely in ignorance of the world beyond the close boundaries of her home: "124 and the field behind it were all the world she knew or wanted" (101). She occasionally complains, "I can't live here. . . . Nobody speaks to us" (14). But she has nowhere to go, no understanding of the world beyond those animated walls, and so she lives in an uneasy truce with these women whose motives and way of life she only partly comprehends.

The reciprocity between the house and its inhabitants changes with each generation: where Baby Suggs knows how to exercise the power of prayer and exorcism to keep spirits in control, if not dispel them, Sethe can practice only an uneasy toleration. Denver, however, makes of the ghost a playmate and companion. She creates a complicated personal mythology around the fragments of the story she knows and accepts the mysterious presence as one of the givens of her strange, lonely life.

A balance of power has been struck in this household between the women who in their various ways accommodate to its strangeness and the spirit who visits them. Motives of appeasement and expiation shape ordinary activity. But that balance is disrupted by two major events: Baby Suggs' death and the appearance of Paul D, another refugee from Sweet Home, a man of Sethe's generation, friend to her lost husband, who has wandered for years finding freedom a matter of nomadic existence and marginal survival on uncertain terms. Suddenly the balance of power and the accommodation are threatened, and the ghost begins a campaign of intimidation to drive Paul D from the house, where it appears he may stay. He brings with him the normality of the outside world, intruding its reality into this little conventional cell where visitations from the other world are more frequent than visits from the town beyond Bluestone Road.

It is shortly after Paul D's arrival that "Beloved" appears, an incarnation of the ghost of the dead baby come now to take a more active role in the struggle for a central place in Sethe's affections and in this home. With Beloved's arrival the house becomes the stage for an escalating battle of wills, a contest in which Beloved seeks to drive out Paul D, subordinate Denver, and have her mother's attentions entirely to herself—a returned baby getting back what is hers.

The idea of "ghosts" loses its boundaries in this novel. Habitation, presence, and fullness are expressed in the very character of inanimate things. The events that have occurred in a place leave a residue of atmosphere. As Beloved observes, the house is "heavy . . . this place is heavy" (54). Similarly, when Sethe goes to the clearing where Baby Suggs preached, she wants to "listen to the spaces that the long-ago singing had left behind" (89).

These people are aware of themselves as living in a force-field, operated on by unseen and unnamed powers. Habitation gives place character, establishing its own invisible but palpable boundaries. Moreover, the character of a place is a matter of relationship between the inhabitant and the spirit of the place. For each of the five main characters 124 assumes a different and peculiar character; the idea of home is shaped and altered by their histories, needs, and various accommodations to the house itself.

During Baby Suggs' best years there, 124 evolved from a way station on the underground railroad, where there were fugitives "folded up tight somewhere: beneath floorboards in a pantry, once in a chimney" (148), to the hospice and haven it became for any black townsperson or itinerant. The years when Baby Suggs owned and ran the house were the time "when 124 was alive." Under her aegis the house was an all-purpose gathering place: a refuge for travelers; a hospital where she nursed Sethe, among others, back to health and wholeness after harrowing escapes; a place where people brought and prepared food, sang, prayed, and nurtured one another. Baby Suggs "had women friends, men friends from all around to share grief with" (96).

Like Baby herself, the house evolves, expanding its influence, widening its hospitable arms to give more and more to the growing community of the freed and needy. As far as Baby is concerned, this is a house the Lord has provided. When Sethe, trying to remind Baby Suggs that there are good white people, points out, "They gave you this house," Baby Suggs replies emphatically, "Nobody *gave* me nothing" (244). The house is hers by divine right; her years as a slave, then as a freedwoman watching her sons grow up in slavery, have paid in full for any goods life has given her thereafter. She accepts the house in a spirit of stewardship and begins the process of transforming the skills she learned in servitude into forms of power to be exercised in the chosen service of her people. Her preaching to them is not about repentance but about repossession of their birthright: "She did not tell them to clean up their lives or to go and sin no more. She did not tell them they were the blessed of the earth, its inheriting meek or its glorybound pure. She told them that the only grace they could have was the grace they could imagine. That if they could not see it, they would not have it" (88). She urges them to love their bodies, their own flesh, reminding them that no one will love it if they do not. Their empowerment must come from themselves; nothing will be given to them, even their own bodies, unless they take possession of them and claim power over them. This is what she has done with the home she has acquired.

But by the time of her death, the event with which the story opens, the house has already "faded," lost much of its vitality, and in Sethe's view, Baby Suggs lies broken in it waiting for death, no longer believing in grace, no longer able to wreak her transformations on fate. The house that was once such a place of refuge has "shut down and put up with the venom of its ghost" (89). Baby Suggs' one remaining desire is to see color; she is "hungry for color." In the middle of a bleak Ohio winter, in a house from which warmth, light, and spiritual vitality have departed, the only vestige of liveliness resides in the bright orange patch on Baby Suggs' quilt with which Sethe tries pathetically to satisfy her yearning.

Sethe's ministrations are far less inspired than Baby's. She does what is necessary to the survival and moderate comfort of the old woman and young girl in her care. She works, cooks, washes Baby's withering body, and preserves the truce with the spirit of the house, quietly harboring painful memories and living on determination and defiance. Sethe lives with memories of Sweet Home that reel themselves in front of her like a private picture show repeated endlessly for her torment and comfort. The farm named Sweet Home "rolled itself out before her in its shameless beauty" (6).

When Baby dies and the house becomes Sethe's, it closes in on itself. Rather than sheltering the flocks, 124 becomes a protective shell around Sethe and Denver, keeping out a world they assume to be hostile. Sethe knows, too, the measure of the loss represented in the quietly deteriorating old house. Unlike Denver, she has memories with which to compare the diminishment and demise of 124: "She remembered when the yard had a fence with a gate that somebody was always latching and unlatching in the time when 124 was busy as a way station. She did not see the white-boys who pulled it down, yanked up posts and smashed the gate leaving 124 desolate and exposed at the very hour when everybody stopped dropping by. The shoulder weeds of Bluestone Road were all that came toward the house" (163).

Sethe has become a toughened woman. Misery has not had for her the benevolent effects it had for Baby Suggs. Like the scarred skin on Sethe's back, her sensitivity and her ability to feel have been reduced as the cost of psychic survival. Unlike Denver, whose sensitivities are heightened by her deprived environment, Sethe girds herself to go on with life with a straightened vision, limited ambitions, and simple survival as a daily goal. She protects herself and Denver, nourishes her memories, and goes on.

Sethe's memories, recorded in a long soliloquy in chapter 20, are a litany of justification. She killed her child for her safety. Killing her, Sethe sealed a bond with the child stronger than life. The strange return of Sethe's ghostly child seems to her a vindication and seems for a time to restore a semblance of family life. And she claims the child as her own. Sethe's primary motive is claiming: "Beloved, she my daughter. She mine. . . . I won't never let her go. . . . Nobody will ever get my milk no more except my own children" (200). She dreams of having the life she missed with her child, planting and sowing with her, teaching her to see and name the natural world. Sethe's ambitions are to have and preserve. Like the steward with the few talents, she has no impulse to multiply but simply to protect and preserve what has been spared to her. The house is hers and the children are hers, and even against the man who enters her life and offers her love her impulse is fiercely to protect and keep them. She has served her term as a slave, has served her term in jail after the murder of her daughter, and now retains only the limited goal of survival without further trouble.

For Denver, neither the house nor the ghost-sister is ringed with the painful associations they have for her mother. Occasionally Denver is driven to a desperation of loneliness, but she develops strategies for coping with this isolation. Accustomed to the peculiarities of her confined and secretive upbringing, she enters into her own pact with both the place and its inhabitant. She regards the house "as a person rather than a structure" (29). In her puzzling world she has worked out a precarious economy of safety based on the half-truths she knows about the past. She knows her mother killed her sister and because of that lives with fear that whatever made her mother do that will return.

> All the time, I'm afraid the thing that happened that made it all right for my mother to kill my sister could happen again. I don't know what it is, I don't know who it is, but maybe there is something else terrible enough to make her do it again. I need to know what that thing might be, but I don't want to. Whatever it is, it comes from outside this house, outside the yard, and it can come right on in the yard if it wants to. So I never leave this house and I watch over the yard, so it can't happen again and my mother won't have to kill me too. Not since Miss Lady Jones' house have I left 124 by myself. Never. (205)

Denver is far more sensitive to the presence in 124 than is her mother, who often does not see or feel the changing atmosphere. Denver's insularity has attuned her finely to the house's moods and to the presence of the invisible child: "Beloved is my sister. I swallowed her blood right along with my mother's milk. The first thing I heard after no hearing anything was the sound of her crawling up the stairs. She was my secret company until Paul D came. He threw her out" (205).

As with her mother and grandmother, Denver lives in an economy of radical loss and pursuit of restoration. What little she has is taken from her without clear promise of restitution. Her sense of a place in the world and her satisfactions depend largely on her own imaginings. As a child she makes a place for herself out in the field, a "green bush house" reminiscent of the clearing where Baby Suggs preached. She engages in "house-play" in a "room" of boxwood bushes behind the house. When Baby Suggs dies, Denver goes there. Like Baby, Denver claims a space for herself and keeps it to herself, harboring her secrets there.

As she grows older, Denver ventures hesitantly into the wider world. She peeks into the windows of Lady Jones's house, where children are taught their lessons, allowing herself only to observe from a distance, knowing too little even to covet what they have; it is "a house other children visited but not her" (102). To Denver, a house is a whole world. She has no comparisons to give her a sense of norms, only life in 124 and in the milieu of all the stories it contains.

When Beloved appears bodily as a member of the household, Denver is able for the first time to define her own role in terms of a meaningful function. Once the secret companion is incarnate and Denver is able to establish an actual relation with her, separation from her mother can begin on terms other than simple escape. Denver sees it has her mission to protect Beloved from her mother this time around. Denver now has a role in the family epic. The fact that it is not Beloved's object to be protected does not prevent Denver from defining the situation in such a way as to give herself this significance. She soon comes to realize that Beloved herself is a force to be reckoned with, dangerous in her own way, and she learns in ambiguous fashion to protect herself from this strange sister even as she presumes to protect her from their murderous mother. Denver takes to sleeping in Baby Suggs' old room, believing that is the "only place she [Beloved] can't get to me in the night" (206–207). Baby Suggs is still, even after her death, part of the household economy or force-field.

But the real spine of Denver's action, the motive of her cloistered existence, is her millennial faith in the return of her father. In her private theology she has been singled out for a particular mission of waiting and protection, holding things together until his return. Her way of making sense of the world has been entirely focused on a past that belongs to another generation and on a future fashioned out of the strands of that past, which is receding into myth year by year with little in the way of lived life to displace it and relativize its importance.

It is only after Beloved's disappearance, when the hold of the ghost of the past on the household is released, that Denver ventures into a wider, more real world and takes her plunge into the ordinary. She leaves home of necessity, having to help Sethe, who is sick from her second ordeal of slow bereavement. Denver's first going out is depicted in a language appropriate to the emotional magnitude of that step: she "stood on the porch of 124 ready to be swallowed up in the world beyond the edge of the porch" (243). Denver finally has an epiphany of normality. She goes to Lady Jones's house and finds herself able to enter a larger world with grace.

As Denver ventures into the larger world, another displacement begins. As her outside life improves, her home life deteriorates. She begins to keep house and care for her mother. The balance of power shifts from mother to daughter, and as it does the process of reconnection with the community begins. Gifts of food are left discreetly at the fence for the sick woman. The tradition of mutual hospitality in the black community reasserts itself. Denver takes a job and begins to learn about the world, first with gratitude, later with dawning recognition of the ironies of inequality that have continued into the generations of freed slaves. She works for gentle white folk with soft blue carpets and china closets, comes in the back door, and attends to their needs so that at the end of the day she can return home to attend to her mother's. In other words, Denver assumes her place in the complex, ambiguous social world of freedom. This is her fall into experience, her liberation from an innocent and protected past into the sorrows of public adult life that are the cost of qualified freedom in a world where that commodity remains precarious.

If the three women represent the evolution of household and family from an economy of desperation into one of a social normality predicated on a new set of constraints as well as release from a past of extremities, Paul D is the agent of that release. His coming creates a disturbance in the field. He is capable of threatening the power of the ghost because he is not of this small world where such power can reign supreme. He is the ghost's competition, and the battle in which she engages him is a pitting of death against life, past against present, the mythic and repetitive against the actual and contingent. He brings his simple hungers for food, sex, and shelter and pits them against the driving, consuming, voracious needs of the baby ghost, breaking open the closed, hermetic circle of women's lives where there "was no room for any other thing or body" (39) and reorienting them to the realities of sex, work, and family. "It took a man," the narrator explains, "Paul D, to shout it off, beat it off, and take its place for himself" (104).

As in a fairy tale, he comes like the prince to free his woman from the thrall of an alien presence. He has been through the requisite trials. Like Sethe and Baby Suggs, Paul D lives haunted by memories of Sweet Home and worse. Paul D's escape story is a harrowing tale of being locked in boxes, nearly drowned in mud, chained by the ankles to a dozen other slaves, wandering homeless for seven years (a biblical number vaguely reminiscent of the wandering Israelites) as nomad and itinerant worker. His way of life is summed up easily: "Move. Walk. Run. Hide. Steal and move on" (66). He keeps his searing memories locked into "the tobacco tin lodged in his chest" (113).

The battle between Paul D and the ghost begins in Oedipal fashion with his first sexual advance toward Sethe, her mother. The house pitches when Paul holds Sethe's breasts. Later, at the carnival, Paul D, Sethe, and Denver become a family. Immediately thereupon Beloved appears. It is as though that vital connection brings to a head the disturbances in the force-field. Paul D is at first defeated by Beloved. He moves out of the house believing he is having "house fits," but he finally recognizes that in some irresistible way she "moved him." It takes Sethe's love, stronger than Beloved's jealousy, to bring him back in. In the interim, he encounters Stamp Paid, another veteran of Sweet Home who, like Denver, is sensitive to the house; he hears voices there, which he believes are voices of the dead. He comes to 124 and cannot knock or go in. Stamp Paid understands Paul D's predicament and assures him that any black house in Cincinnati is open to him. Thus, the novel begins to reintroduce the world beyond Bluestone Road as a congenial place, a web of community ready to incorporate these strays. When Paul D returns, 124 is cleared of Beloved. "He looks toward the house and, surprisingly, it does not look back at him. Unloaded, 124 is just another house needing repair" (264).

In many ghost stories the convention holds that ghosts are bound to inhabit only certain places, returning to them until some unfinished business is resolved. They are bound to the place as they were once bound to their own bodies. Beloved belongs to 124 in just this way; she tells Denver, "I don't want that place [the beyond]. This is the place I am" (123). She is, as Denver perceives her, a "familiar" deeply enmeshed in the fabric of this strange family life until she and the house's other inhabitants are released from their mutual dependence forged of guilt, remorse, and desire for retribution. These accounts are not settled but are dispelled by Paul D's appearance, which signals the restoration of normality as measured by love, sex, and the simple communions of family life. The past is not avenged; it is simply lived beyond. Other elements of normal life are restored: thirty women gather at 124, recollecting their shared memories of the place, and exorcise Beloved with singing. Bodwin, the local abolitionist who gave 124 to Baby Suggs for her home, comes by and confronts Beloved. Thereafter, "124 was quiet."

After Beloved's departure the house is just a house—or almost. Paul D realizes the emptiness of the house: "Something is missing from 124. Something larger than the people who lived there. Something more than Beloved or the red light. He can't put his finger on it, but it seems, for a moment, that just beyond his knowing is the glare of an outside thing that embraces while it accuses" (270–271). The release has been a diminishment, as is every release from a past whose dimensions begin to enlarge into myth. This state of restored normality is not final; it is simply another stage of release into freedom, each stage also a release into a more complex relation with a wider world.

Afterword

One of the most popular shows on the American stage in recent years has been Jane Wagner's one-woman extravaganza starring Lily Tomlin, "The Search for Signs of Intelligent Life in the Universe."[1] For three hours a homeless bag lady on the streets of New York dispenses wisdom accumulated from observing her fellow humans and trying to maintain communication with her "space chums," who are seeking information about earth life. In her crazed state she sees, as lunatic poets have long been supposed to see, the undersides and inner reaches of the lives of the people who brush past her on their planetary journeys. "If evolution was worth its salt," she reflects, "by now it should've evolved something better than survival of the fittest. Yeah, I told 'em I think a better idea would be survival of the wittiest. . . . Seems like evolution has just kinda plateaued out, left mankind with a middle management problem" (113). She reminds us, but without a shred of self-pity, "I wasn't always a bag lady, you know" (19).

A recent novel by Diana O Hehir, *The Bride Who Ran Away*, features an eighty-three-year-old woman, Sybil, who lives out of her car, "a high tan one with a mahogany dashboard which sat on a hill in the diggings outside town" (2).[2] She has "moments of dislocation" during which she is prone to shoplift randomly from the general store, and she wears motley and mismatched clothing, but for all that—and, we suspect, in some way because of all that—she is something of an oracle. One of O Hehir's recent poems features an "old lady under the freeway" who has gone there "to live on a bed of weeds." "My world," she says, "is depths of green, a water of fern." She roasts "shreds of leaf" and "soup in a can." She seems to have discovered some secret that she hoards along with the nail files and pen knives she picks up from "the good / Who fall headlong off the freeway bridge." She is proud, not pathetic, a little bewildering in her curious, unorthodox freedom.[3]

Recently, the case of a homeless woman who had been taken from the streets and who had insisted on her right to return captured the imagination of media audiences for weeks. She was eventually freed, having baffled the courts and raised considerable public discussion not only of what she should have but of what she should be allowed to want.

These homeless heroines put a different slant on our long tradition of heroes whose home is in the woods or under the sky "where the buffalo roams"—voluntary exiles from society who brave the wilderness and its uncertainties in search of adventure, knowledge, wisdom of a kind not to be had within the structures of civilized life. Those American Adams are the ones who have incarnated our desire for innocence regained and something of our fear of entrapment in social niches from which there is no escape. These women inhabit an urban wilderness. Their dispossession is not voluntary; they bear witness not to the power of our collective imagination but to its failure and to our fears of loss, abandonment, and disenfranchisement. Their heroism lies in creative adaptation to what always threatens to become misery and in a kind of insanity that plays at the boundaries between madness and wisdom.

Fascination with the circumstances and consequences of homelessness and rootlessness is the inevitable accompaniment to our long national preoccupation with building and settlement. These conditions are no longer so easily romanticized as the wanderings of Natty Bumppo in the woods, Huck and Jim on the raft, Ishmael on the ship, Mack and the boys in the flophouse on Cannery Row, or Dean Moriarty on the road. The romance of poverty and solitude, like Fitzgerald's "romance of money," has frayed and torn to reveal a sordid reality that fiction and poetry no longer presume to conceal, though writers like Wagner and O Hehir have found ways of inviting readers to contemplate the conditions in which marginal people live from perspectives that defy conventional pity and call us to a deeper, more complex response. But in the midst of distressing evidence that houses and even housing are not and never have been supplied equitably by the democratic system in which we have invested our hopes for equity and abundance, we continue to find a kind of ambiguous heroism among the unhoused and to reaffirm an old American faith in resiliency: people cope. That itself may be a romantic illusion; many are not coping, and it is a matter of national shame that people are dying in our streets for lack of food and shelter.

In a time when three million Americans, many of them families with children, are homeless, and that number is climbing steadily, the notion of the American dream cannot be considered without irony. News media focus increasingly on housing issues, and we are forced to recognize that fewer and fewer Americans can afford houses—or indeed housing of any kind. We are compelled at the same time to remember that large segments of the population, primarily immigrants, laborers, and people of color, have never been able to own homes. The question of home ownership is impossible to disentangle from other forms of empowerment.

As the women's movement, ethnic movements, and various social organizations struggle to change the terms of cultural empowerment, the significance of property and home ownership and the terms under which they can be attained are under constant review. And as we become more aware of the real implications of cultural pluralism and class structures in the United States, our notions of family life come under serious critical scrutiny as well. The housing crisis demands that we reimagine capitalism, rethink the issue of property distribution, and confront the cost of the American dream to those for whom it is more a doomed and ironic fantasy than a hope.

After considering many of the symbolic and political dimensions of houses, I return here to the observation that inhabited space is never neutral; it is "filled with ideologies." The building and habitation of houses in the contemporary United States have much to do with new and more urgent questions of how to find ways for us all to reexamine those ideologies and how to live responsibly on and with the earth. We may need to deescalate our pursuit of creature comforts, to design living spaces that are a little less ambitious in the hope of making them a little more accessible, and to reconsider imaginatively and with compassion Thoreau's salient question, "What is a house?" And perhaps we would do well to add to Thoreau's question a consideration of how the homes we design, build, and buy mirror every aspect of American life and imagination: our diversity, creativity, individuality, and ambition as well as our inequities, greeds, and insularity. As visible testimonies to our collective values, the houses that dot both the fictive and the actual landscape are historic and prophetic texts worthy of careful scrutiny as records of our past and portents of our future.

Notes

INTRODUCTION

1. Ellen Eve Frank, *Literary Architecture*, p. 3. All subsequent page citations are in the text.
2. For some of the classic arguments about gender as a dimension of American mythology, see Annette Kolodney, *The Lay of the Land*, and Ann Douglas, *The Feminization of American Culture*.
3. For discussion of the role of home in education in nineteenth-century New England, see Carl F. Kaestle and Maris A. Vinovskis, "From Apron Strings to ABCs," p. 544.
4. Sigmund Freud, *Introductory Lectures on Psycho-Analysis*, pp. 196, 188.
5. Gaston Bachelard, *The Poetics of Space*, pp. 72, xxxiii.
6. Dolores Hayden, *Redesigning the American Dream*, p. 98.
7. Christopher Alexander, *The Production of Houses*, p. 123.
8. Hayden, *Redesigning the American Dream*, pp. 18, 19.
9. Nathaniel Hawthorne, *Blithedale Romance*, p. 28.
10. David P. Handlin, *The American Home*, p. 82 ff. Handlin elaborates on much of the factual information cited here about nineteenth-century domestic architecture.
11. Rufus W. Griswold, ed., "Willimantic Railroad."
12. Henry James, *The American Scene*, p. 11.
13. Hayden, *Redesigning the American Dream*, p. 8.
14. Tom Wolfe, *From Bauhaus to Our House*, p. 69.
15. Frank Lloyd Wright, *The Natural House*, p. 20.
16. See Buckminster Fuller, *Ideas and Integrities*.
17. W. L. G. Smith, *Life at the South*; cited in Handlin, *The American Home*, p. 81.
18. Walt Whitman, *Leaves of Grass*; cited in Handlin, *The American Home*, p. 69.
19. T. S. Eliot, "East Coker," p. 28.

CHAPTER 1

1. Henry David Thoreau, *Walden and Other Writings*. All subsequent page citations are in the text.
2. Richard N. Masteller and Jean Carwile Masteller, "Rural Architecture in Andrew Jackson Downing and Henry David Thoreau."

3. Andrew Jackson Downing, *The Architecture of Country Houses*, p. 10. All subsequent page citations are in the text.

4. William Howarth, *The Book of Concord*, p. 35. All subsequent page citations are in the text.

5. The note of melancholy sounded here recurs frequently, portending what ultimately emerges as a tragic vision of the inevitable failure of the Thoreauvian ideal, whose standard of heightened moral sensitivity and sustained dialectical consciousness cannot be maintained in a secular capitalistic democracy.

CHAPTER 2

1. Edgar Allan Poe, "The Fall of the House of Usher." All subsequent page citations are in the text.

2. Edgar Allan Poe, "Edgar Allan Poe's Philosophy of Furniture," pp. 158–159.

CHAPTER 3

1. Nathaniel Hawthorne, *The House of the Seven Gables*.

2. Walter Benn Michaels, "Romance and Real Estate."

3. Michaels makes the point that "haunted house stories (like *The House of the Seven Gables*) usually involve some form of anxiety about ownership, inheritance, and legitimacy of title." It is not a very long leap from contemplating these themes as functions of family life and history to understanding how essential they are to that aspect of American experience that has been fundamentally predicated on expropriation. Moreover, he points out, Hawthorne revives in this tale the connections made startlingly explicit by recent historical reevaluations of the evidence between the witchcraft trials and property disputes because he represents the struggle between Pyncheons and Maules as "a conflict between two different modes of economic activity" (ibid., p. 159 ff).

For a thorough discussion of the question of psychic and spiritual inheritance, see Frederick Crews's classic study of Hawthorne's psychology, *The Sins of the Fathers*.

4. Jonathan Edwards, "Images or Shadows of Divine Things," pp. 64, 77, 78.

5. Jonathan Edwards, "Sinners in the Hands of an Angry God," p. 155.

6. Handlin, *The American Home*, pp. 47–48.

7. Ibid., 39.

CHAPTER 4

1. For good general studies of James's uses of architecture in fiction see, for instance, Robert Gale, *The Caught Image*; Richard Gill, *Happy Rural Seat*; R. W. Stallman, *The Houses that James Built*; and Frank, *Literary Architecture*.

2. Curtis Dahl, "Lord Lambeth's America: Architecture in James's 'An International Episode'."

3. Henry James, *The Portrait of a Lady*. All subsequent page citations are in the text.

4. Stallman, *The Houses that James Built*, p. 40.

5. Frank, *Literary Architecture*, p. 172. Frank's chapter on James presents a detailed description of the ways in which James "frames" the various time frames and operative levels of his own consciousness as writer and reader and prototypical character by the same architectural devices used more obviously in the service of staging his stories.

6. Elizabeth Sabiston, "Isabel Archer," p. 39.

7. See Stallman, *The Houses that James Built*, pp. 39–41, for discussion of motifs of imprisonment and rescue.

8. Sabiston, "Isabel Archer," p. 31.

9. See the comparison of Isabel with Pansy in this respect in ibid., p. 43.

10. James's contempt for the unnecessary and excessive decoration characteristic of the late Victorians was shared and excoriated with similar irony by both Wharton and Cather, both of whom employed the conceit of the "overfurnished novel," thereby extending further the useful conceit of the house of fiction.

11. See the elaboration of this analogy in R. W. Stallman, "Some Rooms From 'The Houses that James Built,'" p. 37.

12. Charles R. Anderson, *Person, Place, and Thing in Henry James's Novels*, p. 81.

CHAPTER 5

1. Kate Chopin, *The Awakening and Selected Stories*; Charlotte Perkins Gilman, "The Yellow Wallpaper." All subsequent page citations for both books are in the text.

2. Peggy Skaggs, *Kate Chopin*, pp. 2–3.

3. See Skaggs's chapter on *The Awakening* for further discussion of Mme. Ratignolle and Mlle. Reisz in terms of this polarity.

4. Charlotte Perkins Gilman, *The Home*, p. 23. All subsequent page citations are in the text.

326 • Notes to Pages 147–210

5. Charlotte Perkins Gilman, *The Living of Charlotte Perkins Gilman*, pp. 6–11. All subsequent page citations are in the text.

CHAPTER 6

1. Edith Wharton, *The Age of Innocence*. All subsequent page citations are in the text.

2. William A. Coles, "The Genesis of a Classic," p. xxxiv.

3. For a general discussion of this self-proclaimed American renaissance, see Judith Fryer, *Felicitous Space*, chapter 2.

4. E. F. Ellet, *The New Cyclopedia of Domestic Economy*, p. 45; quoted in Mabel Collins Connelly, *The American Victorian Woman*, p. 104.

5. Edith Wharton and Ogden Codman, *The Decoration of Houses*, introduction, unpaginated. All subsequent page citations are in the text.

6. Edith Wharton, *The Custom of the Country*, p. 73.

7. Coles, "The Genesis," p. xxvii.

8. Ibid., p. xxxv.

9. Fryer, *Felicitous Space*, p. 121.

10. Cited in ibid., p. 65.

11. Coles, "The Genesis," p. xlvii.

CHAPTER 7

1. Willa Cather, *The Professor's House*. All subsequent page citations are in the text.

2. Willa Cather, "The Novel Demeuble," p. 51.

3. Sharon O'Brien, *Willa Cather*, p. 62.

4. The symbolic connection between gender as a confining, culturally constructed category and territory and gender as space more literally considered is a fascinating area of speculation for Cather scholars and biographers. Sharon O'Brien's treatment of both questions is both thorough and provocative (ibid.).

5. Letter from Willa Cather to Mariel Gere, April 25, 1897, cited in ibid., p. 227.

6. For further discussion of the relationship in this and other of Cather's novels among "body, memory, and architecture," see Fryer, *Felicitous Space*.

7. For a more comprehensive discussion of the motif of escape in *The Professor's House*, see Thomas F. Strychacz, "The Ambiguities of Escape in Willa Cather's *The Professor's House*."

8. T. S. Eliot, "East Coker," p. 29.

CHAPTER 8

1. Alfred Kazin, "The Self as History," p. 43.
2. Arthur Mizener, *The Far Side of Paradise*, p. xvii.
3. Ibid., p. 4.
4. David L. Minter, "Dream, Design and Interpretation in *The Great Gatsby*," p. 85. This phrase closely parallels Mizener's characterization of Fitzgerald's perceptions of himself in a psychologically marginalized and oft-uprooted youth.
5. Mizener, *The Far Side*, pp. 13, 14.
6. Minter, "Dream, Design and Interpretation in *The Great Gatsby*," p. 82; F. Scott Fitzgerald, *The Great Gatsby*. All subsequent page citations for the latter book are in the text.
7. It may be similarly relevant here to note that forty acres plus a mule are what former slaves expected after the Civil War.
8. For Lewis's argument, see R. W. B. Lewis, *The American Adam*.

CHAPTER 9

1. William Faulkner, "On Privacy. The American Dream: What Happened to It," p. 61. All subsequent page citations are in the text.
2. William Faulkner, *Absalom, Absalom!* All subsequent page citations are in the text.
3. In *Faulkner's Fictive Architecture*, chapter 4, William Ruzicka links southern architecture to Greek not only in terms of its adaptation of the elements of style in "Greek Revival" but also in terms of the sensibility betokened in that style, which is centralized, exclusionary, geometric, symmetrical, and self-referential; communal and regional rather than imperial; and well suited to the insularity and self-sufficiency of the patriarchal plantation. Sutpen's design follows this pattern in most particulars, and certainly in spirit, though in every respect the virtues the design are intended to evoke and enhance are subverted, the meaning is undermined, and the dream becomes "something like a wing of Versailles glimpsed in a Lilliput's gothic nightmare" (*Requiem for a Nun*, p. 40). Ruzicka also calls attention to the reiterated comparisons between the plan and scale of Sutpen's estate and the plan and scale of Jefferson itself; as Sutpen planned it, the place "would have been almost as large as Jefferson itself at the time" (38). And Sutpen's house, planned by the same architect who designed the courthouse in Jefferson, is described by Miss Rosa as "the size of a court house" (16) and by Jason Compson as "the Spartan shell of the largest edifice in the country, not excepting the courthouse itself" (39).
4. Ibid., p. 46.

5. See ibid., p. 50, for further discussion of the idea of "ontological poverty" as defined by Frederick Wilhelmsen and applied to Sutpen.

6. For a discussion of miscegenation as the divisive element in Sutpen's house and in Southern culture, see Eric J. Sundquist, *Faulkner: The House Divided*, pp. 96–130. Reading Sutpen's saga as historical allegory, Sundquist compares Sutpen in certain respects to Lincoln and the fate of his house, to that of the South, riven paradoxically by the fusions and confusions of miscegenation, and beyond that to the fate of the nation.

7. The two lines of legitimate and illegitimate heritage come together symbolically in Charles Bon's son, Charles Etienne de Saint Valery Bon, whom Clytie brings back to Sutpen's Hundred after the death of his mother. Until adulthood, he lives in Sutpen's house in the ambiguous position of an illegitimate child of miscegenation, sleeping first, ironically, in Judith's bedroom, then in the hall on an elevated cot to distinguish him from the slave, Clytie—Sutpen's child as well, but blacker than he and female, who slept on a pallet on the floor—and then in the attic, with its "spartan arrangements," until he was fourteen and left this home that was only half a home to discover the suppressed half of his identity.

CHAPTER 10

1. Georgia McKinley, "The Crime." All subsequent page citations are in the text.

2. W. D. Weatherill, "The Man Who Loved Levittown." All subsequent page citations are in the text.

3. John Cheever, "The Country Husband." All subsequent page citations are in the text.

CHAPTER 11

1. Marilynne Robinson, *Housekeeping*; Toni Morrison, *Beloved*. All subsequent page citations for both books are in the text.

AFTERWORD

1. Jane Wagner, *The Search for Signs of Intelligent Life in the Universe*. All subsequent page citations are in the text.

2. Diana O Hehir, *The Bride Who Ran Away*. All subsequent page citations are in the text.

3. Diana O Hehir, "The Old Lady Under the Freeway," p. 15.

Bibliography

PRIMARY TEXTS

Cather, Willa. *The Professor's House*. 1925. Reprint. New York: Vintage Books, 1973.

Cheever, John. "The Country Husband." In *Contemporary American Short Stories*, edited by Douglas Angus and Sylvia Angus, 245–274. New York: Fawcett Premier Books, 1967.

Chopin, Kate. *The Awakening and Selected Stories*. Edited by Nina Baym. New York: Modern Library, 1981.

Faulkner, William. *Absalom, Absalom!* New York: Vintage Books, 1964.

Fitzgerald, F. Scott. *The Great Gatsby*. In *Three Novels of F. Scott Fitzgerald*, 3–137. New York: Charles Scribner's Sons, 1953.

Gilman, Charlotte Perkins. "The Yellow Wallpaper." In *The Charlotte Perkins Gilman Reader*, edited by Ann J. Lane, 3–20. New York: Pantheon Books, 1980.

Hawthorne, Nathaniel. *The House of the Seven Gables*. New York: New American Library, 1981.

James, Henry. *The Portrait of a Lady*. New York: Penguin Books, 1983.

McKinley, Georgia. "The Crime." In *Contemporary American Short Stories*, edited by Douglas Angus and Sylvia Angus, 137–153. New York: Fawcett Premier Books, 1967.

Morrison, Toni. *Beloved*. New York: Knopf, 1987.

O Hehir, Diana. *The Bride Who Ran Away*. New York: Washington Square Press, 1988.

Poe, Edgar Allan. "The Fall of the House of Usher." In *The Portable Poe*, edited by Philip Van Doren Stern, 244–267. New York: Penguin Books, 1973.

Robinson, Marilynne. *Housekeeping*. New York: Bantam Books, 1980.

Thoreau, Henry David. *Walden and Other Writings*. Edited by William Howarth. New York: Modern Library, 1981.

Wagner, Jane. *The Search for Signs of Intelligent Life in the Universe*. New York: Harper & Row, 1985.

Weatherill, W. D. "The Man Who Loved Levittown." In *The Man Who Loved Levittown*, 1–17. New York: Bantam Books, 1968.

Wharton, Edith. *The Age of Innocence*. New York: Charles Scribner's Sons, 1968.

OTHER SOURCES

Alexander, Christopher. *A Pattern Language: Towns, Buildings, Construction*. New York: Oxford University Press, 1977.

———. *The Timeless Way of Building*. New York: Oxford University Press, 1979.

Alexander, Christopher, with Howard Davis et al. *The Production of Houses*. New York: Oxford University Press, 1985.

Anderson, Charles R. *Person, Place, and Thing in Henry James's Novels*. Durham, N.C.: Duke University Press, 1977.

Andrews, Wayne. *Architecture, Ambition, and Americans: A Social History of American Architecture*. New York: Free Press, 1978.

Bachelard, Gaston. *The Poetics of Space*. Translated by Maria Jolas. 1958. Reprint. Boston: Beacon Press, 1969.

Beecher, Catherine E., and Harriet Beecher Stowe. *American Woman's Home*. 1869. Reprint. Hartford: Stowe-Day Foundation, 1985.

Cather, Willa. "The Novel Démeublé." In *Not Under Forty*, 43–51. Lincoln: University of Nebraska Press, 1968.

Coles, William A. "The Genesis of a Classic." In Edith Wharton and Ogden Codman, Jr. *The Decoration of Houses*, xxiii-xlix. 1902. Reprint. New York: Norton, 1978.

Crews, Frederick. *The Sins of the Fathers*. Berkeley and Los Angeles: University of California Press, 1966.

Dahl, Curtis. "Lord Lambeth's America: Architecture in James's 'An International Episode.' " *Henry James Review* 5, no. 2 (Winter 1984): 80–95.

Donnelly, Mabel Collins. *The American Victorian Woman: The Myth and the Reality*. Westport, Conn.: Greenwood Press, 1986.

Douglas, Ann. *The Feminization of American Culture*. New York: Knopf, 1977.

Downing, Andrew Jackson. *The Architecture of Country Houses*. 1850. Reprint. New York: Da Capo Press, 1968.

Edwards, Jonathan. "Images or Shadows of Divine Things." In *Basic Writings*, edited by Ola Elizabeth Winslow, 250–253. New York: New American Library, 1966.

———. "Sinners in the Hands of an Angry God." In *Basic Writings*, edited by Ola Elizabeth Winslow. New York: New American Library, 1966.

Eliot, T. S. "East Coker." In *Four Quartets*, 23–32. New York: Harcourt Brace Jovanovich, 1971.

———. "Tradition and the Individual Talent." In *Selected Prose of T. S. Eliot*, edited by Frank Kermode, 37–44. New York: Harcourt Brace Jovanovich, 1975.

Ellet, E. F. *The New Cyclopedia of Domestic Economy*. Norwich, Conn.: Henry Bill, 1873.

Emerson, Ralph Waldo. "The American Scholar." In *The Selected Writings of Ralph Waldo Emerson*, edited by Brooks Atkinson, 45–63. New York: Modern Library, 1968.

Faulkner, William. "On Privacy. The American Dream: What Happened to It." *Harper's Magazine* (July 1955). Reprinted in *William Faulkner: A Critical Collection*. Edited by Leland H. Cox, 61–72. Detroit: Gale Research, 1982.

Foley, Mary Mix. *The American House*. New York: Harper & Row, 1980.

Frank, Ellen Eve. *Literary Architecture: Essays Toward a Tradition*. Berkeley and Los Angeles: University of California Press, 1979.

Freud, Sigmund. *Introductory Lectures on Psycho-Analysis*. Translated and edited by James Strachey. New York: Norton, 1966.

Fryer, Judith. *Felicitous Space: The Imaginative Structures of Edith Wharton and Willa Cather*. Chapel Hill: University of North Carolina Press, 1986.

Fuller, Buckminster. *Ideas and Integrities*. New York: Macmillan, 1963.

Gale, Robert. *The Caught Image: Figurative Language in the Fiction of Henry James*. Chapel Hill: University of North Carolina Press, 1964.

Gill, Richard. *Happy Rural Seat: The English Country House and the Literary Imagination*. New Haven: Yale University Press, 1972.

Gilman, Charlotte Perkins. *The Home*. 1903. Reprint. Tulsa, Okla: Source Book Press, 1970.

———. *The Living of Charlotte Perkins Gilman: An Autobiography*. 1935. Reprint. Salem, N.H.: Ayer Co., 1987.

Griswold, Rufus, ed. "Willimantic Railroad: Transplanted Bogs." *New England Weekly Gazette*, February 24, 1849.

Handlin, David P. *American Architecture*. London: Thames and Hudson, 1985.

———. *The American Home: Architecture and Society, 1815–1915*. Boston: Little, Brown, 1979.

Hawthorne, Nathaniel. *Blithedale Romance*. New York: Norton, 1958.

Hayden, Dolores. *Redesigning the American Dream: The Future of Housing, Work, and Family Life*. New York: Norton, 1984.

Howarth, William. *The Book of Concord: Thoreau's Life as a Writer*. New York: Viking Press, 1982.

James, Henry. *The American Scene*. 1904. Reprint. Bloomington: Indiana University Press, 1968.

Kaestle, Carl F., and Maris A. Vinovskis. "From Apron Strings to ABCs: Parents, Children, and Schooling in Nineteenth-Century Massachusetts." In *Turning Points: Historical and Sociological Essays on the Family*, edited by John Demos and Sarane Spence Boocock, 539–580. Chicago: University of Chicago Press, 1978.

Kazin, Alfred. "The Self as History: Reflections on Autobiography." In *The American Autobiography*, edited by Albert E. Stone, 31–43. Englewood Cliffs, N.J.: Prentice-Hall, 1981.

Kolodney, Annette. *The Lay of the Land*. Chapel Hill: University of North Carolina Press, 1975.

Levine, Miriam. *A Guide to Writers' Homes in New England*. Cambridge, Mass.: Applewood Books, 1984.

Lewis, R. W. B. *Edith Wharton*. New York: Harper Colophon Books, 1975.

Lothrop, Margaret. *The Wayside: Home of Authors*. New York: American Book Co., 1968.

Masteller, Richard N., and Jean Carwile Masteller. "Rural Architecture in Andrew Jackson Downing and Henry David Thoreau: Pattern Book Parody in Walden." *New England Quarterly* (December 1984): 483–510.

Michaels, Walter Benn. "Romance and Real Estate." In *The American Renaissance Reconsidered*, edited by Walter Benn Michaels, 156–182. Baltimore: Johns Hopkins University Press, 1985.

Minter, David L. "Dream, Design and Interpretation in *The Great Gatsby*." In *Twentieth Century Interpretations of "The Great Gatsby*," edited by Ernest H. Lockridge, 82–89. Englewood Cliffs, N.J.: Prentice-Hall, 1968.

Mizener, Arthur. *The Far Side of Paradise: A Biography of F. Scott Fitzgerald*. Boston: Houghton Mifflin, 1965.

O'Brien, Sharon. *Willa Cather: The Emerging Voice*. New York: Oxford University Press, 1987.

O Hehir, Diana. "The Old Lady Under the Freeway." *Summoned*, 15. Columbia: University of Missouri Press, 1976.

Poe, Edgar Allan. "Edgar Allan Poe's Philosophy of Furniture." *Burton's Gentleman's Magazine* (May 1840). Reprinted in *House and Garden* (November 1983): 157–159, 210.

Ruzicka, William. *Faulkner's Fictive Architecture*. Ann Arbor: UMI Research Press, 1987.

Sabiston, Elizabeth. "Isabel Archer: The Architecture of Consciousness and the International Theme." *Henry James Review* 7, nos. 2–3 (Winter-Spring 1986): 29–47.

Skaggs, Peggy. *Kate Chopin*. Boston: Twayne, 1985.

Smith, W. L. G. *Life at the South: Or, Uncle Tom's Cabin as It Is*. Buffalo, N.Y.: 1852.

Stallman, R. W. *The Houses that James Built*. East Lansing: Michigan University Press, 1961.

————. "Some Rooms from 'The Houses that James Built.' " In *Twentieth Century Interpretations of "The Portrait of a Lady,"* edited by Peter Buitenhuis, 37–44. Englewood Cliffs, NJ: Prentice-Hall, 1968.

Strychacz, Thomas F. "The Ambiguities of Escape in Willa Cather's *The Professor's House.*" *Studies in American Fiction* 14 (1986): 49–61.

Sundquist, Eric J. *Faulkner: The House Divided*. Baltimore: Johns Hopkins University Press, 1983.

Wharton, Edith. *A Backward Glance*. 1933. Reprint. New York: Charles Scribner's Sons, 1964.

————. *The Custom of the Country*. New York: Charles Scribner's Sons, 1913.

Wharton, Edith, and Ogden Codman, Jr. *The Decoration of Houses*. 1902. Reprint. New York: Norton, 1978.

Whitman, Walt. *Leaves of Grass*. Edited by Harold Blodgett and Scully Bradley. New York: 1965.

————. *New York Dissected*. Edited by Emory Holloway and Ralph Adimari. New York: 1936.

Williams, Peter. "Constituting Class and Gender: A Social History of the Home, 1700–1901." In *Class and Space: The Making of Urban Society*, edited by Nigel Thrift and Peter Williams, 154–204. London: Routledge and Kegan Paul, 1987.

Wolfe, Tom. *From Bauhaus to Our House*. New York: Farrar, Straus and Giroux, 1981.

Wright, Frank Lloyd. *The Natural House*. 1954. Reprint. New York: New American Library, 1982.

INDEX

Compositor: BookMasters, Inc.
Text: 11/13 Baskerville
Display: Baskerville
Printer: Edwards Bros.
Binder: Edwards Bros.